The Evaluation of Forensic DNA Evidence

Committee on DNA Forensic Science: An Update

Commission on DNA Forensic Science: An Update

National Research Council

NATIONAL ACADEMY PRESS
Washington, D.C.   1996

National Academy Press • **2101 Constitution Ave., N.W.** • **Washington, D.C. 20418**

NOTICE: The project that is the subject of this report was approved by the Governing Board of the National Research Council, whose members are drawn from the councils of the National Academy of Sciences, the National Academy of Engineering, and the Institute of Medicine. The members of the committee responsible for the report were chosen for their special competences and with regard for appropriate balance. In preparing its report, the committee invited people with different perspectives to present their views. Such invitation does not imply endorsement of those views.

This report has been reviewed by a group other than the authors according to procedures approved by a Report Review Committee consisting of members of the National Academy of Sciences, the National Academy of Engineering, and the Institute of Medicine.

This study by the National Research Council's Virtual Commission on DNA Forensic Science: An Update was sponsored by the National Institute of Justice, the State Justice Institute, the National Science Foundation (Grant No. DMS-9415474), the National Institutes of Health, and the Department of Energy (Grant No. DE-FG02-94ER61782). Supported under Award # 93-IJ-CX-0008 from the National Institute of Justice, Office of Justice Programs, U.S., Department of Justice. Points of view in this document are those of the authors and do not necessarily represent the official position of the US Department of Justice.

COMMITTEE ON DNA FORENSIC SCIENCE: AN UPDATE

JAMES F. CROW, *Chair,* University of Wisconsin, Madison
MARGARET A. BERGER, Brooklyn Law School, Brooklyn, New York
SHARI S. DIAMOND, University of Illinois at Chicago/American Bar
    Foundation
DAVID H. KAYE, Arizona State University, College of Law, Tempe
HAIG H. KAZAZIAN, University of Pennsylvania, Philadelphia
ARNO G. MOTULSKY, University of Washington, Seattle
THOMAS A. NAGYLAKI, University of Chicago, Chicago, Illinois
MASATOSHI NEI, Pennsylvania State University, University Park
GEORGE F. SENSABAUGH, University of California, Berkeley
DAVID O. SIEGMUND, Stanford University, Stanford, California
STEPHEN M. STIGLER, University of Chicago, Chicago, Illinois

Advisor

VICTOR A. McKUSICK, The Johns Hopkins Hospital, Baltimore, Maryland

NRC Staff

ERIC A. FISCHER, Study Director
LEE R. PAULSON, Senior Staff Officer
MIRON L. STRAF, Senior Staff Officer
JOHN R. TUCKER, Senior Staff Officer
PAULETTE A. ADAMS, Senior Project Assistant
NORMAN GROSSBLATT, Editor

Preface

DNA analysis promises to be the most important tool for human identification since Francis Galton developed the use of fingerprints for that purpose. We can confidently predict that, in the not-distant future, persons as closely related as brothers will be routinely distinguished, and DNA profiles will be as fully accepted as fingerprints now are. But that time has not yet arrived, and the winds of controversy have not been stilled. Hence this report.

The technique for DNA profiling first appeared about 10 years ago, and the subject is still young. In the early days there was doubt, both as to the reproducibility and reliability of the methods and as to the appropriateness of simplistic calculations that took no account of possible subdivision of the population. Despite the potential power of the technique, there were serious reservations about its actual use.

In 1989, the National Research Council formed the Committee on DNA Technology in Forensic Science to study this new technique. The committee issued its report in 1992. The report resolved a number of questions, and several of its recommendations were widely adopted. Nevertheless, it generated controversy and criticism. Much of that centered on the "interim ceiling principle," a procedure intended to provide an estimate of a profile frequency that is highly conservative (i.e., favorable to the defendant) and independent of the racial origins of the DNA. The principle was criticized as being arbitrary and unnecessarily conservative, as not taking population genetic theory into account, and as being subject to misuse.

In April 1993, Judge William Sessions, then the Director of the FBI, requested that the NRC do a follow-up study to resolve the controversy and to answer other questions that recent empirical work permitted such a study to address. After a meeting of consultants in June 1993, the NRC decided to form a new committee and on August 30, 1993, I was asked to chair it. After a year's delay, mainly due to funding uncertainties, the committee members were named in August 1994, and the first meeting was held in September of that year. Subsequent meetings were held in November and in January and March of 1995. The main recommendations were agreed on and several revisions of a report were prepared between March and June. The remainder of the time has been spent in editing, revising, reviewing by the NRC Report Review Committee, and printing.

In the report, after an introduction and background material (Chapters 1 and 2), we deal with the question of errors in the laboratory and chain of custody and recommend procedures to minimize them (Chapter 3). We then address the question of population subdivision and propose calculating procedures that take it into account (Chapter 4). We also consider the statistical interpretation of DNA evidence, including statistical problems associated with the use of existing databases (Chapter 5). Finally, we include a review of DNA in the courts since the 1992 report (Chapter 6).

Specific recommendations are numbered and given at the ends of the chapters and are reproduced in the Executive Summary and Overview. Other statements in the text are not intended to have the force of formal recommendations, although we do make a number of suggestions. We agree with some statements of the 1992 report and disagree with others. Statements that are not discussed are neither endorsed nor rejected.

This report is the result of many exchanges by phone, fax, and e-mail among the individual committee members and Eric Fischer. We were greatly assisted throughout the project by Lee Paulson and Paulette Adams. The editor was Norman Grossblatt. During the course of the study we received advice by conversation and correspondence from many people. Some of these are listed at the end of the report, but the list is far from complete. We are indebted to all. We particularly thank those who took part in our public meeting on November 18, 1994.

Financial support for this study was provided by the National Institute of Justice, the State Justice Institute, the National Science Foundation, the National Institutes of Health, and the Department of Energy.

This is a period of rapid progress in developing and testing new methods of DNA analysis and of rapid increase in the size and diversity of databases. The information that has accumulated since the 1992 report permits us to be more confident of our recommendations. Courts have seen estimates of match probability ranging over several orders of magnitude. Our recommendations should lead to much greater agreement among the various estimates. I have no illusion that our report will eliminate the controversy; remaining uncertainties and the adversary system in the courts guarantee its continuance. But I hope that we have substantially narrowed the range of acceptable differences.

James F. Crow
Chairman
Committee on DNA Forensic Science:
An Update

Contents

Note to Readers

This report includes three parts:

Executive Summary. This is intended for those who would like to know our recommendations along with minimal explanations. It will be of interest to those who want to get immediately to the bottom line. After a brief introduction, the conclusions are stated followed by a brief description of the rationale.

Overview. This is intended for readers who are interested in the background for the conclusions and recommendations without the technical explanations in the main body of the report. Our intention is to present the scientific background for the conclusions with a minimum of jargon and technical material. The conclusions and recommendations, which are scattered in the various chapters of the main report, are repeated here for the reader's convenience.

Chapters 1-6. These provide the scientific and technical background for the conclusions and recommendations. They are intended to be a rather thorough review of the basic principles and of the systems used in forensic analysis. They provide background data supporting the conclusions. Although we have tried to write as clearly as possible, the chapters, especially 4 and 5, require some background in statistics and population genetics.

Readers of any of the sections will find it useful to refer to the list of abbreviations (p 212) and the glossary (p 214).

We are not aware of any inconsistencies among the three sections, but the full chapters provide the most accurate reflection of the committee's views.

Executive Summary[1]

INTRODUCTION

Nearly a decade has passed since DNA typing methods were first used in criminal investigations and trials. Law enforcement agencies have committed substantial resources to the technology; prosecutors, defense counsel, and judges have struggled with the terminology and ideas of molecular biology, genetics, and statistics. In 1992, a broad-ranging report released by the National Research Council attempted to explain the basics of the relevant science and technology, to offer suggestions for improving forensic DNA testing and its use in law enforcement, and to quiet the controversy that had followed the introduction of DNA profiling in court. Yet, the report did not eliminate all controversy. Indeed, in propounding what the committee regarded as a moderate position—the *ceiling principle* and the *interim ceiling principle*—the report itself became the target of criticism from scientists and lawyers on both sides of the debate on DNA evidence in the courts. Moreover, some of the statements in the 1992 report have been misinterpreted or misapplied in the courts.

This committee was formed to update and clarify discussion of the principles of *population genetics* and statistics as they apply to DNA evidence. Thus, this second report is much narrower than the 1992 report. Issues such as confidentiality and security, storage of samples for future use, the desirability and legality of

---

[1]Abbreviations, symbols, and technical terms are defined in the list of abbreviations (p 212) and the glossary (p 214). The underlying concepts are explained in the overview and in appropriate chapters in the body of the report.

data banks on convicted felons, and international exchange of information are not in our charge. Rather, this report deals mainly with the computation of probabilities used to evaluate the implications of DNA test results that incriminate suspects. It focuses on situations where the *DNA profile* of a suspect (or sometimes a victim) apparently matches that of the *evidence DNA*. (We use the phrase "evidence DNA" to refer to the sample of biological material, such as blood or semen, usually taken from the crime scene or from the victim.) The central question that the report addresses is this: What information can a forensic scientist, population geneticist, or statistician provide to assist a judge or jury in drawing inferences from the finding of a match?

To answer this question, the committee reviewed the scientific literature and the legal cases and commentary on DNA profiling, and it investigated the various criticisms that have been voiced about population data, statistics, and laboratory error. Much has been learned since the last report. The technology for DNA profiling and the methods for estimating frequencies and related statistics have progressed to the point where the reliability and validity of properly collected and analyzed DNA data should not be in doubt. The new recommendations presented here should pave the way to more effective use of DNA evidence.

This report describes both the science behind DNA profiling and the data on the frequency of profiles in human populations, and it recommends procedures for providing various statistics that may be useful in the courtroom. The procedures are based on population genetics and statistics, and they render the ceiling principle and the interim ceiling principle unnecessary.

This executive summary outlines the structure and contents of the full report, and it gives the recommendations together with abbreviated explanations of the reasons behind them. This summary does not constitute a complete exposition, and it is no substitute for a careful reading of the chapters that follow. As the report will reveal, the committee agrees with many recommendations of the 1992 report but disagrees with others. Since the committee has not attempted to review all the statements and recommendations in the 1992 report, the lack of discussion of any statement should not be interpreted as either endorsing or rejecting that statement.

CONTENTS OF THE REPORT

Overview. The report begins with an extended summary of the chapters that make up the full report. This overview describes the essentials of the subject with a minimum of jargon, statistics, and technical details, and it includes a numerical example that illustrates how the procedures that are discussed and recommended would apply in a typical case. The main report offers fuller explanations, details, and justifications.

Chapter 1. The first chapter describes the 1992 NRC report, the changes since that report, the uses and validity of DNA typing, differences between DNA typing in criminal cases and in civil paternity litigation, reasons for the seemingly contradictory probability estimates that different experts sometimes present in court, and the committee's approach to the issue of "population structure."

Chapter 2. The second chapter describes the genetic and molecular basis of DNA typing. It introduces the fundamental concepts of genetics, and it surveys the genetic systems and the technologies used in DNA profiling.

Chapter 3. The third chapter concerns laboratory performance. Although our focus is on the statistics that can be used to characterize the significance or implications of a match between two DNA samples, these statistics do not float in a vacuum. They relate to specific claims or hypotheses about the origin of the DNA samples. If DNA from an evidence sample and DNA from a suspect share a profile that has a low frequency in the population, this suggests that the samples came from the same person; the lower the frequency, the stronger the evidence. But the possibility remains that the match is only apparent—that an error has occurred and the profiles differ from what the laboratory has reported. Chapter 3 describes ways that errors can arise and how their occurrence might be minimized. It contains recommendations regarding quality control and assurance, laboratory accreditation, proficiency tests, and confirmatory testing.

Chapter 4. Much of the controversy about the forensic use of DNA has involved population genetics. Chapter 4 explains the generally applicable principles, then considers the implications of the fact that the population of the United States includes different groups and subgroups with different mixes of genes. The chapter develops and illustrates procedures for taking this fact into account in computing *random-match probabilities* for an incriminating DNA profile in a population or a subgroup of a population.

Chapter 5. The fifth chapter considers how the estimated frequency of an incriminating DNA profile relates to conclusions about the source of the DNA in the evidence sample. It discusses how the frequencies are interpreted as probabilities and related quantities, the degree of uncertainty in such estimates, and the type of calculations that might indicate that a profile is unique. It concludes that the abundance of data in different ethnic groups within the major races and the methods outlined in Chapters 4 and 5 imply that the 1992 report's suggested ceiling principle and interim ceiling principle are unnecessary. In addition, it makes recommendations to help assure the accuracy of estimates for what are known as *VNTR profiles* and to handle the special situation in which the suspect was identified as a result of a search through a database of DNA profiles of known offenders.

Chapter 6. The sixth and final chapter discusses the legal implications of the conclusions and recommendations. It describes the most important legal rules that affect the use of DNA evidence, identifies the questions of scientific fact that have been disputed in court, reviews case law on the admissibility of DNA evidence, and explains how the conclusions and recommendations might be used in applying and developing the law. The report makes no recommendations on matters of legal policy, but it does suggest that the formulation of such policy might be assisted by behavioral research into the various ways that DNA test results can be presented in the courtroom.

Appendices. A glossary of scientific terms and a list of the literature cited are provided at the end of the report.

RECOMMENDATIONS

Major conclusions and recommendations are given at the end of the chapter in which the subject is discussed. For convenience, the report also lists them as a group at the end of the overview. This executive summary lists the recommendations only and gives some of the reasoning behind them.

Recommendations to Improve Laboratory Performance

Recommendation 3.1. Laboratories should adhere to high quality standards (such as those defined by TWGDAM and the DNA Advisory Board) and make every effort to be accredited for DNA work (by such organizations as ASCLD-LAB).

Recommendation 3.2. Laboratories should participate regularly in proficiency tests, and the results should be available for court proceedings.

Recommendation 3.3. Whenever feasible, forensic samples should be divided into two or more parts at the earliest practicable stage and the unused parts retained to permit additional tests. The used and saved portions should be stored and handled separately. Any additional tests should be performed independently of the first by personnel not involved in the first test and preferably in a different laboratory.

Comment. The committee offers these recommendations to improve laboratory performance rather than to try to estimate the probability that a particular laboratory makes a mistake by reporting that two DNA profiles match when in fact they do not match. Auditing and proficiency testing cannot be expected to give a meaningful estimate of the probability that a particular laboratory has made such an error in a specific case. An unrealistically large number of proficiency tests would be needed to estimate accurately even an historical error rate. For such reasons, proficiency test results should not be combined with the estimated frequency of an incriminating profile to yield the probability that a laboratory would report that DNA from a person selected at random contains the incriminating profile. No amount of effort and improved technology can reduce the error rate to zero, and the best protection a wrongly implicated, innocent person has is the opportunity for an independent retest.

Recommendations for Estimating Random-Match Probabilities

Recommendation 4.1. In general, the calculation of a profile frequency should be made with the product rule. If the race of the person who left the evidence-sample DNA is known, the database for the person's race should be used; if the race is not known, calculations for all the racial groups to which possible suspects belong should be made. For systems such as VNTRs, in which a heterozygous locus can be mistaken for a homozygous one, if an upper bound on the frequency of the genotype at an apparently homozygous locus (single band) is desired, then twice the allele (bin) frequency, 2p, should be used instead of p^2. For systems in which exact genotypes can be determined, $p^2 + p(1 - p)\bar{\theta}$ should be used for the frequency at such a locus instead of p^2. A conservative value of $\bar{\theta}$ for the US population is 0.01; for some small, isolated populations, a value of 0.03 may be more appropriate. For both kinds of systems, $2p_ip_j$ should be used for heterozygotes.

Comment. The formulas referred to and the terminology used in this recommendation are explained in the overview and in Chapter 4. The product rule, which gives the profile frequency in a population as a product of coefficients and *allele frequencies*, rests on the assumption that a population can be treated as a single, randomly mating unit. When there are partially isolated subgroups in a population, the situation is more complex; then a suitably altered model leads to slightly different estimates of the quantities that are multiplied together in the formula for the frequency of the profile in the population.

In most cases, there is no special reason to think that the source of the evidence DNA is a member of a particular ethnic subgroup within a broad racial category, and the product rule is adequate for estimating the frequency of DNA profiles. For example, if DNA is recovered from semen in a case in which a woman hitchhiker on an interstate highway has been raped by a white man, the product rule with the 2p rule can be used with VNTR data from a sample of whites to estimate the frequency of the profile among white males.[2] If the race of the rapist were in doubt, the product rule could still be used and the results given for data on whites, blacks, Hispanics, and east Asians.

Recommendation 4.2. If the particular subpopulation from which the evidence sample came is known, the allele frequencies for the specific subgroup should be used as described in Recommendation 4.1. If allele frequen-

---

[2]The 2p rule involves replacing the quantity p^2 for a *single-banded VNTR locus* with the much larger quantity 2p in the product rule. This substitution accounts for cases in which one VNTR band from a heterozygote is not detected, and the person is mistakenly classified as a homozygote. The substitution also ensures that the estimate of the profile frequency will be larger than an estimate from a more precise formula that accounts for population structure explicitly. The technology for *PCR-based systems,* however, does not have these problems, and the 2p rule is inappropriate for these systems. Therefore, Recommendation 4.1 calls for using $p^2 + p(1 - p)\bar{\theta}$ (rather than 2p) in place of p^2 for such systems.

cies for the subgroup are not available, although data for the full population are, then the calculations should use the population-structure equations 4.10 for each locus, and the resulting values should then be multiplied.

Comment. This recommendation deals with the case in which the person who is the source of the evidence DNA is known to belong to a particular subgroup of a racial category. For example, if the hitchhiker was not on an interstate highway but in the midst of, say, a small village in New England and we had good reason to believe that the rapist was an inhabitant of the village, the product rule could still be used (as described in Recommendation 4.1) if there is a reasonably large database on the villagers.

If specific data on the villagers are lacking, a more complex model could be used to estimate the random-match probability for the incriminating profile on the basis of data on the major population group (whites) that includes the villagers. The equations referred to in the second sentence of Recommendation 4.2 are derived from this model.

Recommendation 4.3. If the person who contributed the evidence sample is from a group or tribe for which no adequate database exists, data from several other groups or tribes thought to be closely related to it should be used. The profile frequency should be calculated as described in Recommendation 4.1 for each group or tribe.

Comment. This recommendation deals with the case in which the person who is the source of the evidence DNA is known to belong to a particular subgroup of a racial category but there are no DNA data on either the subgroup or the population to which the subgroup belongs. It would apply, for example, if a person on an isolated Indian reservation in the Southwest, had been assaulted by a member of the tribe, and there were no data on DNA profiles of the tribe. In that case, the recommendation calls for use of the product rule (as described in Recommendation 4.1) with several other closely related tribes for which adequate databases exist.

Recommendation 4.4. If the possible contributors of the evidence sample include relatives of the suspect, DNA profiles of those relatives should be obtained. If these profiles cannot be obtained, the probability of finding the evidence profile in those relatives should be calculated with Formulae 4.8 or 4.9.

Comment. This recommendation deals with cases in which there is reason to believe that particular relatives of the suspect committed the crime. For example, if the hitchhiker described in the comment to Recommendation 4.2 had accepted a ride in a car containing two brothers and was raped by one of them, but there is doubt as to which one, both should be tested. If one brother cannot be located for testing and the other's DNA matches the evidence DNA, then the probability that a brother of the tested man also would possess the incriminating profile should be computed.

Recommendations on Interpreting the Results of Database Searches, on Binning, and on Establishing the Uniqueness of Profiles

Recommendation 5.1 When the suspect is found by a search of DNA databases, the random-match probability should be multiplied by N, the number of persons in the database.

Comment. Recommendations 4.1-4.3 specify the calculation of the random-match probability for an incriminating DNA profile in a relevant population (or subpopulation). When the defendant has been identified as a suspect from information that is unrelated to the DNA profile, the random-match probability is one statistic that helps to indicate the significance of a match. If the random-match probability is very low, it is unlikely that the samples match just because the defendant, though not the source of the evidence sample, coincidentally happens to share that very rare profile.

But when the defendant has been identified by a search through a large database of DNA profiles rather than by non-DNA evidence, the relevance of the random-match probability is less obvious. There are different ways to take the search process into account. Recommendation 5.1 proposes multiplying the random-match probability (P) by the number of people in the database (N). If the person who left the evidence DNA was not in the database of felons, then the probability that at least one of the profiles in the database would also match the incriminating profile cannot exceed NP.

Recommendation 5.2. If floating bins are used to calculate the random-match probabilities, each bin should coincide with the corresponding match window. If fixed bins are employed, then the fixed bin that has the largest frequency among those overlapped by the match window should be used.

This recommendation applies to the computation of a random-match probability when all or part of the profile involves VNTRs, which are fragments of DNA that are separated in the laboratory according to their lengths. Because the lengths of VNTRs cannot be measured exactly, an *uncertainty window* surrounds each measured VNTR, and two VNTRs are said to *match* when their uncertainty windows overlap. To calculate the frequency of matching VNTR profiles, one must find the proportion of VNTRs that fall within a *match window* around each VNTR in the incriminating profile. *Floating bins* do this exactly, whereas *fixed bins* do this approximately. Although the floating-bin procedure is statistically preferable, certain forms of the fixed-bin procedure usually lead to conservative approximations to the floating bin result.

Recommendation 5.3. Research into the identification and validation of more and better marker systems for forensic analysis should continue with a view to making each profile unique.

Comment. If a sufficient set of DNA characteristics is measured, the resulting DNA profiles can be expected to be unique in all populations. (Only identical twins would share such a profile.) Of course, it is impossible to establish uniqueness by profiling everyone in the world, but theory and experience suggests that this uniqueness is attainable in forensic typing. Indeed, some scientists would argue that the existing panoply of characteristics is already sufficient to permit unique identification in many cases. For example, it has been suggested that a probability much less than the reciprocal of the world population is a good indication of uniqueness. The committee has not attempted to define a specific probability that corresponds to uniqueness, but the report outlines a framework for considering the issue in terms of probabilities, and it urges that research into new and cumulatively more powerful systems continue until a clear consensus emerges that DNA profiles, like dermal fingerprints, are unique.

Recommendation for Research on Juror Comprehension

Recommendation 6.1. Behavioral research should be carried out to identify any conditions that might cause a trier of fact to misinterpret evidence on DNA profiling and to assess how well various ways of presenting expert testimony on DNA can reduce any such misunderstandings.

Comment. Scientifically valid testimony about matching DNA can take many forms. The conceivable alternatives include statements of the *posterior probability* that the defendant is the source of the evidence DNA, qualitative characterizations of this probability, computations of the *likelihood ratio* for the hypothesis that the defendant is the source, qualitative statements of this measure of the strength of the evidence, the currently dominant estimates of profile frequencies or random-match probabilities, and unadorned reports of a match. Courts or legislatures must decide which of these alternatives best meets the needs of the criminal justice system. At present, policymakers must speculate about the ability of jurors to understand the significance of a match as a function of the method of presentation. Solid, empirical research into the extent to which the different methods advance juror understanding is needed.

Overview

This overview describes the essentials of the subject with a minimum of jargon, statistics, and technical details. The aim is to present technical information in nontechnical language, but without distorting the meaning by oversimplifying. Although this overview is intended to be self-contained, we shall refer to relevant sections in the main report for fuller explanations, corroborative details, and justification of recommended procedures. We have included an illustrative example at the end of the overview. The glossary and the list of abbreviations at the end of the report may be useful.

INTRODUCTION

DNA typing, with its extremely high power to differentiate one human being from another, is based on a large body of scientific principles and techniques that are universally accepted. These newer molecular techniques permit the study of human variability at the most basic level, that of the genetic material itself, DNA. Standard techniques of population genetics and statistics can be used to interpret the results of forensic DNA typing. Because of the newness of the techniques and their exquisite discriminating power, the courts have subjected DNA evidence to extensive scrutiny. What at first seemed like daunting complexity in the interpretation of DNA tests has sometimes inhibited the full use of such evidence. An objective of this report is to clarify and explain how DNA evidence can be used in the courtroom.

If the array of DNA markers used for comparison is large enough, the chance that two different persons will share all of them becomes vanishingly small. With appropriate DNA test systems, the uniqueness of any individual on the planet (except an identical twin) is likely to be demonstrable in the near future. In the meantime, the justification for an inference that two identical DNA profiles come from the same person rests on probability calculations that employ principles of population genetics. Such calculations are, of course, subject to uncertainty. When in doubt, we err on the side of conservatism (that is, in favor of the defendant). We also discuss ways of keeping laboratory and other errors to a minimum. We emphasize that DNA analysis, when properly carried out and interpreted, is a very powerful forensic tool.

OUR ASSIGNMENT

This committee was asked to update an earlier report, prepared for the National Research Council (NRC) in 1992. There are two principal reasons why such an update is needed. First, forensic science and techniques have progressed rapidly in recent years. Laboratory standards are higher, and new DNA markers are rapidly being introduced. An abundance of new data on DNA markers in different population groups is now available, allowing estimates of the frequencies of those markers in various populations to be made with greater confidence. Second, some of the statements in the first report have been misinterpreted or misapplied in the courts.

This report deals mainly with two subjects:

The first involves the laboratory determination of DNA profiles. DNA can be obtained in substantial amounts and in good condition, as when blood or tissue is obtained from a person, or it can be in limited amounts, degraded, or contaminated, as in some samples from crime scenes. Even with the best laboratory technique, there is intrinsic, unavoidable variability in the measurements; that introduces uncertainty that can be compounded by poor laboratory technique, faulty equipment, or human error. We consider how such uncertainty can be reduced and the risk of error minimized.

The second subject is the interpretation of a finding that the DNA profile of a suspect (or sometimes a victim) matches that of the evidence DNA, usually taken from the crime scene. The match might happen because the two samples are from the same person. Alternatively it might be that the samples are from different persons and that an error has occurred in the gathering of the evidence or in the laboratory. Finally, it might be that the samples are from different people who happen to have the same DNA profile; the probability of that event can be calculated. If the probability is very low, then either the DNA samples are from the same person or a very unlikely coincidence has occurred.

The interpretation of a matching profile involves at least two types of uncertainty. The first arises because the US population is not homogeneous. Rather it consists of different major races (such as black and white), within which there are various subgroups (e.g., persons of Italian and Finnish ancestry) that are not completely mixed in the "melting pot." The extent of such population structure and how it can be taken into account are in the province of population genetics.

The second uncertainty is statistical. Any calculation depends on the numbers in available databases. How reliable are those numbers and how accurate are the calculations based on them and on population genetic theory? We discuss these questions and give answers based on statistical theory and empirical observations.

Finally, some legal issues are discussed. We consider how the courts have reacted to this new technology, especially since the 1992 NRC report.

That earlier report considered a number of issues that are outside our province. Issues such as confidentiality and security, storage of samples for possible future use, legal aspects of data banks on convicted felons, non-DNA information in data banks, availability and costs of experts, economic and ethical aspects of new DNA information, accountability and public scrutiny, and international exchange of information are not in our charge.

As this report will reveal, we agree with many recommendations of the earlier one but disagree with others. Since we make no attempt to review all the statements and recommendations in the 1992 report, the lack of discussion of such an item should not be interpreted as either endorsing or rejecting it.

DNA TYPING

DNA typing for forensic purposes is based on the same fundamental principles and uses the same techniques that are routinely employed in a wide variety of medical and genetic situations, such as diagnosis and gene mapping. Those methods analyze the DNA itself. That means that a person's genetic makeup can be determined directly, not indirectly through gene products, as was required by earlier methods. DNA is also resistant to many conditions that destroy most other biological compounds, such as proteins. Furthermore, only small amounts of DNA are required; that is especially true if PCR (polymerase chain reaction) methods, to be described later, are employed. For those reasons, direct DNA determinations often give useful results when older methods, such as those employing blood groups and enzymes, do not.

We emphasize that one of the most important benefits of DNA technology is the clearing of falsely-accused innocent suspects. According to the FBI, about a third of those named as the primary suspect in rape cases are excluded by DNA evidence. Cases in which DNA analysis provides evidence of innocence ordinarily do not reach the courts and are therefore less widely known. Prompt exclusions can eliminate a great deal of wasted effort and human anguish.

Before describing the techniques of DNA identification, we first provide some necessary genetic background and a minimum vocabulary.

BASIC GENETIC PRINCIPLES

Each human body contains an enormous number of cells, all descended by successive divisions from a single fertilized egg. The genetic material, DNA, is in the form of microscopic *chromosomes,* located in the inner part of the cell, the *nucleus.* A fertilized egg has 23 pairs of chromosomes, one member of each pair having come from the mother and the other from the father. The two members of a pair are said to be *homologous.* Before cell division, each chromosome splits into two. Because of the precision of chromosome distribution in the cell-division process, each daughter cell receives identical chromosomes, duplicates of the 46 in the parent cell. Thus, each cell in the body should have the same chromosome makeup. This means that cells from various tissues, such as blood, hair, skin, and semen, have the same DNA content and therefore provide the same forensic information. There are some exceptions to the rule of identical chromosomes in every cell, but they do not affect the conclusion that diverse tissues provide the same information.

The most important exception occurs when sperm and eggs are formed. In this process, each reproductive cell receives at random one representative of each pair, or 23 in all. The double number, 46, is restored by fertilization. With the exception of the sex chromosomes, X and Y (the male-determining Y is smaller than the X), the two members of a pair are identical in size and shape. (It might seem puzzling that sperm cells, with only half of the chromosomes, can provide the same information as blood or saliva. The reason is that DNA from many sperm cells is analyzed at once, and collectively all the chromosomes are represented.)

A chromosome is a *very* thin thread of DNA, surrounded by other materials, mainly protein. (DNA stands for deoxyribonucleic acid.) The DNA in a single chromosome, if stretched out, would be an inch or more in length. Remarkably, all that length is packed into a cell nucleus some 1/1,000 inch in diameter. The DNA is compacted by coils within coils.

The DNA thread is actually double, consisting of two strands twisted to form a helix (Figure O.1). Each strand consists of a string of *bases* held together by a sugar-phosphate backbone. The four bases are abbreviated A, T, G, and C (these stand for adenine, thymine, guanine, and cytosine, but we shall employ only the abbreviations). In double-stranded DNA, the bases line up in pairs, an A opposite a T and a G opposite a C:

> C A T T A G A C T G A T
> G T A A T C T G A C T A

Thus, if the sequence of bases on one strand is known, the other is determined.

Prior to cell division, the double strand splits into two single strands, each containing a single base at each position. There are free-floating bases in the cell nucleus, and these attach to each single strand according to the A-T, G-C pairing rule. Then they are tied together and zipped up by enzymes. In this way, each

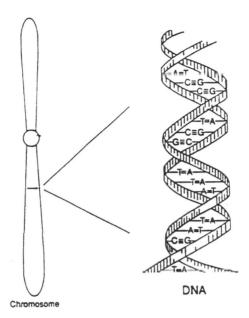

DNA

Chromosome

FIGURE O.1   Diagram of a chromosome, with a small region expanded to show the double-helical structure of DNA. The "steps" of the twisted ladder are four kinds of base pairs, AT, TA, GC, or CG. From NRC (1992).

DNA double helix makes a copy of itself. There are then two identical double strands, each half old and half new, and one goes to each daughter cell. That accounts for the uniformity of DNA makeup throughout the body. The total number of base pairs in a set of 23 chromosomes is about 3 billion.

A *gene* is a stretch of DNA, ranging from a few thousand to tens of thousands of base pairs, that produces a specific product, usually a protein. The order of the four kinds of bases within the gene determines its function. The specific base sequence acts as an encoded message written in three-letter words, each specifying an amino acid (a protein building block). In the diagram above, CAT specifies one amino acid, TAG another, ACT a third, and so on. These amino acids are joined together to make a chain, which folds in various ways to make a three-dimensional protein. The gene product may be detected by laboratory methods, as with blood groups, or by some visible manifestation, such as eye color.

The position that a gene occupies along the DNA thread is its *locus*. In chemical composition, a gene is no different from the rest of the DNA in the chromosome. Only its having a specific sequence of bases, enabling it to encode a specific protein, makes each gene unique. Genes are interspersed among the rest of the DNA and actually compose only a small fraction of the total. Most of the rest has no known function.

Alternative forms of a gene, for example those producing normal and sickle-cell hemoglobin, are called *alleles*. The word *genotype* refers to the gene makeup. A person has two genes at each locus, one maternal, one paternal. If there are two alleles, A and a, at a locus, there are three genotypes, AA, Aa, and aa. The word genotype can be extended to any number of loci. In forensic work, the genotype for the group of analyzed loci is called the DNA *profile*. (We avoid the word fingerprint to prevent confusion with dermal fingerprints.) If the same allele is present in both chromosomes of a pair, the person with that pair is *homozygous*. If the two are different, the person is *heterozygous*. (The corresponding nouns are *homozygote* and *heterozygote*.) Thus, genotypes AA and aa are homozygous and Aa is heterozygous.

Genes on the same chromosome are said to be *linked*, and they tend to be inherited together. They can become unlinked, however, by the process of *crossing over*, which involves breakage of two homologous chromosomes at corresponding sites and exchange of partners (Figure O.2). Genes that are on nonhomologous chromosomes are inherited independently, as are genes far apart on the same chromosome.

Occasionally, an allele may *mutate*; that is, it may suddenly change to another allele, with a changed or lost function. When the gene mutates, the new form is copied as faithfully as the original gene, so a mutant gene is as stable as the gene before it mutated. Most genes mutate very rarely, typically only once in some 100,000 generations, but the rates for different genes differ greatly. Mutations can occur in any part of the body, but our concern is those that occur in the reproductive system and therefore can be transmitted to future generations.

FORENSIC DNA IDENTIFICATION

VNTRs

One group of DNA loci that are used extensively in forensic analysis are those containing Variable Numbers of Tandem Repeats (VNTRs). These are not genes, since they produce no product, and those that are used for forensic determinations have no known effect on the person. That is an advantage, for it means that VNTRs are less likely to be influenced by natural selection, which could lead to different frequencies in different populations. For example, several genes that cause malaria resistance are more common in people of Mediterranean or African ancestry, where malaria has been common.

A typical VNTR region consists of 500 to 10,000 base pairs, comprising many tandemly repeated units, each some 15 to 35 base pairs in length. The exact number of repeats, and hence the length of the VNTR region, varies from one allele to another, and different alleles can be identified by their lengths. VNTR loci are particularly convenient as markers for human identification because they have a very large number of different alleles, often a hundred or more, although

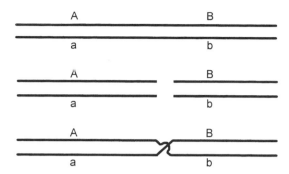

FIGURE O.2   Diagram of crossing over. The chromosomes pair (upper diagram), break at corresponding points (middle), and exchange parts. The result is that alleles A and B, which were formerly on the same chromosome, are now on different chromosomes.

only 15 to 25 can be distinguished practically, as we explain later. (The word allele is traditionally applied to alternative forms of a gene; here we extend the word to include nongenic regions of DNA, such as VNTRs.)

VNTRs also have a very high mutation rate, leading to changes in length. An individual mutation usually changes the length by only one or a few repeating units. The result is a very large number of alleles, no one of which is common. The number of possible genotypes (pairs of alleles) at a locus is much larger than the number of alleles, and when several different loci are combined, the total number of genotypes becomes enormous.

To get an idea of the amount of genetic variability with multiple alleles and multiple loci, consider first a locus with three alleles, A_1, A_2, and A_3. There are three homozygous genotypes, A_1A_1, A_2A_2, and A_3A_3, and three heterozygous ones, A_1A_2, A_1A_3, and A_2A_3. In general, if there are n alleles, there are n homozygous genotypes and $n(n-1)/2$ heterozygous ones. For example, if there are 20 alleles, there are $20 + (20 \times 19)/2 = 210$ genotypes. Four loci with 20 alleles each would have $210 \times 210 \times 210 \times 210$, or about 2 billion possible genotypes.

For a genetic system to be useful for identification, it is not enough that it yield a large number of genotypes. The relative frequencies of the genotypes are also important. The more nearly equal the different frequencies are, the greater the discriminatory power. VNTRs exhibit both characteristics.

DNA Profiling

Genetic types at VNTR loci are determined by a technique called VNTR profiling. Briefly, the technique is as follows (Figure O.3). First, the DNA is extracted from whatever material is to be examined. The DNA is then cut by a specific enzyme into many small fragments, millions in each cell. A tiny fraction of those fragments includes the particular VNTR to be analyzed. The fragmented

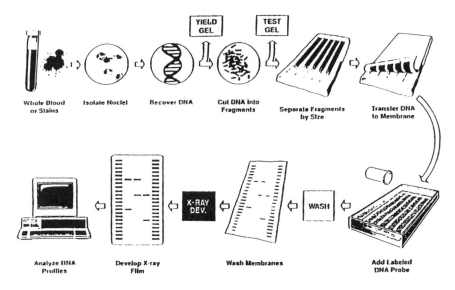

FIGURE O.3   An outline of the DNA profiling process.

DNA is then placed in a small well at one edge of a semisolid gel. Each of the different DNA samples to be analyzed is placed in a different well. Additional wells receive various known DNA samples to serve as controls and fragment-size indicators. Then the gel is placed in an electric field and the DNA migrates away from the wells. The smaller the fragment, the more rapidly it moves. After a suitable time, the electric current is stopped, and the different fragments will have migrated different distances, the shorter ones for greater distances.

In the process, the DNA fragments are *denatured*, meaning that the double strands in each fragment are separated into single strands. The fragments are then transferred by simple blotting to a nylon membrane, which is tougher and easier to handle than the gel and to which the single-stranded fragments adhere. Then a radioactive *probe* is added. A probe is a short section of single-stranded DNA complementary to the specific VNTR of interest, meaning that it has a C where the VNTR has a G, an A where the VNTR has a T, and so on, so that the probe is specifically attracted to this particular VNTR. When the membrane is placed on a photographic film, the radioactive probes take a picture of themselves, producing dark spots on the film at positions corresponding to the particular DNA fragments to which the probe has attached. This photo is called an autoradiograph, or *autorad* for short.

The two DNA samples to be compared (usually from the evidence, E, and from a suspect, S) are placed in separate lanes in the gel, with DNA in several other lanes serving as different kinds of controls. Because of the large number of VNTR alleles, most loci are heterozygous, and there will usually be two bands in each lane. If the two DNA samples, E and S, came from the same individual, the two bands in each lane will be in the same, or nearly the same, positions; if the DNA came from different persons, they will usually be in quite different positions. The sizes of the fragments are estimated by comparison with a "ladder" in which the spots are of known size.

Figure O.4 shows an example. In this case, the question is whether either of two victims, V1 and V2, match a blood stain, called E blood in the figure,

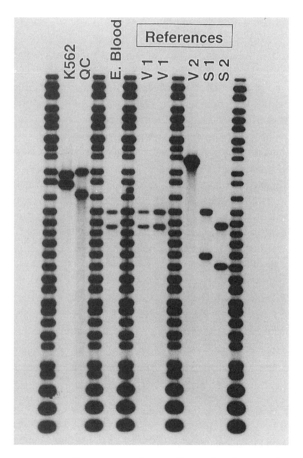

FIGURE O.4   An autorad from an actual case, illustrating fragment-length variation at the D1S7 locus. The lanes from left to right are: (1) standard DNA ladder, used to estimate sizes; (2) K562, a standard cell line with two bands of known size, used as a control; (3) within-laboratory quality control sample; (4) standard ladder; (5) DNA from blood at the crime scene; (6) standard ladder; (7) DNA from the first victim; (8) another sample from the first victim; (9) standard ladder; (10) DNA from the second victim; (11) DNA from the first suspect; (12) DNA from the second suspect; (13) standard ladder. Courtesy of the State of California Department of Justice DNA Laboratory.

that was found on the clothing of suspect S1. S2 is a second suspect in the case. The sizing ladders are in lanes 1, 4, 6, 9, and 13; these are repeated in several lanes to detect possible differences in the rate of migration in different lanes. K562 and QC are other controls. On looking at the figure, one sees that the evidence blood (E blood) is not from V2 (or from S1 or S2), since the bands are in quite different positions. However, it might well be from V1, since the bands in E and V1 are at the same position.

After such an analysis, the radioactive probe is washed off the membrane. Then a new probe, specific for another VNTR locus, is added and the whole process repeated. This is continued for several loci, usually four or more. There is a practical limit, however, since the washing operation may eventually remove some of the DNA fragments, making the bands on the autorad weak or invisible. In the example in Figure O.4, testing at 9 additional loci gave consistent matches between E blood and Victim 1, leaving little doubt as to the source of the blood.

In most laboratories, the sizes of the fragments are measured by a computer, which also does the calculations that are described below.

A DNA fragment from the evidence is declared to match the one from a suspect (or, in the case of Figure O.4, from a victim) if they are within a predetermined relative distance. If the bands do not match, that is the end of the story: the DNA samples did not come from the same individual. If the DNA patterns do match, or appear to match, the analysis is carried farther, as described in the next section.

A difficulty with VNTRs using radioactive probes is the long time required to complete the analysis. One or two weeks are needed for sufficient radiation to make a clear autorad, and, as just described, the different loci are done in succession. As a result, the process takes several weeks. Some newer techniques use luminescent chemicals instead of radioactive ones. As such techniques are perfected and come into wider use, the process will speed up considerably.

Matching and Binning of VNTRs

Because of measurement uncertainty, the estimates of fragment sizes are essentially continuous. The matching process consists of determining whether two bands are close enough to be within the limits of the measurement uncertainty. After the two bands have been determined to match, they are *binned*. In this process, the band is assigned to a size class, known as a bin. Two analytical procedures are the *fixed-bin* and the *floating-bin* methods. The floating-bin method is statistically preferable, but it requires access to a computerized data base. The fixed-bin method is simpler in some ways and easier for the average laboratory to use; hence, it is more widely employed. Only the fixed-bin method is described here, but the reader may refer to Chapter 5 (p 142) for a description of floating-bin procedures.

A match between two different DNA sources (e.g., evidence and suspect DNA) is typically determined in two stages. First is a visual examination. Usually the bands in the two lanes to be compared will be in very similar positions or in clearly different positions. In the latter case, there is no match, and the DNA samples are assumed to have come from different persons. In Figure O.4, only the bands of V1 match the evidence blood. The role of a visual test is that of a preliminary screen, to eliminate obvious mismatches from further study and thereby save time and effort.

The second, measurement-confirmation step is based on the size of the fragment producing the band, as determined by size standards (the standard ladders) on the same autorad (Figure O.4). The recorded size is subject to measurement uncertainty, which is roughly proportional to the fragment size. Based on duplicate measurements of the same sample in different laboratories, roughly 2/3 of the measurements are within 1% of the correct value. In practice, a value larger than 1%, usually 2.5%—although this varies in different laboratories—is used to prevent the possible error of classifying samples from the same person as being different. The measurement with 2.5% of its value added and subtracted yields an *uncertainty window*.

Two bands, say from suspect and evidence, are declared to match if their uncertainty windows overlap; otherwise a nonmatch is declared. Compare the top two diagrams in Figure O.5.

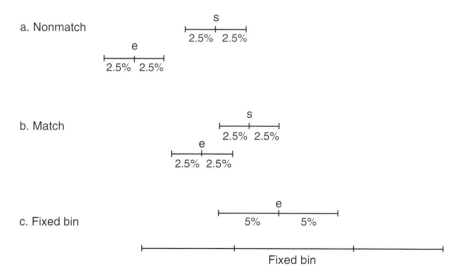

FIGURE O.5   Diagrams showing the extent of the uncertainty windows (a,b) and the match window (c). In the top group, the uncertainty windows do not overlap; in the second they do. The bottom diagram shows the match window of a fragment along with the fixed bin. The match window overlaps bins 10 and 11.

The *match window* is the evidence measurement with 5% of its value added and subtracted. This is compared with the bins in the database (such as those in Table O.1). If the upper and lower values lie within a bin, then the frequency of that bin is used to calculate the probability of a random match. Often, two or more bins will be overlapped by the match window. In Figure O.5, the match window overlaps bins 10 and 11. When that happens, we recommend that the bin with the highest frequency be used. (The 1992 NRC report recommends taking the sum of the frequencies of all overlapped bins, but empirical studies have shown that taking the largest value more closely approximates the more accurate floating-bin method.)

Frequency estimates for very rare alleles have a larger relative uncertainty than do those for more common alleles, because the relative uncertainty is largely

TABLE O.1   Bin (Allele) Frequencies at Two VNTR Loci (D2S44 and D17S79) in the US White Population[a]

D2S44				D17S79			
Bin	Size Range	N	Prop.	Bin	Size Range	N	Prop.
3	0- 871	8	0.005	1	0- 639	16	0.010
4	872- 963	5	0.003	2	640- 772	5	0.003
5	964-1,077	24	0.015	3	773- 871	11	0.007
6	1,078-1,196	38	0.024	4	872-1,077	6	0.004
7	1,197-1,352	73	0.046	6	1,078-1,196	23	0.015
8	1,353-1,507	55	0.035	7	1,197-1,352	348	0.224
9	1,508-1,637	197	0.124	8	1,353-1,507	307	0.198
10	1,638-1,788	170	0.107	9	1,508-1,637	408	0.263
11	1,789-1,924	131	0.083	10	1,638-1,788	309	0.199
12	1,925-2,088	79	0.050	11	1,789-1,924	44	0.028
13	2,089-2,351	131	0.083	12	1,925-2,088	50	0.032
14	2,352-2,522	60	0.038	13	2,089-2,351	16	0.010
15	2,523-2,692	65	0.041	14	2,352-	9	0.006
16	2,693-2,862	63	0.040				
17	2,863-3,033	136	0.086			1,552	0.999
18	3,034-3,329	141	0.089				
19	3,330-3,674	119	0.075				
20	3,675-3,979	36	0.023				
21	3,980-4,323	27	0.017				
22	4,324-5,685	13	0.008				
25	5,686-	13	0.008				
		1,584	1.000				

[a]D2 and D17 indicate that these are on chromosomes 2 and 17. N is the number of genes (twice the number of persons). Each bin includes a range of sizes (in base pairs), grouped so that no bin has fewer than five genes in the data set; this accounts for nonconsecutive bin numbers. Data from FBI (1993), p 439, 530.

determined by the absolute number of alleles in the database. To reduce such uncertainty, it is customary for the data to be *rebinned*. This involves merging all bins with an absolute number fewer than five genes into adjacent bins, so that no bin has fewer than five members. We endorse this practice, not only for fixed bins but also for floating bins, and not only for VNTRs but also for rare alleles in other systems.

Allele (Bin) Frequencies

Databases come from a variety of sources, which we shall discuss later. Each bin is assigned a number, 1 designating the smallest fragments. Table O.1 shows the size range and frequencies of the bins at two loci, D2S44 and D17S79, for the US white population. The first number in the locus designation tells us on which chromosome this locus lies. The second is an arbitrary number that designates the site of the locus on the chromosome. D2S44 is site 44 on chromosome number 2; D17S79 is site 79 on chromosome 17. The data in the table have been rebinned so that no bin has fewer than 5 representatives in the database. D2S44 is more useful for forensic purposes than D17S79 because it has a larger range of sizes, from less than 871 to more than 5,686 base pairs, and because the different bins have more nearly equal frequencies.

Figure O.6 shows a graph of the frequencies of each bin in three populations for D2S44. The top two graphs are from white populations in Georgia and Illinois. Note that the distributions are quite similar. In both states, bin 8 is the commonest; bins 14, 15, and 16 are relatively rare; and the extremes at both ends of the distribution have very low frequencies. Using the Georgia database for an Illinois crime would not introduce much error. In contrast, the distribution for blacks, shown in the bottom graph, is clearly different. That argues for using separate databases for different racial groups. Nevertheless, the most striking feature of the graphs is that the variability among individuals within a population is greater than that between populations.

We have now described procedures for matching and binning and for determining the bin (allele) frequency. We next wish to combine these frequencies to determine the frequency of a multilocus profile. That will be taken up later, in the section on population genetics.

PCR-Based Systems

The polymerase chain reaction (PCR) is a method for greatly amplifying a short segment of DNA, copying the sequence in a way somewhat like that which occurs naturally in the cell (the procedure is described in Chapter 2, p 69). Most PCR-based typing systems allow alleles to be identified as discrete entities, thus avoiding most of the statistical issues that arise in matching and binning of VNTR alleles.

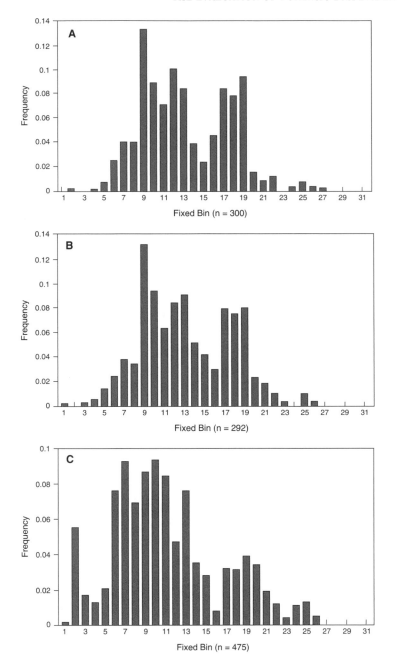

FIGURE O.6   The distribution of bin sizes for locus D2S44. The horizontal axis gives the bin number and the vertical column gives the relative frequency of this bin in the database: (A) Illinois white population, (B) Georgia white population, (C) US black population.

The PCR process has several additional advantages over the procedures used with VNTRs. It is relatively simple and easily carried out in the laboratory. Results are obtained in a short time, often within 24 hours. Because of their almost unlimited capacity for amplification, PCR-based methods permit the analysis of extremely tiny amounts of DNA, thus extending the typing technique to samples too small to be used with other approaches (e.g., DNA from a cigarette butt). Moreover, the small sample size required for PCR analysis makes it easier to set aside portions of samples for duplicate testing to verify results or detect possible errors.

There are also disadvantages. One is that any procedure that uses PCR methodology is susceptible to error by contamination. If the contaminating DNA is present at a level comparable to the target DNA, its amplification can confound the interpretation of typing results, possibly leading to an erroneous conclusion. A second disadvantage is that most PCR loci have fewer alleles than VNTRs. That means that more loci are required to produce the same degree of discrimination of DNA from different persons. Third, some PCR loci are associated with functional genes, which means that they may have been subject to natural selection, possibly leading to greater differences among population subgroups than is found with VNTRs. In developing new systems, it is desirable to choose loci that are not associated with disease-causing genes. These are all problems that can be minimized by proper choice of markers and by care and good technique.

One PCR-based genetic marker, DQA, is widely used. It is quick and reliable, and that makes it particularly useful as a preliminary test. On the average, about 7% of the population have the same DQA type, so that different individuals will be distinguished about 93% of the time. Thus, a wrongly accused person has a good chance of being quickly cleared. Other systems are already in use or are being developed. Eventually, we expect such exact determinations to replace current VNTR methods, with a resulting simplification and speed of analysis and reduction of statistical uncertainties.

One of the most promising of the newer techniques involves amplification of loci containing Short Tandem Repeats (STRs). STRs are scattered throughout the chromosomes in enormous numbers, so that there is an almost unlimited potential for more loci to be discovered and validated for forensic use. Individual STR alleles can usually be individually identified, circumventing the need for matching and binning.

We affirm the statement of the 1992 report that the molecular technology is thoroughly sound and that the results are highly reproducible when appropriate quality-control methods are followed. The uncertainties that we address in this report relate to the effects of possible technical and human errors and the statistical interpretation of population frequencies, not to defects in the methodology itself.

ASSURING LABORATORY ACCURACY

The best assurance of accuracy is careful design and statistical analysis, coupled with scrupulous attention to details. The maintenance of high laboratory standards rests on a foundation of sound quality control and quality assurance. *Quality control* (QC) refers to measures taken to ensure that the DNA typing and interpretation meet a specified standard. *Quality assurance* (QA) refers to steps taken by the laboratory to monitor, verify, and document its performance. Regular proficiency testing and regular auditing of laboratory operations are both essential components of a QA program.

Specific and detailed guidelines on QC and QA have been developed by the Technical Working Group on DNA Analysis Methods (TWGDAM), a group of forensic DNA analysts from government and private laboratories. These guidelines define currently accepted practice. They have been endorsed by the American Society of Crime Laboratory Directors/Laboratory Accreditation Board. These and other organizations provide standards for accreditation. Requirements for accreditation include extensive documentation of all aspects of laboratory operations, proficiency testing, internal and external audits, and a plan to address and correct deficiencies.

The DNA Identification Act of 1994 established a federal framework for setting national standards on quality assurance and proficiency testing. These standards are to be developed by a DNA Advisory Board, appointed by the FBI from a list of nominations made by the National Academy of Sciences and professional societies representing the forensic community. This Advisory Board is now in place and is formulating mechanisms for accreditation and quality control.

We believe that proficiency testing is of great value. These tests can be either open or blind. TWGDAM recommends one fully blind proficiency test per laboratory per year, if such a program can be implemented.

In open proficiency tests, the analyst knows that a test is being conducted. In blind proficiency tests, the analyst does not know that a test is being conducted. A blind test is therefore more likely to detect such errors as might occur in routine operations. However, the logistics of constructing fully blind proficiency tests are formidable. The "evidence" samples have to be submitted through an investigative agency so as to mimic a real case, and unless that is done very convincingly, a laboratory might well suspect that it is being tested.

Whichever kind of test is used, the results are reported and, if errors are made, needed corrective action is taken. Several tests per year are mandated by the various accrediting organizations.

Some commentators have argued that the probability of a laboratory error leading to a reported match for samples from different individuals should be estimated and combined with the probability of randomly drawing a matching profile from the population. We believe this approach to be ill advised. It is difficult to arrive at a meaningful and accurate estimate of the risk of such laboratory errors. For one thing, in this rapidly evolving technology, it is the current practice and not the past record of a laboratory that is relevant, and that necessarily means smaller numbers and consequent statistical uncertainty. For another, the number of proficiency tests required to give an accurate estimate of a low error rate (and it must be low to be acceptable) is enormous and would be outlandishly expensive and disruptive. We believe that such efforts would be badly misplaced and would use resources that could much better be used in other ways, such as improving laboratory standards.

No amount of attention to detail, auditing, and proficiency testing can completely eliminate the risk of error. There is a better approach, one that is in general agreement with the 1992 NRC report: wherever feasible, evidence material should be separated into two or more portions, with one or more portions reserved for possible duplicate tests. Only an independent retest can satisfactorily resolve doubts as to the possibility that the first test was in error. It is usually possible to preserve enough material for possible repeat tests. Even if VNTR tests consume most of the material, it should almost always be possible to reserve enough for independent PCR-based confirmatory tests. The best protection an innocent suspect has from a false match is an independent test, and that opportunity should be made available if at all possible.

Even the strongest evidence will be worthless—or worse, might possibly lead to a false conviction—if the evidence sample did not originate in connection with the crime. Given the great individuating potential of DNA evidence and the relative ease with which it can be mishandled or manipulated by the careless or the unscrupulous, the integrity of the chain of custody is of paramount importance. This means meticulous care, attention to detail, and thorough documentation of every step of the process, from collecting the evidence material to the final laboratory report.

POPULATION GENETICS

If the DNA profile from the evidence sample and that of the suspect match, they may have come from the same person. Alternatively, they might represent a coincidental match between two persons who happen to share the profile. To assess the probability of such a coincidental match, we need to know the frequency of the profile in the population.

Ideally, we would know the frequency of each profile, but short of testing the whole population we cannot know that. We must therefore rely on samples from the population, summarized in a database. Furthermore, the probability of a specific profile is very small, much smaller than the reciprocal of the number of people represented in the database. That means that the great majority of profiles are not found in any database. The analyst must therefore estimate the frequency of a profile from information about the component allele frequencies. That requires some assumptions about the relation between allele frequencies and profile frequencies; it also requires modeling.

Randomly Mating Populations

The simplest assumption relating allele and genotype frequencies is that mates are chosen at random. Perhaps surprisingly, such an assumption provides a good approximation to reality for forensic markers. Of course, matings in the United States are not literally at random; two persons from Oregon are much more likely to be mates than are a person from Oregon and one from Florida. But random-mating genotype proportions occur when mating frequencies are determined by the frequencies of the markers. And if the marker frequencies are the same in Oregon, Florida, and other states, that could lead to random-mating proportions throughout the nation, even though the United States is far from a random-mating unit.

Of course, for some traits the population is not in random-mating proportions. Mates are often chosen for physical and behavioral characteristics. But obviously, VNTRs and other forensic markers are not the basis for choice. For example, people often choose mates with similar height, but unless a forensic marker is closely linked to a possible major gene for height, the forensic genotypes will still be in random-mating proportions.

The simplest way to deal with random mating is to take advantage of the convenient fact that random mating of persons has the same genetic consequences as random combination of eggs and sperm. Suppose that at the A locus, 1/10 of the alleles are A_1 and 1/25 are A_2. Then 1/10 of the eggs carry allele A_1 and of these 1/10 will be fertilized by A_1 sperm, so 1/10 of 1/10, that is $1/10 \times 1/10 = (1/10)^2 = 1/100$ of the fertilized eggs will be of genotype A_1A_1. Similarly 1/25 of the A_1 eggs will be fertilized by A_2 sperm, leading to $(1/10) \times (1/25) = 1/250$ A_1A_2 individuals. However, the A_1A_2 genotype can also be produced, with equal frequency, by A_2 eggs fertilized by A_1 sperm, so the total frequency of A_1A_2 genotypes is twice the product of the allele frequencies, or 1/125. Therefore, the frequencies of the genotypes are:

Homozygote A_1A_1: $(1/10)^2 = 1/100$,
Heterozygote A_1A_2: $2(1/10)(1/25) = 1/125$.

It is conventional in general formulations to use letters instead of numerical fractions. If we designate the frequency of allele A_1 by p_1 and of allele A_2 by p_2 (in this example, $p_1 = 1/10$ and $p_2 = 1/25$), the genotype frequencies are

$$A_1A_1: p_1^2, \qquad\qquad\qquad\qquad\qquad (O.1a)$$
$$A_1A_2: 2p_1p_2. \qquad\qquad\qquad\qquad\qquad (O.1b)$$

Populations in which the genotypes are in random-mating proportions are said to be in Hardy-Weinberg (HW) ratios, named after G. H. Hardy and W. Weinberg, the discoverers of this simple principle.

How well do actual populations agree with HW ratios? One example is given in Table 4.3 (p 94). M and N are two alleles at a blood-group locus. Six studies were done in the white population of New York City, a population that is genetically quite heterogeneous. The data came from blood donors, persons involved in paternity cases, patients, and hospital staff. They involve six studies over a period of almost 10 years. The total number was 6,001 persons, or 12,002 genes. Yet, as the table shows, the overall frequency of heterozygotes is within 1% of its HW expectation. For traits that are not involved in mate selection, the genotypes in actual populations are very close to HW proportions.

With continued random mating, alleles at different loci, even if initially linked on the same chromosome, become separated by crossing over and eventually reach linkage equilibrium (LE). At LE, the frequency of a composite genetic profile is the product of the genotype frequencies at each constituent locus. The rate of approach to LE depends on how close together the loci are on the chromosome. Loci on nonhomologous chromosomes, as almost all forensic loci are, approach LE quickly: the departure from LE is halved each generation. After half a dozen generations, LE can be assumed with sufficient accuracy for forensic purposes. Confirming this, in the large TWGDAM data set, the departure of two-locus pairs from LE in the white population was less than half a percent, and only slightly larger in blacks and Hispanics (Table 4.7, p 110). The deviations from expectations in individual cases were small and in both directions, as expected. Under HW and LE assumptions, the expected proportion of a specific genetic profile can be readily computed by calculating the genotype frequencies at each locus and multiplying them. In the forensic literature, that calculating procedure is called the *product rule*.

For illustration, suppose that at a second locus the two relevant alleles are B_1 and B_2, with frequencies 1/15 and 1/40. Then the frequency of genotype B_1B_2 is $2(1/15)(1/40) = 1/300$. Now, putting this together with the A locus considered above, we find that the frequency of the composite genotype A_1A_1 B_1B_2 is $1/100 \times 1/300 = 1/30,000$. And likewise for more than two loci; genotype frequencies at each locus are multiplied.

Such estimates of the frequency of a particular profile in a population are, of course, subject to uncertainty. Even moderate-sized DNA databases (drawn from samples of several hundred persons) are subject to statistical uncertainty, and in smaller ones, the uncertainty is greater. In addition, the database might not properly represent the population that is relevant to a particular case. Finally, the assumptions of HW and LE, although reasonable approximations for most populations, are not exact. We shall elaborate on this point later, but to anticipate, we believe that it is safe to assume that the uncertainty of a profile frequency calculated by our procedures from adequate databases (at least several hundred persons) is less than a factor of about 10 in either direction. To illustrate, if a profile frequency is calculated to be one in 100 million, it is safe to say that the true value is almost always between one in 10 million and one in a billion.

We now consider modifications of the product-rule calculations to make them more realistic in the face of uncertainties.

Population Structure

The population of the United States is made up of subpopulations descended from different parts of the globe and not fully homogenized. The authors of the 1992 NRC report were concerned that profile frequencies calculated from population averages might be seriously misleading for particular subpopulations. Extensive studies from a wide variety of databases show that there are indeed substantial frequency differences among the major racial and linguistic groups (black, Hispanic, American Indian, east Asian, and white). And within these groups, there is often a statistically significant departure from random proportions. As we said earlier, those departures are usually small, and formulae based on random mating assumptions are usually quite accurate. So, the product rule, although certainly not exact for real populations, is often a very good approximation.

The main reason for departures from random-mating proportions in forensic DNA markers is population structure due to incomplete mixing of ancestral stocks. Suppose that we estimate genotype frequencies in a subgroup by applying the product rule to allele frequencies based on overall population averages. To the extent that the subgroups have different allele frequencies, such an estimate will be too high for heterozygotes and too low for homozygotes. The reason for this is that matings within a subgroup will tend to be between (perhaps distant) relatives, and relatives share alleles. Thus, matings within a subgroup will produce more homozygotes and fewer heterozygotes than if the mates were chosen at random from the whole population.

In contrast to this systematic effect on homozygote and heterozygote frequencies, departures from LE because of population substructure are largely random and are not predictable in direction. Consequently, when several loci are involved, deviations in opposite directions tend to cancel.

Dealing with Subpopulations

The writers of the 1992 NRC report were concerned that there might be important population substructure and recommended an *interim ceiling principle* (discussed later in this overview) to address that concern. We take a different tack. We assume that there is undetected substructure in the population and adjust the product rule accordingly. There is a simple procedure for doing this. Since using the HW rule for heterozygote frequencies provides an overestimate if there is substructure, we employ the product rule as a conservative estimate for heterozygotes. But we need a modification to correct the opposite bias in the homozygote estimates.

For VNTRs, a single band in a lane does not necessarily imply a homozygote. It might be a heterozygote with two alleles too close together to distinguish, or one of the alleles, for any of several reasons, might not be detected. It has become standard practice in such cases to replace p^2, the homozygote frequency as estimated by Equation O.1a (p 26), by 2p, where p is the bin frequency. It is easily shown (Chapter 4, p 105) that this substitution provides a conservative correction for homozygotes. So we follow earlier recommendations (e.g., the 1992 report) to use the product rule for VNTRs and to replace p^2 by 2p for all single bands. This is called the *2p rule*. It is illustrated in the example at the end of this overview.

The 2p rule has been criticized as being more conservative than necessary. However, with VNTRs, double bands greatly outnumber single bands, so the bias is usually not great. We retain the rule for two reasons: It is conservative, and it is thoroughly ingrained in standard forensic practice. We caution, however, that it was intended for criminal cases and might not be appropriate for other applications, such as determining paternity. It should not be used except as a conservative modification for rare alleles when heterozygotes may appear to be homozygotes.

Another rule is applicable when there is no problem in distinguishing homozygotes from heterozygotes, as with most PCR-based systems. The procedure is to replace p^2 with the expression $p^2 + p(1-p)\bar{\theta}$, where $\bar{\theta}$ is an empirically determined measure of population subdivision. The measured value of $\bar{\theta}$ is usually considerably less than 0.01 for forensic markers in the United States, so we recommend 0.01 as a conservative value, except for very small, isolated populations of interrelated people, where 0.03 may be more appropriate.

Persons from the Same Subpopulation

Usually, the subgroup to which the suspect belongs is irrelevant, since we want to calculate the probability of a match on the assumption that the suspect is innocent and the evidence DNA was left by someone else. The proper question is: What is the probability that a randomly chosen person, other than the suspect, has the genetic profile of the evidence DNA? That is the question we have dealt with so far. In some cases, however, it may be known that the suspect(s) is(are) from the same subpopulation as the source of the evidence DNA. An instance would be a crime committed in a small, isolated village, with all potential suspects from the same village. Ideally, the calculation should be based on the allele frequencies in that particular village, but usually such frequencies will not be known.

An alternative is to measure the degree of population subdivision and, using that, to write expressions for the conditional probability that, given the genotype of the first person, a second person from the same subgroup will have that genotype. The appropriate expressions for the match probability are

$$A_1A_1: \text{Prob} = \frac{\left[2\bar{\theta} + (1-\bar{\theta})p_1\right]\left[3\bar{\theta} + (1-\bar{\theta})p_1\right]}{(1+\bar{\theta})(1+2\bar{\theta})}, \tag{O.2a}$$

$$A_1A_2: \text{Prob} = \frac{2\left[\bar{\theta} + (1 - \bar{\theta})p_1\right]\left[\bar{\theta} + (1 - \bar{\theta})p_2\right]}{(1 + \bar{\theta})(1 + 2\bar{\theta})}. \qquad (O.2b)$$

Although these expressions might appear complex, they are actually a straightforward adjustment of the standard HW formulae. Notice that if $\bar{\theta} = 0$, the formulae are p_1^2 and $2p_1p_2$, the HW formulae. As before, p_1 and p_2 are obtained from the frequencies in the database. We suggest 0.01 as a suitable value of $\bar{\theta}$. If the population is very small and isolated, or if a still more conservative estimate is desired, 0.03 can be used.

As an example, consider the A locus already used (p 26), in which $p_1 = 1/10$ and $p_2 = 1/25$. Then the match probability for the heterozygote, A_1A_2, is $2(1/10)(1/25) = 1/125$ or 0.008 when $\bar{\theta} = 0$, 0.0105 when $\bar{\theta} = 0.01$, and 0.0160 when $\bar{\theta} = 0.03$. Clearly, this calculation is more conservative than the simple product rule.

SOME STATISTICAL CONSIDERATIONS

The Reference Database

Ideally, the reference data set, from which profile frequencies are calculated, would be a simple random sample or a scientifically structured random sample from the relevant population. But this can be an impracticable ideal. For one thing, it is not always clear which population is most relevant. Should the sample be local or national? Should it include both sexes? If only males, should it include only those in the ages that commit most crimes? For another thing, random sampling is usually difficult, expensive, and impractical, so we are often forced to rely on convenience samples. Databases come from such diverse sources as blood banks, paternity-testing laboratories, laboratory personnel, clients in genetic-counseling centers, law-enforcement officers, and people charged with crimes. The saving point is that the DNA markers in which we are interested are believed theoretically and observed empirically to be essentially uncorrelated with the rules by which the samples are chosen.

We are confident that these convenience samples are appropriate for forensic uses, mainly for two reasons. First, the loci generally used for identification are usually not parts of functional genes and therefore are unlikely to be correlated with any behavioral or physical traits that might be associated with different subsets of the population. Second, empirical tests have shown only very minor differences among the frequencies of DNA markers from different subpopulations or geographical areas.

Indeed, samples from different subgroups often show statistically significant differences. This is especially true if the sample sizes are large, since in large samples, small differences can be statistically significant. But we are more concerned with the magnitude of the difference and the uncertainty in our calculations than with formal statistical significance. We shall deal with this further on.

Match Probability, Likelihood Ratio, and Two Fallacies

Forensic calculations are conventionally presented in one of two ways: the probability of a random match (called the *match probability*), calculated from the frequencies of DNA markers in the database; and the *likelihood ratio* (LR). The LR is the ratio of the probability of a match if the DNA in the evidence sample and that from the suspect came from the same person to the probability of a match if they came from different persons. Since the probability of a match when the samples came from the same person is one (unless there has been a mistake), the likelihood ratio is simply the reciprocal of the match probability.

A likelihood ratio of 1,000 says that the profile match is 1,000 times as likely if the DNA samples came from the same person as it would be if they came from two randomly chosen members of the population. It does *not* say that if the DNA samples match then they are 1,000 times as likely to have come from the same person as from different persons. It is important to keep this distinction straight. The misstatement, a logical reversal of the first, is an example of "the prosecutor's fallacy."

Although in the simplest cases the match probability and the likelihood ratio provide the same information (because one is the reciprocal of the other), there are cases in which the likelihood ratio is conceptually simpler. One such case happens with a mixed sample. This is illustrated in Chapter 5 (p 129) with an example in which the evidence sample has four bands, two of which are shared with the suspect. The match-probability approach, used in the 1992 NRC report, ignores some of the data, whereas a complete analysis is easily obtained by using the LR.

The second fallacy is "the defendant's fallacy." That is to assume that in a given population, anyone with the same profile as the evidence sample is as likely to have left the sample as is the suspect. If 100 persons in a metropolitan area are expected to have the same DNA profile as the evidence sample, it is a fallacy to conclude that the probability that the suspect contributed the sample is only 1/100. The suspect was originally identified by other evidence; such evidence does not exist for the 99 other persons expected to have the same profile. However, if the suspect was found through a search of a large DNA database, that changes the situation, as we shall soon discuss.

Bayes's Theorem

The reason that the prosecutor's fallacy is inviting is that, even though it gives a wrong answer, it purports to answer the question in which the court is really interested—namely, what is the probability that the evidence sample and the suspect sample came from the same person? Neither the match probability nor the likelihood ratio gives this. Yet, the latter can be used to obtain this probability, provided we are willing to assume a value for the *prior probability* that the two samples have a common source. The prior probability that the two samples came from the same person is the probability of that event based on evidence other than the DNA.

The principle is more easily expressed if stated as odds rather than probability. (Odds are the ratio of the probability that an event will occur to the probability that it will not: Odds = Prob/(1 − Prob); if the probability is 2/3, the odds in favor are 2/1, or as conventionally written, 2:1.) Specifically, the final (*posterior*) odds that the suspect and evidence DNA came from the same person are the prior odds multiplied by the likelihood ratio (LR):

$$\text{Posterior odds} = \text{Prior odds} \times \text{LR}.$$

In other words, whatever you believe the odds to be without the DNA evidence, they are multiplied by LR when the DNA evidence is included. Although this rule (Bayes's Theorem) is routinely used in paternity cases, it has hardly ever been used in criminal cases not involving proof of paternity.

Since the prior odds are hardly ever known even approximately and are usually subjective, a practice that has been advocated is to give posterior odds (or probabilities) for a range of prior odds (or probabilities). If the likelihood ratio is very high, uncertainty about the value of the prior probability may make little difference in the court's decision.

Suppose that the LR is one million. If the prior odds are 1:10, the posterior odds are 100,000:1; if the prior odds are 1:100, the posterior odds are still 10,000:1.

Suspect Identified by Database Search

A special circumstance arises when the suspect is identified not by an eyewitness or by circumstantial evidence but rather by a search through a large DNA database. If the only reason that the person becomes a suspect is that his DNA profile turned up in a database, the calculations must be modified. There are several approaches, of which we discuss two. The first, advocated by the 1992 NRC report, is to base probability calculations solely on loci not used in the search. That is a sound procedure, but it wastes information, and if too many loci are used for identification of the suspect, not enough might be left for an adequate subsequent analysis. That will become less of a problem as STRs and other systems with many loci become more widely used.

A second procedure is to apply a simple correction: Multiply the match probability by the size of the database searched. This is the procedure we recommend.

The analysis assumes that the database, although perhaps large, is nevertheless a small fraction of the whole population. At present, that is the usual situation. However, as the databases grow large enough to be a substantial fraction of the population, a more complicated calculation is required. Although such a calculation can be straightforward, it is best handled on a case-by-case basis.

Uniqueness

Another issue—one that has not been resolved by the courts—is uniqueness. The 1992 NRC report said: "Regardless of the calculated frequency, an expert should—given . . . the relatively small number of loci used and the available population data—avoid assertions in court that a particular genotype is unique in the population." Some courts have held that statements that a profile is unique are improper. Yet, with existing databases and *a fortiori* with larger numbers of loci, likelihood ratios much higher than the population of the world are often found. An LR of 60 billion is more than 10 times the world population. Should a profile that rare be regarded as unique?

The definition of uniqueness is outside our province. It is for the courts to decide, but in case such a decision is to be made, we show how to do the relevant calculations. Before a suspect has been profiled, the probability that at least one other person in a population of N unrelated persons has the profile of the evidence DNA is at most NP, where P is the probability of the profile. Then the probability that the profile is unique is at least $1 - NP$.

Suppose the calculated profile probability $P = 1/(60 \text{ billion})$ and the world population N is taken as 6 billion. Then $NP = 1/10$. The probability that the profile is unique, except possibly for relatives, is at least about 9/10.

Uncertainty About Estimated Frequencies

Match probabilities are estimated from a database, and such calculations are subject to uncertainties. The accuracy of the estimate will depend on the genetic model, the actual allele frequencies, and the size of the database. In Chapter 5 (p 146) we explain how to compute confidence limits on the probabilities, if the databases are regarded as random samples from the populations they represent. That, however, includes only part of the uncertainty. Remaining is the uncertainty due, not to the small sample size, but to the possibilities that the database is not representative of the population of interest or that the mathematical model might not be fully appropriate. We therefore take a more realistic, empirical approach. As mentioned earlier, the uncertainty of a profile-frequency calculation that uses our methods and an adequate database (at least several hundred persons) is less than about 10-fold in either direction. We now explain where this conclusion comes from.

We used the published data and graphs assembled from around the world by the FBI to determine the extent of error if an *incorrect* database is used. That should provide an upper limit for the uncertainty with the *correct* database. For example, suppose a crime is committed in Colorado by a man known to be white.

In the absence of a local database, a national white database is used. Graphs (examples are Figures 5.3 and 5.4, p 150 and 152) show that the individual values that are possibly incorrectly estimated lie within 10-fold above and below the "correct" value. We conclude that it is reasonable to regard calculated multilocus match probabilities as accurate within a factor of 10 either way. This is true for various subsets within the white, black, Hispanic, and east Asian populations. However, if the database from the wrong racial group is used, the error may be larger (Figure 5.5, p 153). That argues for the use of the correct racial database if that can be ascertained; otherwise, calculations should be made for all relevant racial groups, i.e., those to which possible suspects belong. The databases should be large enough to have some statistical accuracy (at least a few hundred persons), and alleles represented fewer than five times should be rebinned (grouped so that no bin has fewer than five).

Additional information comes from comparison of profiles within the databases. An early study used FBI and Lifecodes data for blacks, whites, Southeast Hispanics, and Southwest Hispanics. Among 7,628,360 pairs of profiles from within those databases, no four- or five-locus matching profiles were found, and only one three-locus match was seen. A newer and more extensive analysis, compiling data from numerous TWGDAM sources, summarized a large number of profiles from white, black, and Hispanic databases. Of 58 million pairwise comparisons within racial groups, only two possible four-locus matches were found, and none were found for five or six loci.

We conclude that, when several loci are used, the probability of a coincidental match is very small and that properly calculated match probabilities are correct within a factor of about 10 either way. If the calculated probability of a random match between the suspect and evidence DNA is 1/(100 million), we can say with confidence that the correct value is very likely between 1/(10 million) and 1/(1 billion).

PCR-Based Tests

As already mentioned, PCR-based tests have a number of advantages. They include the ability to identify individual alleles, as well as simplicity and quick turn-around. But there are disadvantages. Most of the loci used have a small number of alleles, so that many more loci are required for the same statistical power as provided by a few VNTRs. STRs are also based on repeating units, have a high mutation rate (although not as high as some VNTRs), have a fairly large number of alleles, and are usually capable of unique allelic identification. With 12 STR loci, there is discriminatory power comparable to that of four or five VNTRs, and comparisons between geographical and racial groups show similarities and differences comparable to those of VNTRs.

The quantity $\bar{\theta}$, which we use as a measure of population substructure, is determined largely by the population history rather than by the frequency of the alleles involved. It is also very small, less than about 0.01 in the United States. There has not been the extensive sampling of subpopulations and geographical areas for PCR-based systems that has been done with VNTRs. New data show low values of $\bar{\theta}$ and good agreement with IIW and LE. The uncertainty range appears to be about the same as that for VNTRs. We therefore believe that STRs can take their place along with VNTRs as forensic tools. They circumvent most of the matching and binning problems that VNTRs entail.

THE CEILING PRINCIPLES

The most controversial recommendations of the 1992 NRC report are the ceiling principle and the interim ceiling principle. They were intended to place a lower limit on the size of the profile frequency by setting threshold values for allele frequencies used in calculations. The ceiling principle calls for sampling 100 persons from each of 15-20 genetically homogeneous populations spanning the racial and ethnic diversity of groups represented in the United States. For each allele, the highest frequency among the groups sampled, or 5%, whichever is larger, would be used. Then the product rule would be applied to those values to determine the profile frequency. But the data needed for applying this principle have not been gathered. We share the view of those who criticize it on practical and statistical grounds and who see no scientific justification for its use.

The 1992 report recommended further that until the ceiling principle could be put into effect, an interim ceiling principle be applied. In contrast to the ceiling principle, the interim ceiling principle has been widely used, and sometimes misused. The rule says: "In applying the multiplication [product] rule, the 95% upper confidence limit of the frequency of each allele should be calculated for separate US 'racial' groups and the highest of these values or 10% (whichever is larger) should be used. Data on at least three major 'races' (e.g., Caucasians, blacks, Hispanics, east Asians, and American Indians) should be analyzed."

The interim ceiling principle has the advantage that in any particular case it gives the same answer irrespective of the racial group. That is also a disadvantage, for it does not permit the use of well-established differences in frequencies among different races; the method is inflexible and cannot be adjusted to the circumstances of a particular case. The interim ceiling principle has been widely criticized for other reasons as well, and we summarize the criticisms in Chapter 5 (p 157). We agree with those criticisms.

Our view is that sufficient data have been gathered to establish that neither ceiling principle is needed. We have given alternative procedures, all of which are conservative but less arbitrary.

Although we recommend other procedures and believe that the interim ceiling principle is not needed, we recognize that it has been used and some will probably continue to use it. To anticipate this possibility, we offer several suggestions in

Chapter 5 that will make the principle more workable and less susceptible to creative misapplications.

DNA IN THE COURTS

Prior to 1992, there was controversy over our two main issues, laboratory error and population substructure. The 1992 NRC report was intended to resolve the controversy, but the arguments went on. One reason is that the scientific community has not spoken with one voice; defense and prosecution witnesses have given highly divergent statistical estimates or have disagreed as to the validity of all estimates. For this reason, some courts have held that the analyses are not admissible in court. The courts, however, have accepted the soundness of the typing procedures, especially for VNTRs. The major disagreement in the courts has been over population substructure and possible technical or human errors. The interim ceiling principle, in particular, has also been the subject of considerable disagreement. We hope that our report will ease the acceptance of DNA analysis in the courts and reduce the controversy.

We shall not summarize the various court findings and opinions here. The interested reader can find this information in Chapter 6, which also discusses the implications that our recommendations could have on the production and introduction of DNA evidence in court proceedings.

CONCLUSIONS AND RECOMMENDATIONS

Conclusions and recommendations are given at the ends of the chapters in which the relevant subject is discussed. For convenience, they are repeated here.

Admissibility of DNA Evidence (Chapter 2)

DNA analysis is one of the greatest technical achievements for criminal investigation since the discovery of fingerprints. Methods of DNA profiling are firmly grounded in molecular technology. When profiling is done with appropriate care, the results are highly reproducible. In particular, the methods are almost certain to exclude an innocent suspect.

One of the most widely used techniques involves VNTRs. These loci are extremely variable, but individual alleles cannot be distinguished, because of intrinsic measurement variability, and the analysis requires statistical procedures. The laboratory procedure involves radioactivity and requires a month or more for full analysis. PCR-based methods are prompt, require only a small amount of material, and can yield unambiguous identification of individual alleles.

The state of the profiling technology and the methods for estimating frequencies and related statistics have progressed to the point where the admissibility of properly collected and analyzed DNA data should not be in doubt. We expect continued development of new and better methods and hope for their prompt validation, so that they can quickly be brought into use.

Laboratory Errors (Chapter 3)

The occurrence of errors can be minimized by scrupulous care in evidence-collecting, sample-handling, laboratory procedures, and case review. Detailed guidelines for QC and QA (quality control and quality assurance), which are updated regularly, are produced by several organizations, including TWGDAM. ASCLD-LAB is established as an accrediting agency. The 1992 NRC report recommended that a National Committee on Forensic DNA Typing (NCFDT) be formed to oversee the setting of DNA-analysis standards. The DNA Identification Act of 1994 gives this responsibility to a DNA Advisory Board appointed by the FBI. We recognize the need for guidelines and standards, and for accreditation by appropriate organizations.

Recommendation 3.1. Laboratories should adhere to high quality standards (such as those defined by TWGDAM and the DNA Advisory Board) and make every effort to be accredited for DNA work (by such organizations as ASCLD-LAB).

Proficiency Tests

Regular proficiency tests, both within the laboratory and by external examiners, are one of the best ways of assuring high standards. To the extent that it is feasible, some of the tests should be blind.

Recommendation 3.2: Laboratories should participate regularly in proficiency tests, and the results should be available for court proceedings.

Duplicate Tests

We recognize that no amount of care and proficiency testing can eliminate the possibility of error. However, duplicate tests, performed as independently as possible, can reduce the risk of error enormously. The best protection that an innocent suspect has against an error that could lead to a false conviction is the opportunity for an independent retest.

Recommendation 3.3: Whenever feasible, forensic samples should be divided into two or more parts at the earliest practicable stage and the unused parts retained to permit additional tests. The used and saved portions should be stored and handled separately. Any additional tests should be performed independently of the first by personnel not involved in the first test and preferably in a different laboratory.

Population Genetics (Chapter 4)

Sufficient data now exist for various groups and subgroups within the United States that analysts should present the best estimates for profile frequencies. For VNTRs, using the 2p rule for single bands and HW for double bands is generally conservative for an individual locus. For multiple loci, departures from linkage equilibrium are not great enough to cause errors comparable to those from uncertainty of allele frequencies estimated from databases.

With appropriate consideration of the data, the principles in this report can be applied to PCR-based tests. For those in which exact genotypes can be determined, the 2p rule should not be used. A conservative estimate is given by using the HW relation for heterozygotes and a conservative value of $\bar{\theta}$ in Equation 4.4a for homozygotes.

Recommendation 4.1: In general, the calculation of a profile frequency should be made with the product rule. If the race of the person who left the evidence-sample DNA is known, the database for the person's race should be used; if the race is not known, calculations for all racial groups to which possible suspects belong should be made. For systems such as VNTRs, in which a heterozygous locus can be mistaken for a homozygous one, if an upper bound on the genotypic frequency at an apparently homozygous locus (single band) is desired, then twice the allele (bin) frequency, 2p, should be used instead of p^2. For systems in which exact genotypes can be determined, $p^2 + p(1-p)\bar{\theta}$ should be used for the frequency at such a locus instead of p^2. A conservative value of $\bar{\theta}$ for the US population is 0.01; for some small, isolated populations, a value of 0.03 may be more appropriate. For both kinds of systems, $2p_ip_j$ should be used for heterozygotes.

A more conservative value of $\bar{\theta} = 0.03$ might be chosen for PCR-based systems in view of the greater uncertainty of calculations for such systems because of less extensive and less varied population data than for VNTRs.

Evidence DNA and Suspect from the Same Subgroup

Sometimes there is evidence that the suspect and other possible sources of the sample belong to the same subgroup. That can happen, e.g., if they are all members of an isolated village. In this case, a modification of the procedure is desirable.

Recommendation 4.2: If the particular subpopulation from which the evidence sample came is known, the allele frequencies for the specific subgroup should be used as described in Recommendation 4.1. If allele frequencies for the subgroup are not available, although data for the full population are, then the calculations should use the population-structure Equations 4.10 for each locus, and the resulting values should then be multiplied.

Insufficient Data

For some groups—and several American Indian and Inuit tribes are in this category—there are insufficient data to estimate frequencies reliably, and even the overall average might be unreliable. In this case, data from other, related groups provide the best information. The groups chosen should be the most closely related for which adequate databases exist. These might be chosen because of geographical proximity, or a physical anthropologist might be consulted. There should be a limit on the number of such subgroups analyzed to prevent inclusion of more remote groups less relevant to the case.

Recommendation 4.3: If the person who contributed the evidence sample is from a group or tribe for which no adequate database exists, data from several other groups or tribes thought to be closely related to it should be used. The profile frequency should be calculated as described in Recommendation 4.1 for each group or tribe.

Dealing with Relatives

In some instances, there is evidence that one or more relatives of the suspect are possible perpetrators.

Recommendation 4.4: If the possible contributors of the evidence sample include relatives of the suspect, DNA profiles of those relatives should be obtained. If these profiles cannot be obtained, the probability of finding the evidence profile in those relatives should be calculated with Formulae 4.8 or 4.9.

Statistical Issues (Chapter 5)

Confidence limits for profile probabilities, based on allele frequencies and the size of the database, can be calculated by methods explained in this report. We recognize, however, that confidence limits address only part of the uncertainty. For a more realistic estimate, we examined empirical data from the comparison of different subpopulations and of subpopulations within the whole. The empirical studies show that the differences between the frequencies of the individual profiles estimated by the product rule from different adequate subpopulation databases (at least several hundred persons) are within a factor of about 10 of each other, and that provides a guide to the uncertainty of the determination for a single profile. For very small estimated profile frequencies, the uncertainty can be greater, both because of the greater relative uncertainty of individually small probabilities and because more loci are likely to be multiplied. But with very small probabilities, even a larger relative error is not likely to change the conclusion.

Database Searches

If the suspect is identified through a DNA database search, the interpretation of the match probability and likelihood ratio given in Chapter 4 should be modified.

Recommendation 5.1: When the suspect is found by a search of DNA databases, the random-match probability should be multiplied by N, the number of persons in the database.

If one wishes to describe the impact of the DNA evidence under the hypothesis that the source of the evidence sample is someone in the database, then the likelihood ratio should be divided by N. As databases become more extensive, another problem may arise. If the database searched includes a large proportion of the population, the analysis must take that into account. In the extreme case, a search of the whole population should, of course, provide a definitive answer.

Uniqueness

With an increasing number of loci available for forensic analysis, we are approaching the time when each person's profile is unique (except for identical twins and possibly other close relatives). Suppose that, in a population of N unrelated persons, a given DNA profile has probability P. The probability (before a suspect has been profiled) that the *particular* profile observed in the evidence sample is not unique is at most NP.

A lower bound on the probability that *every* person is unique depends on the population size, the number of loci, and the heterozygosity of the individual loci. Neglecting population structure and close relatives, 10 loci with a geometric mean heterozygosity of 95% give a probability greater than about 0.999 that no two unrelated persons in the world have the same profile. Once it is decided what level of probability constitutes uniqueness, appropriate calculations can readily be made.

We expect that the calculation in the first paragraph will be the one more often employed.

Matching and Binning

VNTR data are essentially continuous, and, in principle, a continuous model should be used to analyze them. The methods generally used, however, involve taking measurement uncertainty into account by determining a match window. Two procedures for determining match probabilities are the floating-bin and the fixed-bin methods. The floating-bin method is statistically preferable but requires access to a computerized database. The fixed-bin method is more widely used and understood, and the necessary data tables are widely and readily available. When our fixed-bin recommendation is followed, the two methods lead to very similar results. Both methods are acceptable.

Recommendation 5.2: If floating bins are used to calculate the random-match probabilities, each bin should coincide with the corresponding match window. If fixed bins are employed, then the fixed bin that has the largest frequency among those overlapped by the match window should be used.

Ceiling Principles

The abundance of data in different ethnic groups within the major races and the genetically and statistically sound methods recommended in this report imply that both the ceiling principle and the interim ceiling principle are unnecessary.

Further Research

The rapid rate of discovery of new markers in connection with human gene-mapping should lead to many new markers that are highly polymorphic, mutable, and selectively neutral, but which, unlike VNTRs, can be amplified by PCR and for which individual alleles can usually be distinguished unambiguously with none of the statistical problems associated with matching and binning. Furthermore, radioactive probes need not be used with many other markers, so identification can be prompt and problems associated with using radioactive materials can be avoided. It should soon be possible to have systems so powerful that no statistical and population analyses will be needed, and (except possibly for close relatives) each person in a population can be uniquely identified.

Recommendation 5.3: Research into the identification and validation of more and better marker systems for forensic analysis should continue with a view to making each profile unique.

Legal Issues (Chapter 6)

In assimilating scientific developments, the legal system necessarily lags behind the scientific world. Before making use of evidence derived from scientific advances, courts must scrutinize the proposed testimony to determine its suitability for use at trial, and controversy within the scientific community often is regarded as grounds for the exclusion of the scientific evidence. Although some controversies that have come to closure in the scientific literature continue to limit the presentation of DNA evidence in some jurisdictions, courts are making more use of the ongoing research into the population genetics of DNA profiles. We hope that our review of the research will contribute to this process.

Our conclusions and recommendations for reducing the risk of laboratory error, for applying human population genetics to DNA profiles, and for handling uncertainties in estimates of profile frequencies and match probabilities might affect the application of the rules for the discovery and admission of evidence in court. Many suggestions can be offered to make our recommendations most effective: for example, that every jurisdiction should make it possible for all defendants to have broad discovery and independent experts; that accreditation, proficiency testing, and the opportunity for independent testing (whenever feasible) should be prerequisites to the admission of laboratory findings; that in resolving disputes over the adequacy or interpretation of DNA tests, the power of the court to appoint its own experts should be exercised more frequently; and that experts should not be barred from presenting any scientifically acceptable estimate of a random-match probability. We have chosen, however, to make no formal recommendations on such matters of legal policy; we do, however, make a recommendation concerning scientific evidence—namely, the need for behavioral research that will assist legal decision makers in developing standards for communicating about DNA in the courtroom.

Recommendation 6.1: Behavioral research should be carried out to identify any conditions that might cause a trier of fact to misinterpret evidence on DNA profiling and to assess how well various ways of presenting expert testimony on DNA can reduce such misunderstandings.

We trust that our efforts to explain the state of the forensic science and some of the social-science findings that are pertinent to resolving these issues will contribute to better-informed judgments by courts and legislatures.

ILLUSTRATIVE EXAMPLE

A Typical Case

As an illustration, we have chosen an example that involves VNTR loci. The methods used for the other systems are very similar, except that they usually do not involve the complications of matching and binning, so the more complicated situation is better for illustration. We shall analyze the same data in several ways.

Suppose that samples of blood are obtained from a crime scene and DNA from two suspects, 1 and 2. We should like to know whether the profile of either suspect matches the profile of the evidence DNA.

First we isolate the DNA from the three samples, making sure that all three have been handled separately and that each step in the chain of custody has been checked and documented. The DNA is first cut into small segments by an enzyme, Hae III. The fragments from the evidence sample (E) and from the two suspects (S1 and S2) are placed in small wells in the gel, each sample in a separate lane. Along with these three are a number of controls, as illustrated in Figure O.4, each with its own lane. The laboratory has been careful not to put any of the three DNA samples into adjacent lanes to prevent possible leakage of DNA into the wrong lane.

After being placed in an electric field for a carefully determined time, the DNA in all the lanes is transferred by blotting to a nylon membrane (stronger and easier to handle than the gel). Then a radioactive probe that is specific for locus D2S44 is flooded onto the membrane. The probe adheres to the corresponding region in the DNA sample, and any nonadhering probes are washed off. The membrane is then placed in contact with a photographic film to prepare an autorad. Figure O.7 illustrates the result in this case.

The rough size of the fragment can be determined from the scale in the figure. In practice, the scale is a ladder, a group of DNA fragments that differ from each other in increments of approximately 1,000 base pairs (the ladder can be seen in Figure O.4) It is immediately apparent (Figure O.7) that E and S1 match as far as the eye can tell, but that S2 is clearly different. That alone is sufficient to exclude S2 as a suspect. The sizes of the six bands are determined by comparison with the ladder. This operation is ordinarily done by a computer programmed to scan the autorad and measure the sizes of the bands.

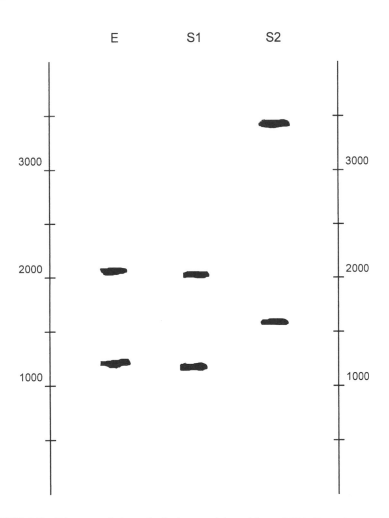

FIGURE O.7   Diagram of a hypothetical autorad for evidence DNA (E) and two suspects (S1 and S2). Note that E and S1 appear to match, whereas S2 is clearly not the source of the evidence DNA. The numbers at the two sides are numbers of base pairs.

TABLE O.2   The Uncertainty Windows for a VNTR Marker (Probe D2S44) in an Illustrative Example

Source	Band	Size	2.5%	Uncertainty Window
E	Larger	1,901	48	1,853-1,949
	Smaller	1,137	28	1,109-1,165
S1	Larger	1,876	47	1,829-1,923
	Smaller	1,125	28	1,097-1,153
S2	Larger	3,455	86	3,369-3,541
	Smaller	1,505	38	1,467-1,543

The calculations (or computer output) are shown in Table O.2. The measured value of each band is given, along with upper and lower limits of the uncertainty window, which spans the range from 2.5% below to 2.5% above the measured value. Comparing the uncertainty window of S1 and E for the smaller band, we see that the windows overlap; the upper limit of S1, 1,153, is within the range, 1,109 to 1,165, of E. Likewise, the uncertainty windows of the larger bands also overlap. In contrast, the uncertainty windows for the two bands from S2 do not overlap any of the evidence bands. So our visual impression is confirmed by the measurements. S2 is cleared, whereas S1 remains as a possible source of the evidence DNA.

The next step is to compute the size of the match window (Table O.3), which will be used to find the frequency of this marker in a relevant database of DNA marker frequencies. This is the measurement E plus and minus 5% of

TABLE O.3   Match Windows and Frequencies for Several VNTR Markers in an Illustrative Example

Locus	Band	Size	5%	Match Window	Bin(s)	Freq.
D2S44	Larger	1,901	95	1,806-1,996	11, 12	0.083
	Smaller	1,137	57	1,080-1,194	6	0.024
D17S79	Larger	1,685	84	1,601-1,769	9, 10	0.263
	Smaller	1,120	56	1,064-1,176	4, 6	0.015
D1S7	Single				14	0.068
D4S139	Larger				10	0.072
	Smaller				13	0.131
D10S28	Larger				9	0.047
	Smaller				16	0.065

Probability of a random match, 5 loci:
P = 2(0.083)(0.024) × 2(0.263)(0.015) × 2(0.068) × 2(0.072)(0.131) × 2(0.047)(0.065)
  = 1/(2 billion)
Uncertainty range: 1/(200 million) to 1/(20 billion)

its value. So for the larger band the limits are $1,901 - 95$ and $1,901 + 95$, or 1,806 to 1,996. We then look at a bin-frequency table, shown in Table O.1 (p 20). The table shows that the lower limit, 1,806, lies in bin 11, and the upper limit, 1,996, is in bin 12. Notice that the frequency of the alleles in bin 11 is 0.083 and that in bin 12 is 0.050, so we take the larger value, 0.083. This is shown as the frequency in the rightmost column of Table O.3.

Continuing, we find the size of the smaller band of E is 1,137, and its lower and upper limits are 1,080 and 1,194. Both of these values are within bin 6 in Table O.1. Its frequency is 0.024, shown in the right column of Table O.3.

Now the membrane is "stripped," meaning that the probes are washed off. Then the membrane is flooded with a new set of probes, this time specific for locus D17S79. Assume that the measurements of E are 1,685 and 1,120, and that the uncertainty windows of E and S1 again overlap. The ± 5% match window for the larger band is 1,601 to 1,769, and comparing this with Table O.1 shows that the match window overlaps bins 9 and 10, of which 9 has the higher frequency, 0.263. In the same way, the match window for the smaller band overlaps bands 4 and 6, and the larger frequency is 0.015.

Again, the membrane is stripped and a new probe specific for D1S7 is added. This time, there is only one band. The individual is either homozygous, or heterozygous and the second band did not appear on the gel. So we apply the 2p rule, doubling the frequency from 0.068 to 0.136. Now the process is continued through two more probes, D4S139 and D10S28, with the frequencies shown in the Table O.3. (If you wish, you may verify these numbers from Table 4.5, p 101, which also shows frequencies for black and Southeastern Hispanic databases.)

The next step is to compute the probability that a randomly chosen person has the same profile as the evidence sample, E. For this, we use the product rule with the 2p rule for the single band. For each double band, we compute twice the product of the two frequencies. For the single band, we use twice the allele frequency. Thus, going down through the table, the probability is

$$2(0.083)(.024) \times 2(0.263)(0.015) \times 2(0.068) \times 2(0.072)(0.131) \times 2(0.047)(0.065)$$
$$= 4.9 \times 10^{-10}, \text{ or about 1 in 2 billion.}$$

The maximum uncertainty of this estimate is about 10-fold in either direction, so the true value is estimated to lie between 1 in 200 million and 1 in 20 billion.

Suspect Found by Searching a Database

In the example above, we assumed that the suspect was found through an eyewitness, circumstantial evidence, or from some other information linking him to the crime. Now assume that the suspect was found by searching a database. If the database consists of 10,000 profiles, we follow the rule of multiplying the calculated probability by that number. Thus, the match probability, instead of one in 2 billion, is 10,000 times greater, or one in 200,000.

Suspect and Evidence from the Same Subpopulation

It might be that the crime took place in a very small, isolated village, and the source of the evidence and suspect are both known to be from that village. In that case, we use the modified Equation O.2b.

Consider first D2S44, in which $p_1 = 0.083$ and $p_2 = 0.024$. Suppose that the village is very small and that we wish to be very conservative, so we take $\bar{\theta} = 0.03$. The probability from Equation O.2b is

$$\frac{2 \times [0.03 + (0.97 \times 0.083)] \times [0.03 + (0.97 \times 0.024)]}{1.03 \times 1.06} = 0.010786.$$

Continuing in the same way through the other four loci, using Equation O.2a for D1S7, and multiplying the results gives about 1/(600 million).

A PCR-Based System

We shall not give a specific example for a PCR-based system. The reason is that the situation is simpler, since there is usually no matching and binning. The detailed procedures are specific for each system and will not be repeated here. The techniques in general (e.g., for STRs) are the same as for VNTRs. They involve positions of bands in gels and photographs of the bands. The methods often use chemical stains rather than radioactive probes; that saves time. The allele frequency is determined directly from the database, and the calculations of match probabilities and likelihood ratios are exactly the same as those just illustrated.

1

Introduction

Whether the practical results to be derived from his researches will repay the pains he has bestowed upon them we must take leave to doubt. It will be long before a British jury will consent to convict a man upon the evidence of his finger prints; and however perfect in theory the identification may be, it will not be easy to submit it in a form that will amount to legal evidence.

—From an 1892 review in *The Athenaeum* of
Finger Prints, by Sir Francis Galton

DNA technology makes possible the study of human variability at the most basic level—the level of genetic material, DNA. Previous methods using blood groups and proteins have analyzed gene products, rather than DNA itself. In addition to providing more direct genetic information, DNA can withstand environmental conditions that destroy proteins, so old, badly degraded samples of bodily fluids still can provide abundant information. If the array of DNA segments (markers) used for comparison is large enough, the probability that two unrelated persons (or even close relatives, except identical twins) will share all of them is vanishingly small. The techniques for analyzing DNA are already very powerful; they will become more so.

DNA analysis is only one of a group of techniques that make use of new and increasingly sophisticated advances in science and technology. Some of the subjects involved are epidemiology, survey research, economics, and toxicology. Increasingly, the methods are technical and statistical, as with forensic DNA analysis. The issues are at the interface of science and law, and involve the difficult problem of accommodating the different traditions in the two areas. For a discussion of scientific and legal issues involved in the use of scientific evidence in the courts, see Federal Judicial Center (1994).

THE 1992 NATIONAL RESEARCH COUNCIL REPORT

DNA techniques began to be used in criminal cases in the United States in 1988. The emergence of numerous scientific and legal issues led to the formation in 1989 of the National Research Council Committee on DNA Technology in Forensic Science. That committee's report, issued in 1992 (NRC 1992), affirmed the value of DNA typing for forensic analysis and hailed it as a major advance in the field of criminal investigation. In an introductory statement, the committee wrote:

> We recommend that the use of DNA analysis for forensic purposes, including the resolution of both criminal and civil cases, be continued while improvements and changes suggested in this report are being made. There is no need for a general moratorium on the use of the results of DNA typing either in investigation or in the courts.

To improve the quality of DNA-typing information and its presentation in court, the report recommended various policies and practices, including

• Completion of adequate research into the properties of typing methods to determine the circumstances under which they yield reliable and valid results (p 8, 61-63).[1]

• Formulation and adherence to rigorous protocols (p 8, 97ff).

• Creation of a national committee on forensic DNA typing to evaluate scientific and technical issues arising in the development and refinement of DNA-typing technology (p 8, 70-72).

• Studies of the relative frequencies of distinct DNA alleles in 15-20 relatively homogeneous subpopulations (p 14, 90, 94).

• A ceiling principle using, as a basis of calculation, the highest allele frequency in any subgroup or 5%, whichever is higher (p 14, 95).

• A more conservative "interim ceiling principle" with a 10% minimum until the ceiling principle can be implemented (p 14, 91-93).

• Proficiency testing to measure error rates and to help interpret test results (p 15, 88-89).

• Quality-assurance and quality-control programs (p 16, 97-109).

• Mechanisms for accreditation of laboratories (p 17, 23, 100-101).

• Increased funding for research, education, and development (p 17, 153).

• Judicial notice of the scientific underpinnings of DNA typing (p 23, 133).

• Financial support for expert witnesses (p 23, 148-149).

• Databases and records freely available to all parties (p 23, 26, 93-95).

---

[1]Page references indicate where the topics are discussed in the 1992 NRC report.

• An end to occasional expert testimony that DNA typing is infallible and that the DNA genotypes detected by examining a small number of loci are unique (p 26, 92).

Many of the recommendations of the 1992 NRC report have been implemented. Some of the perceived difficulties at the time, such as insufficient information on the differences among various population subgroups, have been largely remedied. Studies of different subgroups, although not done exactly in the manner advocated by the report, have been extensive. New techniques and improvements in old ones have increased the power and reliability of DNA data.

Nevertheless, controversy over the forensic applications of DNA has continued, and the report has been strongly criticized (Balazs 1993; Devlin, Risch, and Roeder 1993, 1994; Kaye 1993; Morton, Collins, and Balazs 1993; Collins and Morton 1994). The most contentious issues have involved statistics, population genetics, and possible laboratory errors in DNA profiling. In 1994, the National Research Council established the present committee to update the 1992 report.

THE COMMITTEE'S TASK

The committee's task statement reads:

The committee will perform a study updating the previous NRC report, *DNA Technology in Forensic Science*. The study will emphasize statistical and population genetics issues in the use of DNA evidence. The committee will review relevant studies and data, especially those that have accumulated since the previous report. It will seek input from appropriate experts, including those in the legal and forensics communities, and will encourage the submission of cases from the courts. Among the issues examined will be the extent of population subdivision and the degree to which this information can or should be taken into account in the calculation of probabilities or likelihood ratios. The committee will review and explain the major alternative approaches to statistical evaluation of DNA evidence, along with their assumptions, merits, and limitations. It will also specifically rectify those statements regarding statistical and population genetics issues in the previous report that have been seriously misinterpreted or led to unintended procedures.

Thus, a number of issues addressed by the 1992 report are outside our province. Such issues as confidentiality and security, storage of samples for possible future use, legal aspects of data banks on convicted felons, non-DNA information in data banks, availability and costs of experts, economic and ethical aspects of new DNA information, accountability and public scrutiny, and international exchange of information are not in our charge.

The major issues addressed in this report are in three groups:

• *The accuracy of laboratory determinations.* How reliable is genetic typing? What are the sources of error? How can errors be detected and corrected? Can their rates be determined? How can the incidence of errors be reduced? Should calculation of the probability that an uninvolved person has the same profile as the evidence DNA include an estimate of the laboratory error rate?

• *The accuracy of calculations based on population-genetics theory and the available databases.* How representative are the databases, which originate from convenience samples rather than random samples? How is variability among the various groups in the US population best taken into account in estimating the population frequency of a DNA profile?

• *Statistical assessments of similarities in DNA profiles.* What quantities should be used to assess the forensic significance of a profile match between two samples? How accurate are these assessments? Are the calculations best presented as frequencies, probabilities, or likelihood ratios?

Those three sets of questions are related. All fall within the committee's task of analyzing "statistical and population genetics issues in the use of DNA evidence," and of reviewing "major alternative approaches to statistical evaluation of DNA evidence." To help answer the questions, we discuss the current state of scientific knowledge of forensic DNA-typing methods (Chapter 2), ways of ensuring high standards of laboratory performance (Chapter 3), population-genetics theory and applications (Chapter 4), statistical analysis (Chapter 5), and legal considerations (Chapter 6).

In the remainder of this chapter, we elaborate on some of the developments that have occurred since the 1992 NRC report and on the scope of our review and recommendations. In addition, we attempt to clarify various preliminary points about forensic DNA typing before undertaking a more detailed analysis of the methodological and statistical issues in later chapters.

As will be seen in this report, we agree with many of the findings and recommendations of the 1992 report but disagree with others. Statements and recommendations on which we do not comment are neither endorsed nor rejected.

THE VALIDITY OF DNA TYPING

The techniques of DNA typing outlined in Chapter 2 are fully recognized by the scientific community. To the extent that there are disagreements over the use of these techniques to produce evidence in court, the differences in scientific opinions usually arise when the DNA profile of an evidence sample (as from a crime scene) and that of a sample from a particular person (such as a suspect) appear to be the same. (Although much of DNA analysis involves comparing a sample from a crime scene with one from a suspect, useful comparisons can also be made with DNA from other sources, for example, a victim or a third party who happened to be present at the scene of a crime.) In general, there are three explanations for a finding that two profiles are indistinguishable: the samples came from the same person, the samples came from different persons who happen to have the same DNA profile, and the samples came from different persons but were handled or analyzed erroneously by the investigators or the laboratory.

At the time of the 1992 NRC report, there were various approaches to assessing the first and second possibilities. Although current information is much more extensive, opinions still differ as to how best to make probability calculations that take advantage of the great power of DNA analysis while being scrupulously careful to protect an innocent person from conviction. We hope in this report to narrow the differences.

THE USE OF DNA FOR EXCLUSION

The use of DNA techniques to exclude a suspect as the source of DNA has not been a subject of controversy. In a sense, exclusion and failure to exclude are two sides of the same coin, because the laboratory procedures are the same. But there are two important differences:

• Exclusion—declaring that two DNA samples do not match and therefore did not come from the same person—does not require any information about frequencies of DNA types in the population. Therefore, issues of population genetics are not of concern for exclusion. However, in a failure to exclude, these issues complicate the calculation of chance matches of DNA from different persons.

• Technical and human errors will occur no matter how reliable the procedures and how careful the operators. Although there are more ways of making errors that produce false exclusions than false matches, courts regard the latter, which could lead to a false conviction, as much more serious than the former, which could lead to a false acquittal.

There have been various estimates of the proportion of innocent prime suspects in major crimes. FBI (1993a) reports that in one-third of the rape cases that were examined, the named suspect was eliminated by DNA tests. Undoubtedly the true proportions differ for different crimes and in different circumstances. Nonetheless, DNA testing provides a great opportunity for the falsely accused, and for the courts, because it permits a prompt resolution of a case before it comes to court, saving a great deal of expense and reducing unnecessary anxiety. Furthermore, a number of convicted persons, some of whom have spent as long as 10 years in prison, have been exculpated by DNA testing.[2]

Because cases in which a suspect is excluded by nonmatching DNA almost never come to court, experts from testing laboratories usually testify for the prosecution. In exceptional cases, the prosecution, relying on other evidence,

---

[2]Scores of convicted felons are petitioning courts to allow tests to be performed on preserved samples, and more than seventeen of those exonerated by post-conviction DNA testing have been released. See Developments. . . (1995).

proceeds in the face of nonmatching DNA profiles, and the laboratory experts testify for the defense.[3] In all cases, the job of the laboratory is the same: to analyze the DNA in samples and to interpret the results accurately and without prejudice for or against either party.

CHANGES SINCE THE 1992 NRC REPORT

Population Data

A major change in the last four years has been in the amount of available population data on DNA frequencies in different groups and different geographical regions (see Chapters 4 and 5). Although considerable information was available at the time of the 1992 NRC report, the writers of that report believed that the data were too sparse and the methods for detection of population subdivision too weak to permit reliable calculations of coincidental-match probabilities. In particular, they feared that subsets of the population might have unusual allele frequencies that would not be revealed in an overall population average or not be well represented in the databases used to estimate frequencies. The 1992 report therefore recommended the use of an ad hoc approach for the calculation of an upper bound on the frequencies that would be found in any real population; this approach used what was termed the "ceiling principle." The report recommended that population frequency data be collected on homogeneous populations from 15-20 racial and ethnic groups. The highest frequency of a marker in any population, or 5%—whichever was higher, was to be used for calculation. Until the highest frequencies were available, an "interim ceiling principle" was to be used. That would assign to each marker the highest frequency value found in any population database (adjusted upward to allow for statistical uncertainty) or 10%—whichever was higher. The result would be a composite profile frequency that did not depend on a specific racial or ethnic database and would practically always exceed the frequency calculated from the database of the reference populations.

The ceiling principles have been strongly criticized by many statisticians, forensic scientists, and population geneticists (Cohen 1992; Weir 1992a, 1993a; Balazs 1993; Devlin, Risch, and Roeder 1993, 1994; Morton, Collins, and Balazs 1993; Collins and Morton 1994; Morton 1994), and supported by others (Lempert 1993; Lander and Budowle 1994). Most courts that have discussed it have accepted it as a way of providing a "conservative" estimate. Conservative estimates deliberately undervalue the weight of the evidence against a defendant. Statistically accurate estimates, based as they are on uncertain assumptions and measurements, can yield results that overvalue the weight of evidence against

---

[3]For example, State v. Hammond, 221 Conn. 264, 604 A.2d 793 (1992).

the defendant, even though on average they produce values that are closer to the true frequency than those produced by conservative estimates.

As detailed in Chapters 4 and 5, information is now available from a number of relevant populations, so that experts can usually base estimates on an appropriate database. Indeed, the 1992 committee might not have intended to preclude such estimates, at least if accompanied by interim ceiling figures. In this context, Lander (a member of that committee) and Budowle (1994) state:

> Most importantly, the report failed to state clearly enough that the ceiling principle was intended as an ultra-conservative calculation, which did not bar experts from providing their own "best estimates" based on the product rule. The failure was responsible for the major misunderstanding of the report. Ironically, it would have been easy to correct.

Technical Improvements

A second change since 1992 is mainly incremental. Individually small but collectively important procedural modifications have improved the technical quality of the DNA-testing process. One has only to compare DNA autoradiographs (see Chapter 2) made five years ago with those of today. Computer analysis and better equipment improve efficiency and can increase measurement accuracy. Perhaps most important, DNA-laboratory analysts have gained experience, not just in individual laboratories but collectively across the field. A mistake whose cause is discovered is not likely to be repeated. Laboratory quality-assurance programs are better developed, and there are now organizations that provide standards and conduct proficiency tests. These are discussed in Chapter 3.

A common technique of forensic DNA testing uses loci that contain variable-number tandem repeats (VNTRs), explained in Chapter 2. These are still of primary importance and are the major topic of our discussion, although we discuss other kinds of genetic markers as well. The standard VNTR system entails data that are subject to imprecision of measurement, so that very similar DNA patterns cannot be reliably distinguished; we discuss these problems in Chapter 5. Furthermore, most current VNTR methods require radioactive materials, and the procedures are slow; it can take six weeks or more for a complete analysis. Chemiluminescent systems can reduce the time, since waiting for sufficient radioactive decay is unnecessary, and these systems are coming into use. Increasingly, more-rapid methods are being used, and these usually permit precise identification of genes. Although this change is gradual, we are approaching a time when analysis will be quicker, cheaper, and less problematic than current methods. We foresee a time when each person can be identified uniquely (except for identical twins).

PATERNITY TESTING

Paternity testing has traditionally used blood groups and protein markers, but these have been supplemented if not largely supplanted by the much more powerful DNA methods. The basic procedures are the same for paternity testing as for crime investigation (Walker 1983; AABB 1994), and the experience of paternity-testing laboratories can be valuable in the criminal context as well. Indeed, parentage testing sometimes provides evidence in a criminal proceeding.[4] The laboratories can provide information of use in forensic analysis. For example, a discrepancy between mother and child can offer information about error rates or mutation (see Chapter 2). Many laboratories do both forensic and paternity analysis.

Nevertheless, the two applications are different in important respects. Paternity testing involves analysis of the genetic relations of child, mother, and putative father; crime investigations usually involve the genetically simpler question of whether two DNA samples came from the same person. Mutation (see Chapter 2) is a factor to be taken into account in paternity testing; it is not an issue in identity testing. In cases brought to establish paternity for child support, inheritance, custody, and other purposes, the law gives the claims of the parties roughly equal weight and uses a civil, rather than the higher criminal, standard of proof. The 1992 NRC report's recommendations for conservative population and statistical analyses of data were motivated by the legal requirement of proof beyond a reasonable doubt applied in criminal trials. Those recommendations are therefore inappropriate for civil cases. In particular, the report did not propose either of the ceiling principles for paternity testing, and their use in civil parentage disputes is inappropriate. Likewise, the recommendations in the present report apply to criminal forensic tests and not to civil disputes.

REGULATORY OVERSIGHT

The 1992 NRC report (p 70-72) recommended the formation of a National Committee on Forensic DNA Typing (NCFDT), to provide advice on scientific and technical issues as they arise. The NCFDT would have consisted "primarily of molecular geneticists, population geneticists, forensic scientists, and additional members knowledgeable in law and ethics" to be convened under an appropriate government agency. Two suggested agencies were the National Institutes of Health and the National Institute of Standards and Technology.

Neither agency has accepted or been given the responsibility and funding. Instead, the DNA Identification Act of 1994 (42 USC §14131, 1995) provides for a DNA advisory board to be appointed by the Federal Bureau of Investigation from nominations submitted by the National Academy of Sciences and other organizations. The board, which is now in place, will set standards for DNA testing and provide advice on other DNA-forensic matters. This makes it unlikely that the proposed NCFDT will come into being. We expect the new DNA

---

[4]E.g., State v Spann, 130 N.J. 484, 617 A.2d 247 (1993); Commonwealth v Curnin, 409 Mass. 218, 565 N.E.2d 440 (1991).

Advisory Board to issue guidelines for quality-assurance and proficiency tests that testing laboratories will be expected to follow. Laboratories will not be able to obtain federal laboratory-development funds unless they demonstrate compliance with the standards set by the advisory board.

SEEMINGLY CONTRADICTORY NUMBERS

The uncertainties of assumptions about population structure and about population databases and a desire to be conservative have led some experts to produce widely different probability estimates for the same profile. In court one expert might give an estimate of one in many millions for the probability of a random DNA match and another an estimate of one in a few thousand—larger by a factor of 1,000, or more (for an example, see Weir and Gaut [1993]; other examples are given in Chapter 6). Such discrepancies have led some courts to conclude that the data and methods are unreliable. However, probability estimates, particularly the higher values, are intended to be conservative, sometimes extremely so.

Experts are likely to differ far more in their degree of conservatism than in their best (statistically unbiased) point estimates. If two experts give *conservative* estimates that differ widely, they might both be correct; they often differ not in their expertise, but in their conservatism. For instance, if A says that the distance from Los Angeles to New York is more than 1,000 miles and B says that it is more than 2,000 miles, both are correct; if C says that it is more than 100 miles, this, too, is correct, but excessively conservative and, as a result, much less informative. It might also be misleading, for example, if this gross underestimate led a person to think that he could drive from Los Angeles to New York on one tankful of gasoline. Extreme differences arise if one expert relies solely on direct counts of genetic types in the database and uses no population genetics theory whereas the other makes assumptions grounded in theory. The two experts' best estimates, if both were to use this theory, are likely to be fairly close.

In fact, some have proposed that profile probabilities should be estimated from direct counts of profiles in the database. One problem is that there are trillions of possible five-locus profiles, the overwhelming majority of which are not found in any database. How does one interpret all those zero profile frequencies? One suggestion is to assign an arbitrary value determined by an upper 95% confidence limit. For a database of 100 individuals, this leads to a value of 0.03 for this upper limit; for a database of 1,000, this upper limit is 0.003. The 1992 NRC report suggests that the upper 95% confidence limit be used not only for the zero class, but also instead of the face value estimate for other frequencies as well. However, the report goes on to say that "such estimates do not take advantage of the full potential of the genetic approach." We emphatically agree with this statement.

Even under the assumption that the database is a random sample, the direct-counting procedure is excessively conservative, giving values several orders of magnitude greater than even the most conservative estimates based on genetic assumptions. It does not make use of knowledge of the nature of the markers, of standard population genetic theory, and of population data. It therefore throws out a great deal of relevant information that should be used. For these and other reasons, we reject the counting method (see Chapter 5).

VERY SMALL PROBABILITIES

If a testing laboratory uses genetic markers at four or five VNTR loci, the probability that two unrelated persons have identical DNA profiles might well be calculated to be one in millions, or billions, or even less. The smaller the probability, the stronger is the argument that the DNA samples came from the same person. Some have argued that such a small probability—much smaller than could ever be measured directly—lacks validity because it is outside the range of previous observations. Yet they might accept as meaningful the statement that the probability that two persons get the same bridge hand in two independent deals from a well-shuffled deck is about one in 600 billion, a number far outside anyone's bridge experience and 100 times the world population.

The proper concern is not whether the probability is large or small, but how accurate it is. Probabilities are not untrustworthy simply because they are small. In most cases, given comparable non-DNA evidence, a judge or jury would probably reach the same conclusion if the probability of a random match were one in 100,000 or one in 100 million.

Because of the scientific approach of statisticians and population geneticists, treatment of DNA evidence has become a question of probabilities. But some other kinds of evidence are traditionally treated in absolute terms. The probative value of DNA evidence is probably greater than that of most scientific evidence that does not rely on statistical presentations, such as firearms, poisoning, and handwriting analysis. We urge that the offering of statistical evidence with DNA profiles not be regarded as something unusual and mysterious. In fact, because much of science is quantitative, the DNA precedent might point the way to more scientific treatment of other kinds of evidence.

FINGERPRINTS AND UNIQUENESS

The history of fingerprints offers some instructive parallels with DNA typing (Stigler 1995). Francis Galton, the first to put fingerprinting on a sound basis, did an analysis 100 years ago that is remarkably modern in its approach. He worked out a system for classifying, filing, and retrieving. He showed that a person's fingerprints do not change over time. He invented an analysis that circumvented the fact that small parts of a fingerprint are not strictly independent. He also found that fingerprints of relatives were similar, although not identical, and that there were no unique racial patterns.

Galton concluded that, given a particular fingerprint pattern on a specified digit, such as the left index finger, the probability that a second specified person would have a matching pattern on the same digit was less than the reciprocal of 40 times the world population at that time, and hence the probability that a pattern identical to the given one occurred on the same finger of anyone else in the population of the world would be less than 1/40. When prints from several fingers are compared, the probability that all will match becomes very small. This means, Galton said, that if two sets of prints are identical they must have come from the same person.

Although Galton paid careful attention to probabilities, his successors usually have not; but see Stoney and Thornton (1986). It is now simply accepted that fingerprint patterns are unique.

The 1992 NRC report (p 92) stated that "an expert should—given the relatively small number of loci used and the available population data—avoid assertions in court that a particular genotype is unique in the population." Yet, what meaning should be attached to a profile frequency that is considerably less than the reciprocal of the world population? Given a person with a profile the frequency of which is estimated at only one-tenth the reciprocal of the world population, the probability that no one else in the world has this profile is about 9/10. Should this person be regarded as unique? If not, how high should the probability be for the profile to be regarded as unique? That is for society or the courts, not the present committee, to decide, but we discuss these issues in Chapter 5. Given that such a decision might be made, we show how to do the requisite calculations.

DESIGNATING POPULATION GROUPS AND SUBGROUPS

There is no generally agreed-on vocabulary for treating human diversity. Major groups are sometimes designated as *races*, and at other times as *ethnic* groups. *Ethnic group* is also used to designate subgroups of major groups. The 1992 NRC report used *ethnic group* both ways. Furthermore, groups are mixed, all the classifications are fuzzy at the borders, and the criteria for membership are variable. For such reasons, some assert that the word *race* is meaningless (Brace 1995). But the word is commonly used and generally understood, and we need a vocabulary.

For convenience, uniformity, and clarity, in this report we designate the major groups in the United States—white (Caucasian), black (African American), Hispanic, east Asian (Oriental), and American Indian (Native American)—as *races* or *racial groups*. We recognize that most populations are mixed, that the definitions are to some extent arbitrary, and that they are sometimes more linguistic (e.g., Hispanic) than biological. In fact, people often select their own classification. Nevertheless, there are reproducible differences among the races in the frequencies of DNA profiles used in forensic settings, and these must be taken into account if errors are to be minimized.

Groups within the races—such as Finnish and Italian within whites and different tribes among American Indians—will be designated as *subgroups*. A subgroup can be small, such as the members of a small community descended from a handful of ancestors, or large, such as all those whose ancestors came from a large European country. Because it has different meanings, *ethnic group* will not be used unless its meaning is clear from context.

Today, there are extensive data on DNA-type frequencies in diverse populations around the United States and in many parts of the world. The data are divided by race and geography and sometimes by ancestry within a race. The sources are varied; they include blood banks, paternity-testing laboratories, hospitals, clinics, genetic centers, and law-enforcement agencies. Although the use of such convenience sampling has been questioned, the degree of similarity between data sets from different sources and different geographical regions supports their general reliability. Furthermore, the VNTR markers used for forensics have no known effects, so there is no reason to think that they would be associated with such characteristics as a person's occupation or criminal behavior.

As emphasized in the 1992 report, the United States is not a homogeneous melting pot. In Chapter 4, we specifically address the problems arising from the fact that the population is composed of local communities of different ancestries, not completely mixed. Because it is difficult to find pure local groups in the United States, we rely more on data from ancestral areas. For example, rather than looking for populations of Danish or Swiss Americans, which are mixed with other populations, we look at data from Denmark and Switzerland. These will differ more from each other than will their American relatives, who have to various degrees had their differences reduced by admixture. The study of European groups should lead to an overestimate of the differences among white ethnic groups in the United States and so permit conservative calculations.

The 1992 report assumed for the sake of discussion that population structure exists. We go further: We are sure that as population databases increase in numbers, virtually all populations will show some statistically significant departures from random mating proportions. Although statistically significant, many of the differences will be small enough to be practically unimportant.

THE NATURE OF OUR RECOMMENDATIONS

To deal with uncertainties about population structure, the 1992 NRC report recommended a ceiling principle and an interim ceiling principle. We replace those ad hoc recommendations with the explicit assumption that population substructure exists and recommend formulae that take it into account. We consider special cases, such as relatives of a suspect or instances in which a suspect and an evidence sample are known to come from the same subgroup. We also discuss the uncertainties of the various calculations.

We discuss but do not propose rules for addressing laboratory error. Laboratory procedures have become more standardized since the last report, largely because of the work of the Technical Working Group on DNA Analysis and Methods (TWGDAM 1991-1995). In addition, DNA-typing and proficiency tests are now common. TWGDAM and the FBI's new DNA Advisory Board can modify their recommendations as technical changes and experience warrant. Rather than make specific technical recommendations, and especially rather than try to anticipate changes, we prefer to leave the detailed recommendations to those groups and trust professional scrutiny and the legal system to call attention to shortcomings. Laboratories now use a variety of testing procedures; in particular, DNA-amplification methods are common and new markers are coming into use. We affirm the importance of laboratories' adhering to high standards, of following the guidelines, and of participating in quality-assurance and accreditation programs.

We make no attempt to prescribe social or legal policy. Such prescriptions inevitably involve considerations beyond scientific soundness. Nevertheless, we recognize the connection between our scientific assessments and the efforts of the legal system to develop rules for using forensic DNA analyses; we describe the relationship between our conclusions about scientific issues and the admissibility and weight of DNA evidence in Chapter 6.

Finally, we recognize that technical advances in this field are very rapid. We can expect in the near future methods that are more reliable, less expensive, and less time-consuming than those in use today. We also expect more rapid and more efficient development of population databases that makes use of DNA already in storage. We urge as rapid development of new systems as is consistent with their validation before they are put into general use.

2

Genetic and Molecular Basis of DNA Typing

This chapter describes the two principal kinds of genetic systems used in forensic DNA typing. Both take advantage of the great molecular variability in the human population, which makes it very unlikely that two unrelated persons have the same DNA profile. The first kind involves highly variable chromosomal regions that differ in length; the length measures are imprecise, so statistical procedures are needed to address the uncertainty. In the second kind, genetic variability is less, but the gene determination is usually unambiguous. Before describing the systems, we set forth some principles of genetics and molecular biology necessary for understanding them.

FUNDAMENTALS OF GENETICS[1]

In higher organisms, the genetic material is organized into microscopic structures called *chromosomes*. A fertilized human egg has 46 chromosomes (23 pairs), which, with appropriate staining and microscopic techniques, are visible in the cell nucleus. The two members of a pair are *homologous*. One member of each pair comes from the sperm and the other from the egg. Through the process of chromosomal duplication and separation (*mitosis*) at the time of cell

---

[1]Introductions to genetics and molecular biology are available in various textbooks. Mange and Mange (1994) have written an easy-to-read, yet quite complete elementary textbook of human genetics. The basics of forensic DNA technology are given by Kirby (1992). For more details, see Ballantyne et al. (1989), Lee and Gaensslen (1990), Pena et al. (1993), Saferstein (1993), and Weir (1995b). A clear summary of the general principles and techniques is given in the Summary and Chapters 1 and 2 of the 1992 report (NRC 1992).

division, the two daughter cells and the parent all are identical in chromosomal content, and, with a few exceptions, all the cells in the body should have chromosomes identical with those of the fertilized egg. The process sometimes errs: some cells have too many or too few chromosomes, and some differentiated tissues (such as liver) might have some cells with a different chromosome number (Therman and Susman 1993). But for the most part, cells throughout the body are identical in chromosomal composition.[2] The most important exception occurs in the development of the reproductive cells. During formation of sperms and eggs, the process of reduction division (*meiosis*)—a chromosomal duplication followed by two cell divisions—halves the number of chromosomes from 46 to 23. Thus, sperms and eggs have only one member of each chromosome pair. The double number, 46, is restored by fertilization. A cell (or organism) with two sets of chromosomes is *diploid*. A cell, such as an egg, with one set is *haploid*.

Chromosomes vary greatly in size, but the two members of a homologous pair (one maternal and one paternal) are identical in microscopic appearance, except for the sex-chromosome pair, X and Y, in which the male-determining Y is much smaller than the X. A set of 23 chromosomes with the genetic information they contain is termed the *genome*.

A chromosome is a very thin thread of DNA, surrounded by other materials, mainly protein. If straightened out, an average chromosome would be an inch or more long. But it is arranged as coils within coils and so can be packed into a cell only a thousandth of an inch in diameter. The DNA thread is not visible in an ordinary microscope, and a stained chromosome is more rod-like than thread-like during the mitotic stages when it is most visible.

The DNA thread is actually double—two strands coiled around each other like a twisted rope ladder with stiff wooden steps (Figure 2.1). The basic chemical unit of DNA is the nucleotide, consisting of a base (a half-step in the ladder) and a sugar-phosphate complex (the adjacent section of the rope). There are four kinds of bases, designated A, G, T, and C; A stands for adenine, G for guanine, T for thymine, and C for cytosine. The nucleotides of one DNA strand pair up in a specific fashion with those of the other to form the ladder; because of their specific size and complementary shape, T always pairs with A, and G with C. A DNA strand has a chemical directionality that is defined by the antisymmetry of the chemical connections between the successive sugars and phosphates in the two strands. In double-stranded DNA, the two strands run in opposite directions.

Because of the pairing rule just described, if we know the sequence of nucleotides on one strand, we automatically know the sequence on the other strand. A short segment of double-stranded DNA is shown below; the arrows indicate opposite directionality of the two strands.

---

[2]More important for our purpose, tissues with different numbers of chromosomes (except for some malignancies) have the same DNA content as diploid cells.

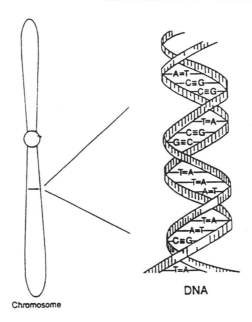

DNA

Chromosome

FIGURE 2.1   Diagram of the double-helical structure of DNA in the chromosome. From NRC (1992).

$$TAGCTTACGCC \rightarrow \qquad\qquad (1)$$

$$\leftarrow ATCGAATGCGG \qquad\qquad (2)$$

Note that a T is always opposite an A and a G opposite a C. Because the chemical bonds holding the two bases (half-steps) together are weak, the two members of a base pair easily come apart; when that happens, the DNA ladder separates into two single strands. If a short single-strand segment, such as (1), is free in the cell, it will tend to pair with its complement, (2), even if the complement is part of a much longer piece of DNA. This process, termed hybridization, can occur in vitro and is one of the key properties that make DNA typing possible. In the laboratory, the two strands of DNA are easily separated by heat and rejoin at lower temperatures, so the process can be manipulated by such simple procedures as changing the temperature; chemical treatments can also be used.

The total DNA in a genome amounts to about 3 billion nucleotide pairs; because there are 23 chromosomes per genome, the average length of a chromosome is about 130 million nucleotide pairs. A gene is a segment of DNA, ranging from a few thousand to more than a hundred thousand nucleotide pairs, that contains the information for the structure of a functional product, usually a protein. The specific sequence of nucleotides in a gene acts as an encoded message that is translated into the specific amino acid sequence of a polypeptide or protein.

The gene product might be detected only chemically or might lead to a visible trait, such as eye pigment. An alteration (*mutation*) of the gene might compromise the gene function and result in a disease, such as cystic fibrosis. The position on the chromosome where a particular gene resides is its *locus*.

Alternative forms of a gene, such as those producing normal and sickle-cell hemoglobin, are called *alleles*. If the same allele is present in both chromosomes of a pair, the person is *homozygous*; if the two alleles are different, the person is *heterozygous*. (The corresponding nouns are *homozygote* and *heterozygote*.) A person's genetic makeup is the *genotype*. Genotype can refer to a single gene locus with two alleles, A and a, in which case the three possible genotypes are AA, Aa, and aa; or it can be extended to several loci or even to the entire set of genes. In forensic analysis, the genotype for the group of analyzed loci is called the DNA *profile*. (The word *fingerprint* is sometimes used, but to avoid confusion with dermal fingerprints we shall use the word *profile*.)

The number of human genes is thought to be between 50,000 and 100,000; the number is quite uncertain. It is known, however, that genes make up only a small fraction of all the DNA in the genome. Even functional genes, especially larger ones, contain noncoding regions (*introns*). In fact, the great bulk of DNA has no known function. The chromosomal segments used most often in forensic analysis are usually in nonfunctional regions.

The sequence of nucleotides in the genome determines the genetic difference between one person and another. But the DNA of different persons is actually very similar. Corresponding sequences from the same genes in two people differ by an average of less than one nucleotide in 1,000 (Li and Sadler 1991). Yet the total number of nucleotides in a haploid genome is so large, about 3 billion, that any two people (unless they are identical twins) differ on the average in several million nucleotides. Most of the differences are outside the coding regions (genes), so the average number of nucleotide differences in the functional regions between two unrelated persons is much less. Nevertheless, the number of differences in the functional regions is large enough to account for the genetic diversity in the human population that is so apparent in such things as body shape, hair color, and facial appearance.

Before a cell divides, each chromosome is copied. In this process, the two strands of DNA in a short stretch separate, and each single strand copies its opposite, according to the A-T, G-C rule. The process proceeds, zipper-like, along the chromosome until there are two double strands where there was one before. (The entire chromosome is not actually copied sequentially from end to end—this would require more time than the interval between cell divisions; rather, there are multiple starting points along the chromosome.) When the cell divides, the two identical chromosomes, each half-old and half-new, go into separate daughter cells and ensure the genetic identity of the two cells.

Genes that are on the same chromosome are *linked*; that is, they tend to be inherited together. However, during the formation of a sperm or egg, the two members of a chromosomal pair line up side by side and randomly exchange parts, a process called *crossing over* or *recombination*. Therefore, genes that were once on the same chromosome might eventually be on a partner chromosome (Figure 2.2). Genes that are very close to one another on the same chromosome might remain associated for many generations before they are separated. Genes that are on nonhomologous chromosomes are inherited independently, as are genes far apart on the same chromosome. The allelic combinations eventually become randomized in the population, quickly if the loci are on nonhomologous chromosomes or far apart on the same chromosome, more slowly if the loci are closer together.

The process of DNA copying, although nearly exact, is not perfect, so a gene is sometimes changed to another form. This mistake, which can also happen in other ways (e.g., because of radiation and some chemicals), is called a *mutation*. Ordinarily this occurs very rarely; the probability of a typical gene's mutating is 1/100,000 or less per generation.[3]

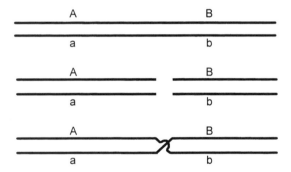

FIGURE 2.2   The exchange of parts between homologous chromosomes (crossing over). The chromosomes pair (upper), break at corresponding points (middle), and exchange parts (lower). The result is that genes that were formerly on the same strand are separated, and vice versa. For example, alleles A and B, which were formerly on the same chromosome, are now on homologous chromosomes, and A and b, formerly separated, are now together. (This shows only the two strands that participate in the event. Needless to say, the actual molecular details of the process are more complicated.)

---

[3]The human body has an enormous number of cells. Rarely, mutations occur in the body cells during development or later, after the organism has formed. Such so-called somatic mutations play an important role in the causation of cancer, but they are not a problem in forensic testing because the tiny fraction of mutant cells in a tissue sample are swamped by the much larger number of nonmutant cells. There is a remote possibility that a mutation might occur so early in embryonic development that DNA in eggs or sperm might differ from that in blood from the same person. We are not aware of any such instance in forensic work, although rare occurrences have been observed by researchers. Regardless, when any sample shows a three-allele pattern at one locus but not at others, additional testing should be done to resolve the uncertainty. If it should occur, it could lead to the conclusion that two samples of DNA from the same person came from two different persons.

In view of the identical DNA composition in most cells, analysis of DNA from various tissues yields the same results. This is an important feature of DNA profiling because it means that cells from various parts of the body (such as blood, semen, skin, hair, and saliva) can be used.

VNTR TYPING

The regions of DNA that have most often been used in forensic analysis have no product and no known function. They are known as minisatellites or *variable-number tandem repeats* (VNTRs). VNTR regions are not genes, and our interest in them is solely related to their use for identifying individuals. We therefore refer to them as *markers*.

In these regions, usually ranging from 500 to 10,000 nucleotide pairs, a core sequence of some 15-35 base pairs is repeated many times consecutively along the chromosome. In a VNTR, the number of repeats varies from person to person. At a given marker locus, sequences with different numbers of repeated units are called *alleles*, even though the word was originally applied to functional genes.

Because different alleles consist of different numbers of repeats, VNTR alleles can be identified by their lengths. If DNA fragments of different lengths are placed on a semisolid medium (gel) in an electric field, they migrate at different rates; different-sized fragments can therefore be identified by the distance they travel between electrodes in such a gel.

The VNTR loci chosen for forensic use are on different chromosomes, or sometimes very far apart on the same chromosome, so they are independently inherited. VNTR loci are particularly convenient for identification because they have a very large number of alleles, often a hundred or more.

One reason for the great variability of VNTRs is their high mutation rate, as much as 1% per generation (Jeffreys and Pena 1993). The repeated units predispose the chromosomes to mistakes in the process of replication and crossing over, thus increasing or decreasing the length (Armour and Jeffreys 1992; Olaisen et al. 1993). The large number of alleles means that the number of possible genotypes is enormous. For example, at a locus with 20 alleles, there are 20 homozygous genotypes, in addition to $(20 \times 19)/2 = 190$ heterozygous ones, for a total of 210. With four such loci, the number of genotypes is 210^4 or about 2 billion. With five loci, this number becomes more than 400 billion. The corresponding number of genotypes at a locus with 50 alleles is 1,275; the number for four such loci exceeds 2 trillion.

Another advantage of VNTRs for forensic work is that none of the alleles is very common. The different alleles are much more similar in frequency than multiple alleles of most genes. That is undoubtedly due to the high mutation rate and to the fact that most mutations increase or decrease the length of a VNTR by only one or a few units.

The essentials of the typing procedure are as follows (FBI 1990). The details vary somewhat from laboratory to laboratory; in a well-run operation, there are tests and checks at each stage to prevent errors. The technique is illustrated in Figure 2.3. First, the DNA is extracted from the source material and put into solution; the procedure differs according to whether the source is blood,[4] saliva, hair, semen, or other tissue. A portion of the DNA solution is tested to determine whether the amount and quality of DNA are sufficient for the analysis to be continued.

The next step involves cutting the DNA into small fragments. This is done with a *restriction enzyme* that recognizes a specific short DNA sequence and cuts the molecule at that point. For example, the enzyme HaeIII, widely used in forensic work, finds the sequence GGCC (CCGG on the other strand that is paired with it) wherever it exists and cuts both strands of the DNA between the G and the C. Thus, the DNA is cut into small pieces whose lengths are determined by the distances between successive GGCC sequences. This four-base sequence occurs millions of times in the genome, so the total DNA is chopped up into millions of fragments. Of course, the use of this enzyme generally requires that there be no GGCC sequences within any VNTR marker that will be analyzed; when such sequences are present, there are breaks within the VNTR leading to fragments of other sizes, and the analysis becomes more complicated.

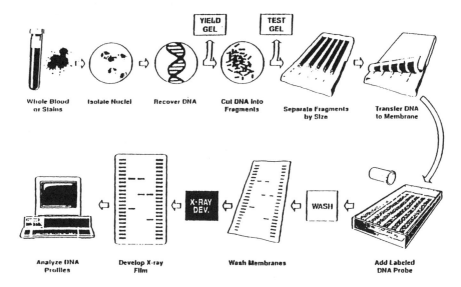

FIGURE 2.3   An outline of the DNA profiling process. The figure illustrates a procedure for VNTR analysis of DNA extracted from whole blood. However, nuclei are not usually isolated as a separate step in DNA typing.

---

[4]Because red blood cells have no nuclei, they have no DNA. But white blood cells do have nuclei and are numerous enough for a small amount of blood usually to be sufficient for an analysis.

The collection of fragments is then placed into a well on a flat gel, and the gel is placed in an electric field. After an appropriate length of time, the fragments migrate different distances in the electric field, depending mainly on their sizes, the smaller ones migrating more rapidly. This process is called *electrophoresis*. At this stage, the fragments are invisible. They are then chemically treated to separate the double strands into single ones.

Because the gels are difficult to work with, the single-stranded fragments are then transferred directly to a nylon membrane, to which they adhere. This process is called *Southern blotting*, named after its inventor. The fragments are then in the same positions on the membrane as they were on the gel. The next step is to flood the membrane with a single-stranded *probe*, a short segment of single-stranded DNA chosen to be complementary to a specific VNTR. The probe will hybridize with the DNA fragment that contains the target VNTR sequence and adhere to it. Any probe that does not bind to this specific DNA sequence is washed off. The probe also contains radioactive atoms. The nylon membrane is then placed on an x-ray film, and emissions from the probe expose the film at locations along the membrane where the probe has adhered to the VNTR. The film with its pictures of the radioactive spots is called an *autoradiograph*, or *autorad*. The process requires several days for sufficient radioactive decay to produce a visible band on the film.

Corresponding fragments from different persons differ in the number of repeat units; hence, the sizes of the fragments vary. That is reflected in their migrating at different rates in the electric field and showing up as bands in different positions on the autorad.

The number of different repeat units in VNTR markers can be very large. As a consequence, determining the exact number of repeats is beyond the resolving power of the usual laboratory technology, and analysis must allow for the resulting imprecision of the measurement. If two bands are visible on an autorad, the person is heterozygous. But if the bands occur in indistinguishable positions, so that only one is visible, the person is presumed to be homozygous. That causes no difficulty; treating a group of indistinguishable alleles as a single allele is a standard practice in traditional genetics.

Forensic VNTR DNA analysis involves testing at several loci, usually four or five, but often more. The analyst follows the procedure described above for one class of radioactive DNA (one probe). After an autoradiograph has been produced for one radioactive probe, this probe is washed off (stripped), another DNA probe targeting another VNTR locus on another chromosome is applied, and the procedure is repeated. The whole process is repeated for each of the multiple probes. Because it takes several days for sufficient radioactivity to be emitted to produce a visible band on the film, the entire process of four or five probes takes several weeks.

The position of a radioactively labeled band on the membrane is an indication of the size of the VNTR, usually expressed as the number of nucleotide pairs.

Because of measurement uncertainty, the size of a band is not known exactly, and it is necessary to take this uncertainty into account in analyzing autorads (see Chapter 5).

Figure 2.4 shows an autorad for one locus (D1S7) in an actual case. (In this notation, the first number, 1 in this case, indicates that this locus is on chromosome

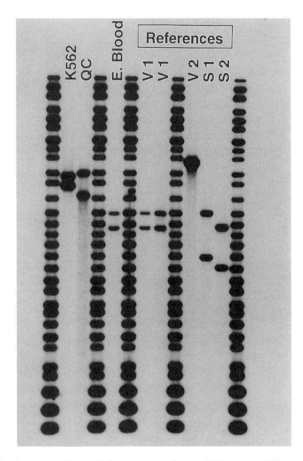

FIGURE 2.4   An autoradiograph from an actual case. This autorad illustrates restriction fragment-length variation at the D1S7 locus. The lanes from left to right are: (1) standard DNA fragment sizing ladder; (2) K562, a standard cell line with two bands of known molecular weight; (3) within-laboratory blind quality-control sample; (4) standard DNA-fragment sizing ladder; (5) DNA from the evidence blood stain; (6) standard DNA-fragment sizing ladder; (7) DNA from the first victim; (8) another sample from the first victim; (9) standard DNA-fragment sizing ladder; (10) DNA from the second victim; (11) DNA from the first suspect; (12) DNA from the second suspect; (13) standard DNA-fragment sizing ladder. Courtesy of the State of California Department of Justice DNA Laboratory.

number one.) Suspects S1 and S2 were charged with having beaten to death two victims, V1 and V2. Blood stains (E blood) were found on the clothing of S1. K562 is from a human cell line and is a widely used laboratory standard. Lanes 1, 4, 6, 9, and 13 show standard DNA fragments used as a molecular-weight sizing ladder. Using multiple lanes for the sizing ladder allows more accurate sizing of the DNA fragments. The quality-control lane (QC) is a blood stain given to the analyst at the beginning of the case, to be processed in parallel with the evidence sample; it is a blind test for the analyst and must meet laboratory specifications. In this particular case, full testing using 10 loci gave consistent matches between E blood and Victim 1.

Bands of similar size are often grouped into *bins*, sets of VNTR alleles of similar size. The usual width of a bin is about 10% of the mean size of the VNTR segment at the center of the bin. The alleles within a bin are treated as though they are a single allele. The words *homozygous* and *heterozygous* then apply to persons whose DNA falls into the same or different bins.

The presence of a single band in a lane might mean that the person is homozygous, but the person could also be heterozygous and the second band for some reason is not visible. Two bands might be so close together that they appear as one on the gel, a second band might be too faint to see (sometimes a problem with degraded material), or the second band might be from an allele so large or small as to fall outside the size range that can be distinguished by electrophoresis. There is a rule for dealing with this situation, and we discuss it in Chapter 4.

In an effort to avoid the use of radioactivity, some laboratories are beginning to use luminescent molecules as labels on their probes. An added benefit of this approach is that analysis of each probe can be completed within a single working day. As these methods are perfected and become more widespread, the time required for an analysis will be greatly reduced and the problems of disposal of radioactive waste circumvented.

PCR-BASED METHODS

The polymerase chain reaction (PCR) is a laboratory process for copying a chosen short segment of DNA millions of times. The process is similar to the mechanism by which DNA duplicates itself normally. The PCR process consists of three steps. First, each double-stranded segment is separated into two strands by heating. Second, these single-stranded segments are hybridized with primers, short DNA segments (20-30 nucleotides in length) that complement and define the target sequence to be amplified. Third, in the presence of the enzyme DNA polymerase, and the four nucleotide building blocks (A, C, G, and T), each primer serves as the starting point for the replication of the target sequence. A copy of the complement of each of the separated strands is made, so that there are two double-stranded DNA segments. This three-step cycle is repeated, usually 20-35 times. The two strands produce four copies; the four, eight copies; and so on until the number of copies of the original DNA is enormous. The main difference between this procedure and the normal cellular process is that the PCR process is limited to the amplification of a small DNA region. This region is usually not more than 1,000 nucleotides in length, so PCR methods cannot, at least at present, be used for large DNA regions, such as most VNTRs. There is a possibility that this limitation may soon be removed (Barnes 1994).

The PCR process is relatively simple and is easily carried out in the laboratory. Results can be obtained within a short time, often within 24 hours, in contrast with the several weeks required for a complete VNTR analysis. Because the amplification is almost unlimited, PCR-based methods make possible the analysis of very tiny amounts of DNA. This advantage makes the technique particularly useful for forensic analysis, in that the amount of DNA in some forensic samples, such as single shed hairs or saliva traces on cigarette butts, is minute. The technique extends DNA typing to evidence samples that at present cannot be typed with other approaches. Moreover, the small amount of DNA required for PCR analysis makes it easier to set aside portions of samples for repeat testing in the same or another laboratory. Amplification of samples that contain degraded DNA is also possible; this allows DNA typing of old and decayed samples, remains of fire and accident victims, decayed bodies, and so on.

There is another advantage of PCR-based methods. They usually permit an exact identification of each allele, in which case there are no measurement uncertainties. Thus, the calculations and statistical analysis associated with matching and binning of VNTRs are not needed. Nevertheless, ambiguity can sometimes arise if there are mutations that alter individual repeats, and binning or some other adjustment may be required.

Given those advantages, it is not surprising that PCR-based typing is widely and increasingly used in forensic DNA laboratories in this country and abroad. Many forensic laboratories carry out PCR-based typing along with VNTR typing. Some laboratories, particularly smaller ones, have gone exclusively to PCR techniques.

Once the amount of DNA is amplified by PCR methods, the analysis proceeds in essentially the same way as with VNTRs. There are minor procedural modifications, but the general procedures are the same—identification of fragments of different size by their migration in an electric field.

Another class of repeated units is STRs, short tandem repeats of a few nucleotide units. These are very common and are distributed widely throughout the genome (Edwards et al. 1992; Hammond et al. 1994). Because the total length is short, STRs can be amplified with PCR. Alleles differing in size can be resolved to the scale of single bases with both manual and automated sequencing technologies. Moreover, it has proved possible to co-amplify STRs at multiple loci, allowing significant increases in the speed of test processing (Klimpton et al. 1993; Hammond et al. 1994). They do not have as many alleles per locus as VNTRs, but that is compensated by the very large number of loci that are potentially usable. As more STRs are developed and validated, this system is coming into wide use.

Any procedure that uses PCR is susceptible to error caused by contamination leading to amplification of the wrong DNA. The amplification process is so efficient that a few stray molecules of contaminating DNA can be amplified along with the intended DNA. Most such mistakes are readily detected after the PCR analysis is completed because the contaminating DNA yields a weak pattern that differs from the predominant pattern. Most undetected contamination is likely to lead to a false-negative result; that is, a nonmatch might be declared when a match actually exists. Nevertheless, false-positive results are also possible, in which the profile from an evidence sample is falsely declared to match the genetic type of another person. That could happen, for example, if by mistake the same amplified sample were used twice in a given analysis, instead of two different samples. Procedures for minimizing the occurrence of errors are discussed in Chapter 3.

A second disadvantage of most markers used in PCR-based typing is that they have fewer alleles than VNTRs and the distribution of allele frequencies is not as flat. Hence, more loci are required to produce the same amount of information about the likelihood that two persons share a profile. Furthermore, some of these loci are functional (they are genes, not just markers). Those are more likely to be subject to natural selection and therefore might not conform strictly to some of the population-genetics assumptions used in evaluating the significance of a match (discussed in Chapter 4). In the future, loci that are brought on as markers should be chosen so as not to be linked to important disease-producing genes, so that the markers can more confidently be treated as neutral, and to provide greater assurance of genetic privacy. In fact, some three-base repeating units are the cause of severe human diseases (Wrogemann et al. 1993; Sutherland and Richards 1995), and even some VNTRs might have disease associations (Krontiris 1995). These are not used in forensics, however.

One application of PCR in forensic work has used the DQA locus (the gene is called DQA, its product, DQα) (Blake et al. 1992; Comey et al. 1993). In distinction to VNTRs, the alleles at this locus code for a protein. This locus is part of the histocompatibility complex, a group of highly variable genes responsible for recognizing foreign tissue. Eight alleles at the DQA locus have been identified, although only six are commonly used in forensic work. The different alleles can be distinguished by specific probes. With these six alleles there are 21 possible genotypes; six homozygous and 15 heterozygous.

Analysis of DQA uses the same DNA hybridization technique as VNTR analysis. In this case, probes specific for individual alleles are placed in designated locations on a membrane (because the probes, rather than the DNA to be typed, are fixed on the membrane, this is called a *reverse* blot). The amplified DNA is then added, and the DNA from whatever DQA alleles are present hybridizes with the appropriate probe. A stain reaction specific for double-stranded DNA shows up as a colored spot on the membrane wherever specific hybridization occurs. The positions of the colored spots on the membrane strip indicate which alleles are present.

The DQA system has several advantages. It is quick and reliable, so it is useful as a preliminary test. It can also be used, with other markers, as part of a more detailed DNA profile. In practice, a substantial fraction of suspects are cleared by DNA evidence, and prompt exclusion by the DQA test is obviously preferable to waiting months for results of a VNTR test. On the average, the DQA genotype of a given person is identical with that of about 7% of the population at large, so an innocent person can expect to be cleared in short order 93% of the time. This high probability might not be achieved if the sample includes DNA from more than one individual.

Another system that is beginning to be widely used is the Amplitype poly-marker (PM) DNA system. This system analyzes loci simultaneously: LDLR (low-density-lipoprotein receptor), GYPA (glycophorin A, the MN blood-groups), HBGG (hemoglobin gamma globin), D7S8 (an anonymous genetic marker on chromosome 7), and GC (group-specific component). There are two or three distinguishable alleles at each locus. The system has been validated with tests for robustness with respect to environmental insults (Herrin et al. 1994; Budowle, Lindsay, et al. 1995), and there is substantial information on population frequencies, which is discussed in Chapter 4.

Other PCR-based techniques have been or are being developed. For example, D1S80 is a VNTR in which the largest allele is less than 1,000 bp long. Its value for forensic analysis has been validated in a number of tests (Sajantila et al. 1992; Herrin et al. 1994; Budowle, Baechtel, et al. 1995; Cosso and Reynolds 1995). The locus consists of a 16-base unit that is repeated a variable number of times. There are more than 30 distinguishable alleles. The size classes are fully discrete, so usually each allele can be distinguished unambiguously. However, some ambiguous alleles are caused by insertion or deletion of a single base and these complicate the analysis.

Another class of genetic marker is mitochondrial DNA. Mitochondria are microscopic particles found in the cell, but outside the nucleus, so they are not associated with the chromosomes. The transmission of mitochondria is from mother to child; the sperm has very little material other than chromosomes. Ordinarily, all the mitochondrial particles in the cell are identical. There is no problem distinguishing heterozygotes from homozygotes, since only one kind of DNA is present. Since mitochondrial DNA is always transmitted through the female, all the children of one woman have identical mitochondrial DNA. Therefore, siblings, maternal half-siblings, and others related through female lines are as much alike in their mitochondrial DNA as identical twins. Mitochondrial DNA is particularly useful for associating persons related through their maternal lineage, for example, for associating skeletal remains to a family.

A highly variable region of mitochondrial DNA is used for forensic analysis.

The techniques have been validated, and there is a growing body of frequency data. For a detailed account of the methodology and validation, see Wilson et al. (1993). A disadvantage for forensic use is that siblings cannot be distinguished, nor can other maternally related relatives, such as cousins related through sisters. Since mitochondria are inherited independently of the chromosomes, mitochondrial information can be combined with nuclear data to yield probabilities of a random match (see Chapter 4).

A promising technique is minisatellite repeat mapping, or digital typing, which, apart from length variation, detects sequence differences within the base sequences repeated in VNTRs (Jeffreys et al. 1991; Armour and Jeffreys 1992; Monckton et al. 1993). Although technical limitations still need to be overcome before this system can be used in forensic analysis, it could have a particular advantage, in that it uses the same loci that have already been extensively studied in various populations and subpopulations.

Table 2.1 summarizes the most widely used systems.

CONCLUSIONS

DNA analysis is one of the greatest technical achievements for criminal investigation since the discovery of fingerprints. Methods of DNA profiling are firmly grounded in molecular technology. When profiling is done with appropriate care, the results are highly reproducible. In particular, the methods are almost certain to exclude an innocent suspect.

One of the most widely used techniques today involves VNTRs. These loci are extremely variable, but individual alleles cannot be distinguished, because of intrinsic measurement variability, and the analysis requires statistical procedures. It involves radioactivity and requires a month or more for full analysis. PCR-based methods are prompt, require only a small amount of material, and can yield unambiguous identification of individual alleles. Various PCR methods, particularly STRs, are increasingly being used.

The state of the profiling technology and the methods for estimating frequencies and related statistics have progressed to the point where the admissibility of properly collected and analyzed DNA data should not be in doubt. We expect continued development of new and better methods and hope for prompt validation so that they can quickly be brought into use.

TABLE 2.1   Genetic Markers Used in Forensic Identification

Nature of Variation at Locus

Locus Example	Method of Detection	Number of Alleles	Diversity[a]
Variable Number Tandem Repeat (VNTR)[b]			
D2S44 (core repeat 31 bp)	Intact DNA digested with restriction enzyme, producing fragments that are separated by gel electrophoresis; alleles detected by Southern blotting followed by probing with locus-specific radioactive or chemiluminescent probe	At least 75 (size range 700-8500 bp); allele size distribution continuous	ca. 95% in all populations studied
D1S80 (core repeat 16 bp)	Amplification of allelic sequences by PCR; discrete allelic products separated by electrophoresis and visualized directly	ca. 30 (size range 350-1000 bp); alleles can be discretely distinguished	80-90%, depending on population
Short Tandem Repeat (STR)[c]			
HUMTHO1 (tetranucleotide repeat)	Amplification of allelic sequences by PCR; discrete allelic products separated by electrophoresis on sequencing gels and visualized directly	8 (size range 179-203 bp); alleles can be discretely distinguished	70-85%, depending on population
Simple Sequence Variation[d]			
DQA (an expressed gene in the histocompatibility complex)	Amplification of allelic sequences by PCR; discrete alleles detected by sequence-specific probes	8 (6 used in DQA kit)	85-95%, depending on population
Polymarker (a set of 5 loci)	Amplification of allelic sequences by PCR; discrete alleles detected by sequence-specific probes	Loci are bi- or tri-allelic; 972 genotypic combinations	37-65%, depending on locus and population
Mitochondrial DNA Control Region (D-loop)	Amplification of control-region sequence and sequence determination	Hundreds of sequence variants known	Greater than 95%

[a]In a randomly mating diploid population, diversity is the same as heterozygosity. In general, including haploid mitochondria, the value is $1 - \Sigma_i p_i^2$ (for explanation, see Chapter 4).

[b]VNTR loci contain repeated core sequence elements, typically 15-35 bp in length. Alleles differ in number of repeats and are differentiated on the basis of size.

[c]STR loci are like VNTR loci except that the repeated core sequence elements are 2-6 bp in length. Alleles differ in number of repeats and are differentiated on the basis of size.

[d]Nucleotide substitution in a defined segment of a sequence.

3

Ensuring High Standards of Laboratory Performance

If DNA from an evidence sample and DNA from a suspect or victim share a profile that has a low frequency in the population, this suggests that the two DNA samples came from the same person; the lower the frequency, the stronger the evidence. But the possibility remains that the match is only apparent—that an error has occurred and the true profile of one of the sources differs from that reported by the laboratory. We describe here ways that laboratory errors, particularly errors that might falsely incriminate a suspect, can arise, how their occurrence might be minimized, and how to take into account the fact that the error rate can never be reduced to zero.

Although this report focuses mainly on methods for computing the frequencies of profiles in various populations and the uncertainty in estimates of such quantities (Chapters 4 and 5), it is important to understand that those estimates will be of little value if there has been an error in determining that the two DNA profiles match. A reported match in DNA samples that is the result of error in the handling or analysis of the samples could lead to the conviction of an innocent person, and an erroneously reported exclusion could also have serious consequences. Although there are more ways for an error to lead to a false exclusion than a false match, the US system of justice is more concerned with the latter, since it regards false conviction as worse than false acquittal.

We recognize that some risk of error is inevitable, as in any human endeavor, whatever efforts a laboratory takes to eliminate mistakes. Nonetheless, safeguards can be built into the system to prevent both types of errors and to identify and correct them. It is important that forensic laboratories use strict quality-control standards to minimize the risk of error.

QUALITY CONTROL AND QUALITY ASSURANCE IN THE LABORATORY

The maintenance of high laboratory standards rests on a foundation of sound quality control (QC) and quality assurance (QA). *Quality control* and *quality assurance* refer to related but distinct components of a laboratory's effort to deliver a quality product (ANSI/ASQC A3-1978). *Quality control* refers to measures that are taken to ensure that the product, in this case a DNA-typing result and its interpretation, meets a specified standard of quality. *Quality assurance* refers to measures that are taken by a laboratory to monitor, verify, and document its performance. Regular proficiency testing and regular auditing of laboratory operations are both essential components of QA programs. QA thus serves as a functional check on QC in a laboratory. Demonstration that a laboratory is meeting its QC objectives provides confidence in the quality of its product.

Current QC and QA Guidelines

The 1992 report (NRC 1992) outlined many features of desirable QC and QA as part of a proposed regulatory program (p 104-105):

• "Individual analysts have education, training, and experience commensurate with the analysis performed and testimony provided.

• "Analysts have a thorough understanding of the principles, use, and limitations of methods and procedures applied to the tests performed.

• "Analysts successfully complete periodic proficiency tests and their equipment and procedures meet specified criteria.

• "Reagents and equipment are properly maintained and monitored.

• "Procedures used are generally accepted in the field and supported by published, reviewed data that were gathered and recorded in a scientific manner.

• "Appropriate controls are specified in procedures and are used.

• "New technical procedures are thoroughly tested to demonstrate their efficacy and reliability for examining evidence material before being implemented in casework.

• "Clearly written and well-understood procedures exist for handling and preserving the integrity of evidence, for laboratory safety, and for laboratory security.

• "Each laboratory participates in a program of external proficiency testing that periodically measures the capability of its analysts and the reliability of its analytic results.

• "Case records—such as notes, worksheets, autoradiographs, and population data banks—and other data or records that support examiners' conclusions are prepared, retained by the laboratory, and made available for inspection on court order after review of the reasonableness of a request."

Although not QC or QA features, the following are listed as desirable aspects of a regulatory program (NRC 1992, p 105):

• "Redundancy of programs is avoided, so that unnecessary duplication of effort and costs can be eliminated.
• "The program is widely accepted by the forensic-science community.
• "The program is applicable to federal, state, local, and private laboratories.
• "The program is enforceable—i.e., . . . failure to meet its requirements will prevent a laboratory from continuing to perform DNA typing tests until compliance is demonstrated.
• "The program can be implemented within a relatively short time.
• "The program involves appropriate experts in forensic science, molecular biology, and population genetics."

This list substantially summarizes more-detailed and more-specific guidelines developed by the Technical Working Group on DNA Analysis Methods (TWG-DAM), a group composed of forensic DNA analysts from government and private laboratories around the United States and Canada. TWGDAM meets several times a year to discuss problems, report on cooperative studies, and share procedures and experiences. It has published guidelines and reports that address various aspects of forensic DNA analysis and laboratory procedure (TWGDAM 1989, 1990a,b, 1991, 1994b,c, 1995). The most recent guidelines define current accepted standards of practice for forensic DNA laboratories in North America.

The crime laboratory accreditation program sponsored by the Laboratory Accreditation Board of the American Association of Crime Laboratory Directors (ASCLD-LAB) requires extensive documentation of all aspects of laboratory operations (including the education, training, and experience of personnel; the specification and calibration of equipment and reagents; the validation and description of analytic methods, the definition of appropriate standards and controls, the procedures for handling samples, and the guidelines for interpreting and reporting data), proficiency testing, internal and external audits of laboratory operations, and a plan to address deficiencies with corrective action and weigh their importance for laboratory competence. The TWGDAM QC and QA guidelines are specifically endorsed by ASCLD-LAB as part of the foundation for accreditation. Laboratories that seek accreditation must submit all their documentation to an accreditation review team and must undergo a week-long site inspection by that team. The site inspection includes a critical evaluation of randomly selected case files to verify that the QC standards as documented are being met. Accredited laboratories must annually certify to ASCLD-LAB that they continue to meet defined standards; they submit proficiency test results to ASCLD-LAB for review. The ASCLD-LAB accreditation program began in 1981; by the end of 1994, 128 forensic laboratories in the United States, one in Canada, and two in Australia had received accreditation. Forensic laboratories in Australia, New

Zealand, Singapore, and Hong Kong were also preparing for ASCLD-LAB accreditation, as was the FBI laboratory in Washington, DC.

The College of American Pathologists (CAP) has recently established a program for laboratory accreditation in molecular pathology, which includes forensic identity-testing and parentage-testing. The program is similar to the ASCLD-LAB program in its requirements for documentation of procedures and of equipment and facilities, QC, QA, etc., and it requires proficiency-testing in the form of participation in an approved program for interlaboratory comparison. As with the ASCLD-LAB program, the accreditation process includes on-site inspection of laboratory operations and records.

The American Society of Crime Laboratory Directors (ASCLD) has published general guidelines for forensic-laboratory management (ASCLD 1987). (Despite the similarity in their names, ASCLD and ASCLD-LAB are separate entities with distinct governing bodies.) The guidelines cover all aspects of forensic analysis and affirm the key element of QA: the responsibility of laboratory managers for all aspects of laboratory operations and performance, including definition and documentation of standards for personnel training, procedures, equipment and facilities, and performance review.

The DNA Identification Act of 1994 establishes a federal framework for setting national standards on QA and proficiency-testing. It authorizes grant funding to be made available to state and local jurisdictions to improve the quality and availability of DNA analysis in forensic laboratories. To be eligible for funding, these jurisdictions must certify that a laboratory will satisfy or exceed QA standards published by the director of FBI; that DNA samples and analyses will be made available only to criminal-justice agencies, courts, and defendants; and that each DNA analyst will undergo external proficiency-testing at intervals not exceeding 180 days. The standards for QA and the standards for testing proficiency of forensic laboratories are to be developed by the DNA Advisory Board (See Chapter 1).

The Role of Proficiency-Testing and Audits

Proficiency-testing and audits are key assessment mechanisms in any program for critical self-evaluation of laboratory performance. Proficiency-testing entails the testing of specimens submitted to the laboratory in the same form as evidence samples. Audits are independent reviews of laboratory operations conducted to determine whether the laboratory is performing according to a defined standard. Both forms of assessment can be conducted internally or externally, that is, by people inside or outside the laboratory. Good QA programs have a mixture of regular internal and external assessment.

The most straightforward form of proficiency-testing is open, or declared. The analyst is presented with a set of samples, typically about five, in a mock case scenario and is asked to determine which samples could have a common source. The analyst is aware that the samples are being used in a proficiency test. Open proficiency-testing evaluates analytical methods and interpretation of results; it identifies systematic problems due to equipment, materials, the laboratory environment (such as contamination), and analyst misjudgment. A benefit of open proficiency-testing conducted by external entities is that many laboratories can test the same set of samples, thus allowing interlaboratory comparison of performance and statistical evaluation of collective results. At present, external proficiency-testing in forensic DNA analysis is offered by three vendors: Collaborative Testing Services, Cellmark Diagnostics (UK), and the College of American Pathologists. All provide summary reports on the results of each proficiency test.

Open proficiency-testing is required under TWGDAM guidelines and is a requirement both for laboratory accreditation by ASCLD-LAB and for board certification of analysts by the American Board of Criminalistics (ABC). TWGDAM specifies that each analyst take at least two proficiency tests per year; the results, including any corrective action for discrepancies, are to be documented. The ASCLD-LAB accreditation program follows TWGDAM in requiring at least two proficiency tests for analysts per year and requires in addition that one of the tests be external. Results are reported by the proficiency-test vendor to ASCLD-LAB as a condition of continuing accreditation. A committee of ASCLD-LAB reviews the discrepancies and may invoke sanctions up to and including suspension of accreditation. ABC similarly requires at least one external proficiency test per year, the results of which are to be reported to ABC.

A second form of proficiency-testing, full-blind proficiency-testing, goes a step beyond open proficiency-testing in that the analyst does not know that a proficiency test is being conducted. It has been argued that full-blind testing provides a truer test of functional proficiency because the analysts will not take extra care in analyzing samples. Whether or not that is so, this form of proficiency-testing evaluates a broader aspect of laboratory operation, from the receipt of the "evidence" at the front desk through analysis and interpretation to final reporting.

The logistics of full-blind proficiency-tests are formidable. The "evidence" samples have to be submitted through an investigative agency in the jurisdiction of the laboratory and have to arrive in the laboratory with case documentation and an identified contact investigator. Without such full cover, a case would likely be recognized as nonroutine, and a blind test suspected. The TWGDAM guidelines recommend one full-blind proficiency test per laboratory per year if such a program can be implemented. The DNA Identification Act of 1994 required that the director of the National Institute of Justice (NIJ) report to Congress on the feasibility of establishing a full-blind proficiency-testing program. The NIJ has reported that, although several of the large laboratory systems conduct blind testing in-house, there is no blind, external, DNA proficiency-testing program generally available to public or private laboratories. The report mentioned some potentially serious issues with blind testing, including the cost of implementation, the risk that DNA data from an innocent donor to the test might end up in criminal DNA databanks, and the chance that the test would impose excessive costs and time demands on law-enforcement agencies. The NIJ has contracted a study to review current testing programs and to examine alternative ways of performing blind tests.

Regular audits of laboratory operations complement proficiency-testing in the monitoring of general laboratory performance. The objective of the audit is to compare a laboratory's performance with its professed quality policies and objectives. Audits cover all phases of laboratory operations related to performance and accordingly touch on matters not covered by proficiency-testing, such as equipment-calibration schedules and case-management records. The TWGDAM QA guidelines recommend audits every two years (TWGDAM 1995) by persons independent of the DNA laboratory operation, preferably including at least one from another organization (typically a laboratory from a jurisdiction in another state).

The objective of both proficiency-testing and auditing is to improve laboratory performance by identifying problems that need to be corrected. Neither is designed to measure error rates.

SAFEGUARDING AGAINST ERROR

Every human activity is associated with some risk of error. There are potential sources of error at every stage in the processing of physical evidence, from collection in the field through laboratory analysis to interpretation of results of analysis. Not all lapses have deleterious consequences; many have no consequences. Many are readily identified and can be corrected. The lapses of most concern, however, are the ones that might lead to a false match. False exclusions are important but are unlikely to lead to false convictions. There is no single solution to the problem of error. To achieve accurate results, care and attention to detail and independent checks must be used at all stages of the analytical process. This section surveys potential sources of error, the consequences of errors, and safeguards to prevent them.

Sample Mishandling and Data-Recording Errors

Mixups or mislabelings of samples or results can occur at any point where evidence is handled or data recorded, that is, from the time of evidence collection in the field to the writing of the final report. The consequences of sample mishandling depend on which samples are mishandled. There are circumstances in which undetected mishandling can lead to false matches; the genetic types of the samples might be determined correctly but the inferred connections among the samples can be incorrect because of sample mixup. Sample mishandling and incorrect recording of data can happen with any kind of physical evidence and are of great concern in all fields of forensic science. The concern regarding mishandling is compounded by the reality that most forensic laboratories have little or no control over the handling of evidence elsewhere. Accordingly, it is desirable to have safeguards not only to protect against mixups in the laboratory but also to detect mixups that might have occurred anywhere in the process.

Safeguards against sample mishandling in the field include proper training of personnel involved in sample collection (such as crime-scene personnel) and submission of complete evidence items (rather than clippings or scrapings) to the laboratory. Mixups in the laboratory as samples are being removed from evidence items for analysis can be minimized by sample-handling policies that allow only one evidence item to be handled at a time. Sample mixup or mislabeling in the analysis stream (for example, transfer of a sample solution to the wrong tube, loading of a sample into the wrong lane on an electrophoresis gel, and misrecording of data) can be minimized by rigorous adherence to defined procedures for sample-handling and data entry.

Redundancy in testing provides a check on sample integrity. Testing of multiple items can serve as a check on consistency of results; inconsistencies among items believed to be of common origin can signal a mixup. For example, demonstration that bloodstains from different evidence items have the same DNA profile is less likely if a sample mixup occurred. Gender testing in cases in which both males and females are involved can also serve as a consistency check and has been used to verify suspected mislabeling. One benefit of the high discriminating power of DNA typing is the detection of sample-mishandling errors that might not have been recognized with classical blood-group and protein-marker testing.

Because an analyst might fail to notice an inconsistent result or a recording error, it is important to have analytical results reviewed by a second person, preferably one not familiar with the origin of the samples or issues in question. An independent reviewer can also catch flaws in analytical reasoning and interpretation. Independent ''second reading'' is common in forensic laboratories and is required by the guidelines (TWGDAM 1991, 1995).

The ultimate safeguard against error due to sample mixup is to provide an opportunity for retesting. In most cases, it is possible to retain portions of the original evidence items and portions of the samples from different stages of the testing. Sample retention is particularly easy when PCR-based typing methods are used for testing. If samples have been retained, questions of error due to mishandling can be resolved by retesting. Allegations of sample mishandling lose credibility if those making the allegation have rejected the opportunity for a retest. Sample retention whenever possible is recommended in the TWGDAM QA guidelines and is standard in many laboratories. As stated in the Guidelines (TWGDAM 1995), ''testing of evidence and evidence samples should be conducted to provide the maximum information with the least consumption of the sample. Whenever possible, a portion of the original sample should be retained or returned to the submitting agency, as established by laboratory policy.''

Even the strongest evidence will be worthless—or worse, could lead to a false conviction—if the evidence sample did not originate in connection with the crime. Given the great individuating potential of DNA evidence and the relative ease with which it can be mishandled or manipulated by the careless or the unscrupulous, the integrity of the chain of custody is of paramount importance.

Faulty Reagents, Equipment, Controls, or Technique

Problems with reagents, equipment, controls, or technique usually lead to failed tests (no results) or to ambiguous test results. Situations in which such problems might lead to a false match or a false exclusion will be uncommon if testing is accompanied by appropriate controls. In any case, adherence to a standard QC program provides safeguards against these kinds of laboratory error. Regular monitoring of reagents and equipment is part of any standard QA program. Use of appropriate QC standards and of positive and negative controls is part of routine testing; failure of the standards and controls to behave as expected in a test signals a problem with the analytical system and might disqualify test results. Moreover, regular monitoring of test outcomes with standards and controls allows recognition of gradually emerging problems with reagents, equipment, controls, standards, and overall procedure that might otherwise be overlooked. For example, almost all North American forensic laboratories that perform VNTR analysis use DNA from the human cell line K562 as a positive typing control; correct sizing of restriction fragments from K562 DNA is prerequisite to accepting a typing result as reportable. Monitoring of K562 fragment-size measurements within a laboratory over time and comparison of measurements between laboratories allow identification of "drift" due to procedural modification, reagent variation, or equipment deterioration.

Inevitably, breakdowns in reagent quality, equipment, controls, or technique occur at times. For example, in the loading of an electrophoresis gel, a sample loaded in one lane might leak into an adjacent lane, which might then appear to contain a mixed sample. Confusion resulting from lane-leakage problems is typically avoided by leaving alternate lanes empty or by placing critical samples in nonadjacent lanes, and this should always be done. In this and other situations involving such lapses, a breakdown is usually readily apparent from the appearance of the results. Review of analytical results by a second analyst who is unfamiliar with the issues in the case protects against lapses of judgment on the part of the primary analyst.

Evidence Contamination

Contamination has been used as an umbrella term to cover any situation in which a foreign material is mixed with an evidence sample. Different kinds of contamination have different consequences for analysis. Contamination with nonbiological materials (gasoline, grit, etc.) or with nonhuman biological materials (microorganisms, plant materials, etc.) can result in test failures but not in genetic typing errors. Part of marker validation includes testing to determine whether the marker can be detected in nonhuman species and if so, whether its presence there might cause confusion in typing. It is generally found that the markers identified by the single locus probes used in forensic VNTR analysis and by PCR-based typing are detected in but a few nonprimate species; if such markers are used, that fact should obviously be taken into account. That is an advantage of DNA typing over enzyme and blood-group testing. Contamination with human material, however, is a possible source of concern for DNA tests.

Three kinds of sample contamination were described in the 1992 National Research Council report (p 65-67) and are briefly summarized here. For each, appropriate safeguards and controls can be built into the analytical system to protect against contamination and to detect it when it does occur.

• *Inadvertent contamination* can occur in the course of sample-handling by investigative or laboratory personnel or by others. The background environment from which the evidence is collected can also cause contamination. The concern about contamination is not peculiar to biological evidence; extraneous evidence (such as a detective's cigarette butt found at the scene) is always a concern. The important consequences of those sorts of contamination are that samples might appear to be mixtures of material from several persons and, in the worst case, that only the contaminating type might be detected. The concern is greater with PCR-based typing methods than with VNTR analysis because PCR can amplify very small amounts of DNA. A false match could occur if the genetic type of the contaminating materials by chance matched the genetic type of a principal (such as a suspect) in the case or, worse, if the contaminant itself came from a suspect in the case. The best safeguard against inadvertent contamination is to have rigorous procedures for sample-handling from field to laboratory. Particular attention should be given to keeping evidence samples separated from reference samples. In VNTR analysis, evidence and reference samples can be kept apart up to the time they are loaded onto the analytical gel. With PCR-based typing, evidence and reference samples can be analyzed separately as well. Contamination from sample-handling or from the background environment can be detected in several ways. Background control samples—samples collected from areas adjacent to bloodstains or other evidence sites—can be used to determine whether background contamination is present. Background control testing is not a new idea; it has long been used in forensic blood-grouping. Knowledge of the genetic types of people who might contribute contaminating material can be used to assess the possibility of contamination from those people. Testing for multiple loci increases the chance of differentiating between contaminant and true sources of a sample. Finally, redundancy in testing provides a consistency check; the chance that multiple samples would all be contaminated the same way is small.

• *Mixed samples* are contaminated by their very nature. Postcoital vaginal swabs, for example, are expected to contain a mixture of semen and vaginal fluids, and shed blood from different persons might run together. Such samples are part of the territory of forensic science and must be dealt with whenever feasible. Sperm DNA can be separated from nonsperm DNA with differential DNA extraction. Detection of sample mixtures of other kinds is generally revealed with genetic typing. Mixtures show the composite of the individual types present; the proportions of the different types reflect the proportions of the contributors to the mixture. Testing samples collected from different areas of a mixed stain can sometimes allow the genetic types of the contributors to be more clearly distinguished.

• *Carryover contamination* is well recognized in PCR testing, although it is not an issue in VNTR analysis. This kind of contamination occurs when a PCR amplification product finds its way into a reaction mix before the target template DNA is added. The carryover product can then be amplified along with the DNA from an evidence sample, and the result can be that an incorrect genetic type is assigned to the evidence sample. A false match can occur if the genetic type of the contaminant matches by chance the genetic type of a principal in the case; in the worst case, the contaminant originates from another party in the case. Primary safeguards against carryover contamination include the use of different work areas for pre-PCR and post-PCR sample-handling, the use of biological safety hoods, the use of dedicated equipment (such as pipetters), and maintenance of a one-way flow of material from pre-PCR to post-PCR work areas so that PCR product cannot come into contact with sample materials. Those safeguards are outlined in the TWGDAM QC and QA guidelines (TWGDAM 1991, 1995). Sterile precautions similar to those used in handling infectious-disease agents in microbiology laboratories may also protect against carryover contamination; many of the contamination issues in PCR work and in infectious-disease microbiology are largely the same. Procedural safeguards can also be used. Genetic typing of evidence samples before the typing of reference samples protects against contamination of the former with the latter. Standard blank controls can be used to detect reagent and work area contamination. If there is any question regarding PCR carryover contamination, retained portions of the evidence item can be tested.

Analyst Bias

An analyst can be biased, consciously or unconsciously, in either direction. Genetic-typing results, however, are usually unambiguous; one cannot make one genetic type look like another simply by wishing it so. In VNTR analysis, patterns must meet empirically defined objective match criteria to be said to match. If enough loci are tested, it is extremely unlikely that two unrelated persons would have indistinguishable VNTR banding patterns.

Bias in forensic science usually leads to sins of omission rather than commission. Possibly exculpating evidence might be ignored or rejected. Contradictory test results or evidence of sample mixture may be discounted. Such bias is relatively easy to detect if test results are reviewed critically. Both TWGDAM and ASCLD-LAB accreditation guidelines stipulate that case files be reviewed internally by a qualified second analyst before a report is released. That not only reveals bias but also reveals mistakes in recording and oversights. Independent review by a defense expert provides even stronger protection against the possibility that bias will lead to a false match. This is most effective if the defense expert is thoroughly familiar with the standard procedures of the testing laboratory so that exceptions from the standard can be noted.

It has been argued that when the analysis of a test result involves subjective judgment, expectations or other biases can influence an analyst's interpretation (Nisbett and Ross 1980). For example, it has been suggested that analysts examining VNTR autoradiographs sometimes interpret faint bands as real or artifactual so as to produce a match with a suspect's profile (Lander 1989; Thompson and Ford 1991, p 140-141; Thompson 1995). The protocols of the next paragraph should greatly reduce such bias, if it exists.

Laboratory procedures should be designed with safeguards to detect bias and to identify cases of true ambiguity. Potential ambiguities should be documented; in particular, any visual overrides of the computer-assisted imaging devices used for making measurements in VNTR analysis must be noted and explained. Internal review can detect cases of bias and true ambiguity as well as oversights and mistakes in recording.

SHOULD AN ERROR RATE BE INCLUDED IN CALCULATIONS?

Some commentators have argued that the rate of profile matching due to laboratory error should be estimated and combined with the random-match probability (calculated with methods described in Chapter 4) to give only a single, summary statistic. But withholding the components of the summary statistic from the judge or jury would deprive the trier of fact of the opportunity to evaluate separately the possibility that the profiles match by coincidence as opposed to the possibility that they are reported to match by reason of laboratory or handling error. We discuss the legal arguments for and against such an exclusionary rule in Chapter 6. Here, we consider whether statistical analysis can provide a meaningful and accurate estimate of the probability of a laboratory or handling error that would produce a reported match between samples of nonmatching DNA.

• The question to be decided is not the general error rate for a laboratory or laboratories over time but rather whether the laboratory doing DNA testing in this particular case made a critical error. The risk of error in any particular case depends on many variables (such as number of samples, redundancy in testing, and analyst proficiency), and there is no simple equation to translate these variables into the probability that a reported match is spurious.

• To estimate accurately, from proficiency test results, the overall rate at which a laboratory declares nonmatching samples to match, as has been suggested, would require a laboratory to undergo an unrealistically large number of proficiency trials. Suppose that two laboratories each have under specific conditions a false-positive error rate of 0.10%—one match per 1,000 nonmatching proficiency trials. To establish that rate accurately, it would be necessary for each laboratory to undergo many thousands of trials. If one laboratory were to pass 1,000 proficiency tests without error, the 95% upper confidence limit for the error rate would be 0.30%. If the other laboratory had made one error, the limit would be 0.47%.[1] Those results are not significantly different statistically. Both laboratories could have a true rate of 0.10%, but a court or jury might regard the laboratory that made no errors in the test as significantly better than the one that made a single error. To put the numbers in context, only the largest forensic laboratories could have performed DNA testing in as many as 1,000 cases; no laboratory performs more proficiency tests than case tests, and none should be expected to.

• The pooling of proficiency-test results across laboratories has been suggested as a means of estimating an "industry-wide" error rate (Koehler et al. 1995). But that could penalize the better laboratories; multiple errors on a single test by one laboratory could substantially affect the overall estimated false-match error rate. Surveys of proficiency test results in the pre-DNA era show that the preponderance of errors originated in a small proportion of laboratories (Sensabaugh and Northey 1985; Sensabaugh 1987). Laboratories that made such errors today would have to document corrective action, which might include suspension of the analysts responsible for the errors (TWGDAM 1991).

• Estimating rates at which nonmatching samples are declared to match from historical performance on proficiency tests is almost certain to yield wrong values. When errors are discovered, they are investigated thoroughly so that corrections can be made. A laboratory is not likely to make the same error again, so the error probability is correspondingly reduced. There has been much publicity about proficiency-trial errors made by Cellmark in 1988 and 1989, the first years of its operation. Two matching errors were made in comparing 125 test samples, for an error rate of 1.6% in that batch. The causes of the two errors were discovered, and sample-handling procedures were modified to prevent their recurrence. There have been no errors in 450 additional tests through 1994. Clearly, an estimate of 0.35% (2/575) is inappropriate as a measure of the chance of error at Cellmark today.

---

[1]For the first case, with no errors, the upper 95% confidence limit, L, was calculated from the equation: $(1 - L)^N = 0.05$, where N is the number of error-free tests. In the case where one error was made in N tests, the equation was $(1 - L)^N + NL(1 - L)^{N-1} = 0.05$. The interpretation of a confidence limit is discussed in Chapter 5.

For all those reasons, we believe that a calculation that combines error rates with match probabilities is inappropriate. The risk of error is properly considered case by case, taking into account the record of the laboratory performing the tests, the extent of redundancy, and the overall quality of the results. However, there is no need to debate differing estimates of false-match error rates when the question of a possible false match can be put to direct test, as discussed in the next section.

RETESTING

A wrongly accused person's best insurance against the possibility of being falsely incriminated is the opportunity to have the testing repeated. Such an opportunity should be provided whenever possible. As we have previously noted, retesting provides an opportunity to identify and correct errors that might have been made during the course of analysis.

Whenever feasible, investigative agencies and testing laboratories should provide for repeat testing. Evidence items should be divided into two or more parts at the earliest possible time, and one or more parts retained for possible repeat testing. Ideally, the division should be made before DNA is extracted, and each part should be handled by different personnel. If division before DNA extraction is not feasible, the division should be made as soon as possible afterward and certainly before any analytical tests are initiated. Retained samples should be stored separately from analyzed samples under conditions that inhibit deteriorative loss, that is, at freezer temperatures and, for intact specimens, in the dry state. If retesting is called for, it should be done by an independent laboratory with different personnel. A defendant who believes that the match is spurious should welcome the opportunity for an independent repeat test. Legal aspects of retesting are discussed in Chapter 6.

CONCLUSIONS AND RECOMMENDATIONS

Laboratory Errors

The occurrence of errors can be minimized by scrupulous care in evidence collecting, sample-handling, laboratory procedures, and case review. Detailed guidelines for QC and QA (quality control and quality assurance), which are updated regularly, are produced by several organizations, including TWGDAM. ASCLD-LAB is established as an accrediting agency. The 1992 NRC report recommended that a National Committee on Forensic DNA Typing (NCFDT) be formed to oversee the setting of DNA-analysis standards. The DNA Identification Act of 1994 gives this responsibility to a DNA Advisory Board appointed by the FBI. We recognize the need for guidelines and standards and for accreditation by appropriate organizations.

Recommendation 3.1: Laboratories should adhere to high quality standards (such as those defined by TWGDAM and the DNA Advisory Board) and make every effort to be accredited for DNA work (by such organizations as ASCLD-LAB).

Proficiency Tests

Regular proficiency tests, both within a laboratory and by external examiners, are one of the best ways of ensuring high standards. To the extent that it is feasible, some of the tests should be blind.

Recommendation 3.2: Laboratories should participate regularly in proficiency tests, and the results should be available for court proceedings.

Duplicate Tests

We recognize that no amount of care and proficiency-testing can eliminate the possibility of error. However, duplicate tests, performed as independently as possible, can reduce the risk of error enormously. The best protection that an innocent suspect has against an error that could lead to a false conviction is the opportunity for an independent retest.

Recommendation 3.3: Whenever feasible, forensic samples should be divided into two or more parts at the earliest practicable stage and the unused parts retained to permit additional tests. The used and saved portions should be stored and handled separately. Any additional tests should be performed independently of the first by personnel not involved in the first test and preferably in a different laboratory.

4

Population Genetics

Much of the controversy about the forensic use of DNA has involved population genetics. In this chapter, we first explain the principles that are generally applicable. We then consider the special problem that arises because the population of the United States includes different population groups and subgroups with different allele frequencies. We develop and illustrate procedures for taking substructure into account in calculating match probabilities. We then show how those procedures can be applied to VNTRs and PCR-based systems.

Consider the comparison of DNA from a crime-scene specimen and from a suspect. (Actually, the evidence DNA need not come from the crime scene, nor the second sample from a suspect, but we use this vocabulary for convenience.) Under current procedures, if the DNA profile from the crime-scene sample reportedly matches that of the suspect, there are two possibilities (aside from error): The DNA at the crime scene came from the suspect or the DNA at the crime scene came from someone else who had the same profile as the suspect. If the DNA profile in question is common in the population, the crime-scene DNA might well have come from someone other than the suspect. If it is rare, the matching of the two DNA profiles is unlikely to be a mere coincidence; the rarer the profile, the less likely it is that the two DNA samples came from different persons.

To assess the probability that DNA from a randomly selected person has the same profile as the evidence DNA, we need to know the frequency of that profile in the population. That frequency is usually determined by comparison with some reference data set. A very small proportion of the trillions of possible profiles are found in any database, so it is necessary to use the frequencies of individual alleles to estimate the frequency of a given profile. That approach necessitates some assumptions about the mating structure of the population, and that is where population genetics comes in.[1]

ALLELE AND GENOTYPE PROPORTIONS

It is conventional in genetics to designate each gene or marker locus with a letter and each allele at that locus with a subscript numeral. So, A_{10} designates the tenth allele at locus A, B_5 the fifth allele at locus B, and so on. When we want a statement to apply to any of the alleles of a given locus, we use a literal subscript, such as i or j. We designate the frequencies (it is customary to use the word *frequency* for relative frequency, meaning proportion) of alleles with the letter p and a corresponding subscript. Thus, the frequency of allele A_3 is p_3 and of allele A_i is p_i. The sum of all the p_i values is 1 because it includes all the possibilities. Symbolically, if Σ stands for summation, $\Sigma p_i = 1$.

At the DQA locus, discussed in Chapter 2, six alleles are customarily used in forensic analysis (Table 4.1). For example, allele $D_{1.1}$ (designated as 1.1 in the table), has a proportion of 0.150, or 15.0%, in the black population; this was computed from the proportions in the right-hand portion of the table. The first six genotypes include the 1.1 allele (the top one has two copies) and adding their frequencies—0.036 + (0.076 + 0.009 + 0.036 + 0.027 + 0.080)/2—yields 0.150. The division by 2 is because in heterozygotes only half the alleles are $D_{1.1}$.

RANDOM MATING AND HARDY-WEINBERG PROPORTIONS

In the simplest population structure, mates are chosen at random. Clearly, the population of the United States does not mate at random; a person from Oregon is more likely to mate with another from Oregon than with one from Florida. Furthermore, people often choose mates according to physical and behavioral attributes, such as height and personality. But they do not choose each other according to the markers used for forensic studies, such as VNTRs and STRs. Rather, the proportion of matings between people with two marker genotypes is determined by their frequencies in the mating population. If the allele frequencies in Oregon and Florida are the same as those in the nation as a whole, then the proportions of genotypes in the two states will be the same as those for the United States, even though the population of the whole country clearly does not mate at random.

We use *random mating* to refer to choice of mates independently of genotype at the relevant loci and independently of ancestry. The expected proportions with

---

[1]An elementary exposition of population genetics is found in Hartl and Clark (1989). A more advanced text, with discussion of many of the formulae used here, is Nei (1987). Practical details of estimation and analysis are given by Weir (1990). See also Weir (1995a).

TABLE 4.1 Observed and Expected Frequencies of DQA Genotypes Based on 224 Blacks and 413 Whites[a]

ALLELES			GENOTYPES		
Allele Frequency %			Observed (Expected) Frequency %		
Allele	Black	White	Genotype	Black	White
1.1	15.0	13.7	**1.1/1.1**	**3.6 (2.3)**	**2.2 (1.9)**
1.2	26.3	19.7	1.1/1.2	7.6 (7.9)	3.6 (5.4)
1.3	4.5	8.5	1.1/1.3	0.9 (1.4)	2.9 (2.3)
2	12.1	10.9	1.1/2	3.6 (3.6)	1.9 (3.0)
3	11.8	20.1	1.1/3	2.7 (3.5)	5.3 (5.5)
4	30.3	27.1	1.1/4	8.0 (9.1)	9.2 (7.4)
			1.2/1.2	**8.5 (6.9)**	**4.6 (3.9)**
			1.2/1.3	2.2 (2.4)	3.4 (3.4)
			1.2/2	4.0 (6.4)	4.6 (4.3)
			1.2/3	7.1 (6.2)	8.2 (7.9)
			1.2/4	14.7 (16.0)	10.4 (10.7)
			1.3/1.3	**0.0 (0.2)**	**1.2 (0.7)**
			1.3/2	2.2 (1.1)	1.5 (1.9)
			1.3/3	1.3 (1.1)	1.7 (3.4)
			1.3/4	2.2 (2.7)	5.1 (4.6)
			2/2	**2.2 (1.5)**	**2.2 (1.2)**
			2/3	1.3 (2.9)	4.8 (4.4)
			2/4	8.5 (7.4)	4.6 (5.9)
			3/3	**0.9 (1.4)**	**4.4 (4.0)**
			3/4	9.4 (7.2)	11.4 (10.9)
			4/4	**8.9 (9.2)**	**6.8 (7.3)**
			Homozygotes	**24.1 (21.5)**	**21.4 (19.0)**
			Heterozygotes	75.7 (78.9)	78.6 (81.0)

[a]Homozygous genotypes in boldface. Data from Maryland State Crime Laboratory (Helmuth, Fildes, et al. 1990).

random mating are called the *Hardy-Weinberg (HW) proportions*, after GH Hardy, a British mathematician, and Wilhelm Weinberg, a German physician. For example, suppose that the proportions of alleles A_1, A_2, and A_3 are p_1, p_2, and p_3, respectively. The proportions of the three alleles among the sperm are given along the top of Table 4.2, and among the eggs, along the left margin. (It is intuitively reasonable and easily demonstrated that random mating is equivalent to combining gametes at random.) The genotypes and their frequencies are given in the interior of the table. The proportion, or frequency, of A_1A_1 homozygotes is thus p_1^2, and the proportion of A_2A_3 (we do not distinguish between A_2A_3 and A_3A_2) heterozygotes is $p_2p_3 + p_3p_2 = 2p_2p_3$.

According to Table 4.1, the proportions of alleles D_2 and D_4 in the white population are 0.109 and 0.271. If we assume HW and treat the sample allele frequencies as if they were the true population frequencies, then the proportion

TABLE 4.2   Hardy-Weinberg Proportions for a Locus with Three Alleles

Alleles (and Frequencies) in Eggs	Alleles (and Frequencies) in Sperm		
	A_1 (p_1)	A_2 (p_2)	A_3 (p_3)
A_1 (p_1)	A_1A_1 (p_1p_1)	A_1A_2 (p_1p_2)	A_1A_3 (p_1p_3)
A_2 (p_2)	A_2A_1 (p_2p_1)	A_2A_2 (p_2p_2)	A_2A_3 (p_2p_3)
A_3 (p_3)	A_3A_1 (p_3p_1)	A_3A_2 (p_3p_2)	A_3A_3 (p_3p_3)

of genotype D_2D_2 would be $(0.109)^2 = 0.012$, or 1.2%; as Table 4.1 shows, the observed fraction in this sample is 2.2%. The proportion of genotype D_2D_4 would be $2(0.109)(0.271) = 0.059$, or 5.9%; the observed value is 4.6%. Neither of those differences is statistically significant. (Note that genotype $D_{1.3}D_{1.3}$ was not found in the black database of 224 persons. With multiple alleles and four or five loci, as with VNTRs, most genotypes are not found in any given database.)

The HW relationship is easily stated symbolically. Using letter subscripts for generality, we let p_i and p_j be the population proportions of two alleles A_i and A_j. If capital letters designate the genotypic proportions, the HW expectations are

$$\text{homozygotes:} \quad A_iA_i: \; P_{ii} = p_i^2, \tag{4.1a}$$
$$\text{heterozygotes:} \quad A_iA_j: \; P_{ij} = 2p_ip_j, \; i \neq j. \tag{4.1b}$$

In words, the simple rule is: The proportion of persons with two copies of the same allele is the square of that allele's frequency, and the proportion of persons with two different alleles is twice the product of the two frequencies.

If for some reason a population does not exhibit HW proportions, as will be the case if mating in the previous generation(s) has not been random, only a single generation of random mating is needed to produce HW proportions. This is clear from Table 4.2, which shows that the proportions of gametes that unite to produce individuals in the next generation depend only on the allele frequencies, not the parental genotypes of the current generation. That property adds greatly to the usefulness of Equations 4.1, because it increases the probability that they are accurate. Populations from different parts of the world with different allele frequencies can be homogenized in a single generation, provided that mating is random. Of course, exactly random mating is very unlikely, but the equations are accurate enough for many practical purposes. In Chapter 5 we give estimates of the degree of uncertainty caused by departures from random mating proportions.

Table 4.1 shows how close actual populations come to HW proportions for DQA. The deviations from HW expectations are not great. In the white population, there is a small but statistically significant excess of homozygotes ($P \approx .03$);

there is an excess in the black population also, but it is not statistically significant.[2] It is not unusual to find a slightly higher proportion of homozygotes than predicted. We consider reasons for that later in the chapter.

In forensic applications, we are often interested in the magnitude of a difference, not just its statistical significance.[3] In the example above, the deficiency in the observed frequency of heterozygotes is greater in the black population than in the white, but only in the latter is it statistically significant. This is because statistical significance depends strongly on sample size: In large samples, quite small differences can be statistically significant but may not be biologically meaningful.

HW Proportions in a Large Sample

The data in Table 4.1 show approximate agreement with HW expectations, but there is some discrepancy. In the black population, the deficiency of heterozygotes is about 4%, and in the white population, it is about 3%. Most of this discrepancy comes from uncertainty introduced because of the sizes of the databases (224 and 413 persons). With larger samples, we would expect the agreement to be better.

---

[2]The usual χ^2 procedure is weak as a test for departure from HW proportions. The following test has considerably more power to detect departures from equilibrium of particular interest in population genetics (Robertson and Hill 1984). In a database of size N, let X_{ij} denote the number of persons of genotype A_iA_j. We assume the model

$$E(X_{ij}) = 2Np_ip_j(1 - \theta) \qquad \text{for } i \neq j;$$
$$E(X_{ii}) = N[p_i^2 + p_i(1 - p_i)\theta] \qquad \text{for } i = j.$$

We want to test the hypothesis that $\theta = 0$ (i.e., HW proportions; see section on subpopulation theory for a discussion of θ). It can be shown that a score test, which can be expected to be particularly powerful in detecting small values of θ, is based on the statistic

$$T = [\Sigma_i (X_{ii}/Q_i) - N]/[N(K - 1)]^{1/2},$$

where K is the number of alleles and Q_i is the maximum likelihood estimate of p_i if $\theta = 0$; in this case, Q_i is the observed proportion of A_i alleles.

An excess of homozygotes will lead to a positive value of T. Provided that N is large enough, the statistic T has approximately a standard normal distribution if $\theta = 0$.

In this case, for the white population in Table 4.1, the X_{ii} values are 413(0.022), 413(0.046), . . . ; the values of p_i are 0.137, 0.197, . . . ; N = 413; and K = 6. Substituting those values into the equation gives T = 1.88, which from a table of the normal probability integral gives P $\approx$ 0.03. For the black population, T = 0.77, giving P $\approx$ 0.22, where P refers to the probability.

[3]The homozygote excess in this data set is larger than is usually found for this locus in more extensive recent studies (such as Rivas et al. 1995). The data in Table 4.1 come from a variety of sources. The data on the black population come mainly from disease-screening programs in California. The data on whites come from a forensic laboratory and from the CEPH (Centre d'Etude du Polymorphisme Humain) collection of family data, stored in France and used for genetic linkage studies.

To examine a much larger sample, we consider data on the M-N blood group locus in the New York City white population for six periods between 1931 and 1969. At this locus, there are two alleles, M and N, and therefore three genotypes, MM, MN, and NN. The data include 6,001 persons (12,002 genes). We chose this locus for three reasons. First, there are only two alleles, and all three genotypes are identified. Second, the allele frequencies are close to 1/2, maximizing the power to detect departures from HW ratios. Finally, the observations are highly reliable technically. They are from A. S. Wiener, the leading blood-group expert of the time. New York City is certainly not a homogeneous population. The persistence of two alleles at intermediate frequencies in many populations suggests that these blood groups are subject to natural selection, but the selection is probably weak, and there are only minor allele-frequency differences among various European countries (Mourant et al. 1976, p 251-260).

These blood-group data (Table 4.3) show that, even in a population as heterogeneous as that of New York City, HW ratios are very closely approximated for traits that are not factors in mate selection. The overall heterozygote frequency is within about 1% of its HW expectation. Agreement with HW expectations should be at least as close for loci, such as most of those used in forensics, that are thought to be selectively neutral.

In the United States, bin frequencies within a racial group are usually similar in different regions. The top two graphs in Figure 4.1 show the similar distribution in white populations in Illinois and Georgia. Comparison of the black and the white populations illustrates a point often made by population geneticists— namely, that differences among individuals within a race are much larger than the differences between races. Nevertheless, the intergroup differences are large

TABLE 4.3   M-N Blood Group Genotypes in New York City Whites[a]

Sample	Total	MM	MN	NN	p_M	p_N	Relative Error
1	236	71	116	49	0.5466	0.4534	0.0083
2	461	132	232	97	0.5380	0.4620	− 0.0123
3	582	166	289	127	0.5335	0.4665	0.0024
4	3,268	1,037	1,623	608	0.5656	0.4344	− 0.0107
5	954	287	481	186	0.5529	0.4471	− 0.0198
6	500	158	249	93	0.5650	0.4350	− 0.0131
Total	6,001	1,851	2,990	1,160	0.5576	0.4424	− 0.0099

[a]The columns show the total number, numbers of the three genotypes, the allele frequencies, and the relative error, computed as follows: The expected number of heterozygotes is $2p_Mp_N \times$ Total. For sample 1 this is $2(0.5466)(0.4534)(236) = 116.975$; relative error $= (116.975 - 116.0)/116.975 = 0.0083$, or 0.83%. The sources of the six convenience samples are (1) parents, (2) mothers, (3) patients and hospital staff, (4) donors and paternity cases, (5) professional donors, (6) paternity cases. Data from Mourant et al. (1976), p 274.

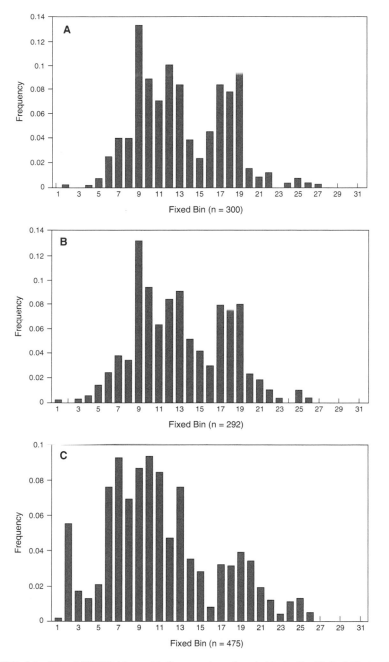

FIGURE 4.1   Fixed VNTR bins with frequencies of each bin in the United States. The locus is D2S44 with the enzyme HAE III: (A) Illinois white population, (B) Georgia white population, (C) US black population. From FBI (1993b), p 52, 51, 185.

enough that the FBI and other forensic laboratories keep separate databases for whites and blacks, and two separate databases for Hispanics, one for those from the eastern United States and another for those from the West.

Exclusion Power of a Locus

The data in Table 4.1 can be used for another purpose. As mentioned in Chapter 2, DQA data can distinguish samples from different individuals 93% of the time, clearing many innocent suspects. The overall probability that two independent persons will have the same DQA genotype is the sum of the squares of the genotype frequencies, as illustrated in Box 4.1.[4]

Box 4.1. Calculating the Exclusion Power of a Locus

We can illustrate the 93% average exclusion power of DQA by reference to the data in Table 4.1. The probability that two randomly chosen persons have a particular genotype is the square of its frequency in the population. The probability that two randomly chosen persons have the same unspecified genotype is the sum of the squares of the frequencies of all the genotypes. Summing the squares of the expected genotype frequencies (in parentheses) for the black population yields $0.023^2 + 0.079^2 + \ldots + 0.092^2 = 0.078$. We used expected rather than observed genotype frequencies to obtain greater statistical precision. For the white population, the value is 0.063. The average is about 0.07. The exclusion power is the probability that the two persons do *not* have the same genotype, or $1 - 0.07 = 0.93$.

If there are n loci, and the sum of squares of the genotype frequencies at locus i is P_i, then the exclusion power is $1 - (P_1 P_2 \ldots P_n)$. Five loci with the power of DQA would give an exclusion power of $1 - (0.07)^5 = 0.999998$.

---

[4]The concept of exclusion power was initially described by Fisher (1951). The calculation of the exclusion power can be simplified, especially if the number of alleles is large, by noting that in HW proportions the unconditional probability of identical genotypes is

$$\sum_i (p_i^2)^2 + \sum_{i,j;i<j} (2p_i p_j)^2 = 2\left(\sum_i p_i^2\right)^2 - \sum_i p_i^4.$$

Each sum on the right has n terms, where n is the number of alleles, rather than n(n + 1)/2, the number of genotypes. Note that the sum in parentheses on the right-hand side is the homozygosity, f_S.

An approximation to the probability of identical genotypes, due to Wong et al. (1987; see also Brenner and Morris 1990), is $2f_S^2 - f_S^3$. This gives the maximum value and is quite accurate for small f_s or when the allele frequencies are roughly equal.

Table 4.4 shows the frequency of bins (the VNTR equivalent of alleles—See Chapter 2) for two VNTR loci. D2S44 has an exclusion power of about 99%. The exclusion power of D17S79 is smaller because it has fewer alleles and more varied bin frequencies; its exclusion power is about 93%.

DEPARTURES FROM HW PROPORTIONS

Clearly, the HW assumption is hardly ever exactly correct. The issue in forensic DNA analysis is whether the departures are large enough to be important. The earlier report (NRC 1992) recommended that databases be tested for agreement with HW expectations and that loci that exhibit statistically significant differences from the expectation be discarded. In our view, that places too much emphasis on formal statistical significance. In practice, statistically significant

TABLE 4.4   Bin (Allele) Frequencies at Two VNTR Loci (D2S44 and D17S79) in US White Population[a]

D2S44				D17S79			
Bin	Size Range	N	Prop.	Bin	Size Range	N	Prop.
3	0- 871	8	0.005	1	0- 639	16	0.010
4	872- 963	5	0.003	2	640- 772	5	0.003
5	964-1,077	24	0.015	3	773- 871	11	0.007
6	1,078-1,196	38	0.024	4	872-1,077	6	0.004
7	1,197-1,352	73	0.046	6	1,078-1,196	23	0.015
8	1,353-1,507	55	0.035	7	1,197-1,352	348	0.224
9	1,508-1,637	197	0.124	8	1,353-1,507	307	0.198
10	1,638-1,788	170	0.107	9	1,508-1,637	408	0.263
11	1,789-1,924	131	0.083	10	1,638-1,788	309	0.199
12	1,925-2,088	79	0.050	11	1,789-1,924	44	0.028
13	2,089-2,351	131	0.083	12	1,925-2,088	50	0.032
14	2,352-2,522	60	0.038	13	2,089-2,351	16	0.010
15	2,523-2,692	65	0.041	14	2,352-	9	0.006
16	2,693-2,862	63	0.040				
17	2,863-3,033	136	0.086			1,552	0.999
18	3,034-3,329	141	0.089				
19	3,330-3,674	119	0.075				
20	3,675-3,979	36	0.023				
21	3,980-4,323	27	0.017				
22	4,324-5,685	13	0.008				
25	5,686-	13	0.008				
		1,584	1.000				

[a]D2 and D17 indicate that these are on chromosomes 2 and 17. N is the number of genes (twice the number of persons). Each bin includes a range of sizes (in base pairs) grouped so that no bin has fewer than five genes in the data set; this accounts for nonconsecutive bin numbers. Data from FBI (1993b), p 439, 530; see Budowle, Monson, et al. (1991).

departures are more likely to be found in large databases because the larger the sample size, the more likely it is that a small (and perhaps unimportant) deviation will be detected; in a small database, even a large departure might not be statistically significant (see Table 4.1 for an example). If the approach recommended in 1992 is followed, the loci with the largest databases, which are the most reliable, would often not be used. As stated earlier, our approach is different. We explicitly assume that departures from HW proportions exist and use a theory that takes them into account. But, as can be seen from the MN data in Table 4.3, we expect the deviations to be small.

Departures from HW proportions in populations can occur for three principal reasons. First, parents might be related, leading to inbreeding. Inbreeding decreases the proportion of heterozygotes, with a compensatory increase in homozygotes.

Second, the population can be subdivided, as in the United States. There are major racial groups (black, Hispanic, American Indian, East Asian, white). Allele frequencies are often sufficiently different between racial groups that it is desirable to have separate databases. Within a race, there is likely to be subdivision. The blending in the melting pot is far from complete, and in the white population, for example, some groups of people reflect to a greater or lesser extent their European origins. A consequence of population subdivision is that mates might have a common origin. Translated into genetic terms, that means that they share some common ancestry—that they are related. Thus, the consequences of population structure are qualitatively the same as those of inbreeding: a decrease of heterozygotes and an increase of homozygotes.[5]

Third, persons with different genotypes might survive and reproduce at different rates. That is called *selection*. We shall not consider this possibility, however, because the VNTR and other loci traditionally used in forensic analysis are chosen specifically because they are thought to be selectively neutral or nearly so. Some, such as DQA, are associated with functional loci that are thought to be selected but show no important departures from HW expectations.

Inbreeding and Kinship

Inbreeding means mating of two persons who are more closely related than if they were chosen at random. The theory of inbreeding was worked out 75 years ago by Sewall Wright, who defined the *inbreeding coefficient, F* (explained in Wright 1951). He gave a simple algorithm for computing F for any degree of

---

[5]There is a theoretical possibility of an increase in heterozygosity. It can happen in a population of first-generation children of different ancestral populations. But such populations are usually mixed with second-generation children, in whom heterozygosity is reduced, and there are other matings. So the effect of population subdivision is to increase homozygosity in the overwhelming majority, if not all, cases.

relationship of parents. The *kinship coefficient*, also designated by F and used to measure degree of relationship between two persons, is the same as the inbreeding coefficient of a (perhaps hypothetical) child.[6] For parent and child, F = 1/4; for sibs, 1/4; for half sibs, 1/8; for uncle (or aunt) and nephew (or niece) 1/8; for first cousins, 1/16; and for second cousins, 1/64.

With inbreeding, the expected proportion of heterozygotes is reduced by a fraction F; that of homozygotes is correspondingly increased. Thus, with inbreeding,

$$A_iA_i: P_{ii} = p_i^2 + p_i(1 - p_i)F, \tag{4.2a}$$
$$A_iA_j: P_{ij} = 2p_ip_j(1 - F). \tag{4.2b}$$

Because F for first cousins is 1/16, a population in which everybody had married a first cousin in the previous generation would be 1/16 less heterozygous than if marriages occurred without regard to family relationships.

Population Subgroups

The white population of the United States is a mixture of people of various origins, mostly European. The black and Hispanic populations also have multiple origins. Matings tend to occur between persons who are likely to share some common ancestry and thus to be somewhat related. Therefore, homozygotes are somewhat more common and heterozygotes less common than if mating were random.

The related problem of greatest concern in forensic applications is that profile frequencies are computed (under the assumption of HW proportions) from the population-average allele frequencies. If there is subdivision, that practice will always lead to an underestimate of homozygous genotype frequencies and usually to an overestimate of heterozygote frequencies.

To understand that, consider a population divided into subpopulations, each in HW proportions. Let p_i denote the frequency of the allele A_i in the entire population. If that entire population mated at random, the frequencies of the genotypes A_iA_i and A_iA_j ($i \neq j$) would be p_i^2 and $2p_ip_j$, respectively. The relationship between those hypothetical genotype frequencies and the actual frequencies of homozygotes, P_{ii}, and heterozygotes, P_{ij}, in the entire population is given by

---

[6]Wright's algorithm is given in standard textbooks (Hartl and Clark 1989, p 238ff; see also Wright 1951). One definition of the inbreeding coefficient is the probability that the two homologous genes in a person are descended from the same gene in a common ancestor. The kinship coefficient of two persons is the corresponding probability of identity by descent of two genes, randomly chosen, one from each person. From those definitions, Wright's algorithm can readily be derived. The algorithm is easily modified for genes on the X-chromosome, but since they constitute such a small fraction of the genome, this is an unnecessary refinement for our purposes.

Wahlund's principle and its extension to multiple alleles and covariances (Nei 1965). That is,

$$P_{ii} = p_i^2 + V_i, \tag{4.3a}$$
$$P_{ij} = 2p_ip_j + 2C_{ij}, \tag{4.3b}$$

where V_i designates the variance of the frequency of A_i and C_{ij} the covariance of the frequencies of A_i and A_j among the subpopulations.[7]

The variance, being the sum of squared quantities, is always positive. The average covariance is negative, because the sum of the variances and covariances over all the alleles must equal zero (because the left-hand terms and first terms on the right, when summed over alleles, must each add to 1). Covariances for specific pairs of alleles, however, might be either positive or negative. In particular, if the allele frequencies are very low and the population is small, they might become positive. If the population is strongly subdivided, the likelihood of positive covariances decreases, because the average value is negative and large.

Thus, to repeat, computing the frequency of a genotype from the population-average allele frequencies, rather than using the average of the actual subpopulation genotype frequencies, will always underestimate the frequency of homozygotes and usually overestimate the frequency of heterozygotes.

As an illustrative example, consider the data in Table 4.5. They come from four white populations—three European and one Canadian. The homozygosities are given in the next-to-bottom line. The weighted average homozygosity for the four populations,[8] with weights proportional to the sizes of the databases, is 0.0759. For the pooled populations, assuming that the total pool mated at random, the homozygosity is 0.0745. As the Wahlund principle states, the average homozy-

---

[7]Suppose that the proportion of persons in subpopulation k is w_k and the frequency of A_i in that subpopulation is $p_{i,k}$. Let the random variable π_i denote the frequency of A_i in each subpopulation. Thus, $\pi_i = p_{i,k}$ with probability w_k, and the average value of π_i is

$$p_i = E(\pi_i) = \sum_k w_k p_{i,k}.$$

Then

$$P_{ii} = E(\pi_i^2) = p_i^2 + V_i,$$
$$P_{ij} = E(2\pi_i\pi_j) = 2p_ip_j + 2C_{ij},$$

where

$$V_i = Var(\pi_i) = \sum_k w_k(p_{i,k} - p_i)^2,$$

$$C_{ij} = Cov(\pi_i, \pi_j) = \sum_k w_k(p_{i,k} - p_i)(p_{j,k} - p_j).$$

[8]The weighted average homozygosity of the subpopulations, assuming random mating within subpopulations, is $\sum_{i,k} w_k p_{i,k}^2$, where w_k is the proportion of persons in the k-th subpopulation and $p_{i,k}$ is the frequency of allele A_i in the k-th subpopulation. The expected homozygosity if the entire population mated at random is $\sum_i p_i^2$, where $p_i = \sum_k w_k p_{i,k}$.

TABLE 4.5   Bin (Allele) Frequencies and Proportions in Four Populations and Their Weighted Averages[a]

Bin	Canadian n_i	p_i	Swiss n_i	p_i	French n_i	p_i	Spanish n_i	p_i	Total n_i	p_i
1	0	0.000	0	0.000	0	0.000	0	0.000	0	0.000
2	1	0.001	0	0.000	1	0.002	1	0.002	3	0.001
3	1	0.001	1	0.001	0	0.000	3	0.005	5	0.002
4	5	0.005	1	0.001	3	0.005	2	0.004	11	0.004
5	8	0.009	13	0.016	3	0.005	6	0.004	30	0.011
6	21	0.023	16	0.020	10	0.016	7	0.014	54	0.019
7	35	0.038	48	0.060	26	0.042	23	0.045	132	0.046
8	41	0.045	30	0.037	24	0.039	17	0.033	112	0.039
9	130	0.142	100	0.124	68	0.110	52	0.102	350	0.123
10	78	0.085	73	0.091	67	0.109	43	0.085	261	0.092
11	72	0.079	67	0.083	35	0.057	48	0.094	222	0.078
12	81	0.088	60	0.075	43	0.070	24	0.047	208	0.073
13	81	0.088	59	0.073	56	0.091	50	0.098	246	0.086
14	23	0.025	24	0.030	29	0.047	18	0.035	94	0.033
15	19	0.021	38	0.047	14	0.023	19	0.037	90	0.032
16	44	0.048	40	0.050	27	0.044	22	0.043	133	0.047
17	98	0.107	71	0.088	72	0.117	61	0.120	302	0.106
18	69	0.075	64	0.080	53	0.086	36	0.071	222	0.078
19	64	0.070	61	0.076	48	0.078	36	0.071	209	0.073
20	18	0.020	12	0.015	10	0.016	18	0.035	58	0.020
21	11	0.012	11	0.014	11	0.018	13	0.026	46	0.016
22	5	0.005	7	0.009	8	0.013	3	0.006	23	0.008
23	0	0.000	2	0.002	0	0.000	0	0.000	2	0.001
24	1	0.001	2	0.002	0	0.000	3	0.006	6	0.002
25	7	0.008	2	0.002	5	0.008	0	0.000	14	0.005
26	3	0.003	2	0.002	3	0.005	2	0.004	10	0.004
27	0	0.000	0	0.000	0	0.000	0	0.000	0	0.000
28	0	0.000	0	0.000	0	0.000	1	0.002	1	0.000
Total (2N)	916	0.999	804	0.998	616	1.001	508	0.998	2,844	0.999
Hom. $= \Sigma p_i^2$	0.079		0.073		0.077		0.073		0.074	

$$f_S = 0.0759 \qquad f_T = 0.0745 \qquad \bar{\theta} = 0.0015$$

[a]The bins are numbered (see Table 4.3). The number at the bottom is the total number of genes (twice the number of persons). The locus is D2S44, and the enzyme is Hae III. Data from FBI (1993b), p 461, 464-468. Three French populations were pooled.

gosity of the subpopulations is greater and the heterozygosity less than those of the pooled population.

The striking feature of the table is not the greater heterozygosity of the pooled population, which is expected, but the smallness of the difference. The four populations and the composite all differ from HW proportions only very slightly. The data on M-N blood groups (Table 4.3) suggest that this is not surprising.

SUBPOPULATION THEORY

We can deal with a structured population by using a theory that is very similar to that of inbreeding. We shall reserve the symbol F for inbreeding caused by a specified degree of relationship of the parents, such as cousins. The symbol θ is sometimes used in forensic science, so we employ it to designate the effects of population subdivision. The following formulae, which are analogous to those for inbreeding, define a parameter θ_{ij} for each genotype A_iA_j. These formulae do not require that the subpopulations mate at random or even that they be distinct.

$$A_iA_i: P_{ii} = p_i^2 + p_i(1 - p_i)\theta_{ii}, \tag{4.4a}$$
$$A_iA_j: P_{ij} = 2p_ip_j(1 - \theta_{ij}), \ i \neq j. \tag{4.4b}$$

In general, the parameters θ_{ij} may be positive or negative. However, substituting the inequalities $P_{ii} \leq p_i$ and $P_{ij} \leq 1$ into equations 4.4a and 4.4b, respectively, demonstrates that $\theta_{ij} \leq 1$ for every i and j.

Let f_0 denote the actual homozygosity in the entire population, and let $h_0 = 1 - f_0$ denote the corresponding heterozygosity. If the population were divided into distinct subpopulations and mating were random within each subpopulation, we would designate f_0 and h_0 by f_S and h_S, respectively. If mating were random within the entire population, these quantities would become f_T and h_T, respectively.

The average of the parameters θ_{ij} over all genotypes is precisely Wright's (1951) fixation index F_{IT}:

$$\bar{\theta} = \frac{f_0 - f_T}{1 - f_T} = \frac{h_T - h_0}{h_T} = F_{IT}. \tag{4.5}$$

For an elementary explanation of Equation 4.5 for equal subpopulation numbers, see Hartl and Clark (1989, p 293); Nei (1987, p 162) presents a more detailed treatment. We also provide an alternative and more general derivation (Appendix 4A).

It is clear that $\bar{\theta}$ is a composite quantity, averaged over all genotypes, whereas Equations 4.4 involve θ_{ii} and θ_{ij} for individual genotypes. In general, $\bar{\theta}$ may be positive or negative, but $\bar{\theta} \leq 1$. However, if the local populations are mating at random or if there is local inbreeding, then the true value of $\bar{\theta}$ is positive. In empirical data, if statistical uncertainties are taken into account, $\bar{\theta}$ is almost always positive or very small. For selectively neutral loci, population values of θ_{ij} for particular genotypes may be negative only temporarily, except in highly unusual situations. Of course, point estimates from samples, which are quite inaccurate, may be negative even when the true value is positive (Weir and Cockerham 1984; Nei 1987; Chakraborty and Danker-Hopfe 1991).

Most of the forensic literature posits distinct subpopulations in HW proportions. In that case, comparison of Equations 4.4 with Equations 4.3 shows that θ_{ii} and θ_{ij} are given by

$$\theta_{ii} = V_i/[p_i(1 - p_i)], \tag{4.6a}$$

$$\theta_{ij} = -C_{ij}/(p_i p_j). \tag{4.6b}$$

Because variances are always greater than or equal to zero, we now have $\theta_{ii} \geq$ 0. However, θ_{ij} can be either positive or negative, although its average value is positive, because the average value of the covariance is negative.

Now $\bar{\theta}$ becomes

$$\bar{\theta} = \frac{f_S - f_T}{1 - f_T} = \frac{h_T - h_S}{h_T} = F_{ST}, \tag{4.7}$$

which must be nonnegative. The symbols F_{ST} (Wright 1951), G_{ST} (Nei 1973, 1977), and θ (Cockerham 1969, 1973; Weir 1990) have very similar meanings and for our purposes can be regarded as interchangeable (Chakraborty and Danker-Hopfe 1991). According to Equation 4.7, if the subpopulations are distinct and in HW proportions, then $\bar{\theta} = F_{ST}$.

Table 4.5 shows that the frequencies in the four populations are quite similar. Furthermore, the values agree well with those from the United States in Table 4.4. The value of $\bar{\theta}$ is about 0.0015, as shown in Box 4.2.

We chose European populations in the example because they are likely to differ more than the US subpopulations descended from those European countries. The original differences are diminished in the United States by mixing with other groups, so we would expect $\bar{\theta}$ calculated for white populations in the United States to be smaller than $\bar{\theta}$ calculated for European and Canadian populations.

We can use Tables 4.4 and 4.5 for another comparison. Treating the composite European and Canadian populations as one randomly mating subpopulation and the US population as the other, $\bar{\theta}$ turns out to be 0.0004. These are, of course, estimates for particular databases, and the estimate is subject to random fluctuation.

If mating is random in each subpopulation, then $\bar{\theta}$ in Equation 4.7 depends only on the allelic (rather than the genotypic) frequencies. In that case, $\bar{\theta}$ can be

---

Box 4.2.   Calculating $\bar{\theta}$: An Example

From Equation 4.7, we have $\bar{\theta} = (f_S - f_T)/(1 - f_T)$. Positing local random mating, we obtain the expected homozygote frequencies by squaring each allele frequency in Table 4.5 and summing the frequencies for each population. The four values are then averaged using weights proportional to the sizes of the databases to give f_S. Then f_T is calculated as the sum of the squares of the allele frequencies for the pooled data. We obtain $f_S = 0.0759$ and $f_T = 0.0745$, so $\bar{\theta} = (0.0759 - 0.0745)/(1 - 0.0745) = 0.0015$.

A glance at Equation 4.7 tells us that $\bar{\theta}$ cannot be large if f_S and f_T are small, as they must be for loci with a large number of alleles, each of low frequency.

estimated more accurately, because allele frequencies are subject to smaller sampling fluctuations than are genotype frequencies. There are several statistical methods for estimating $\bar{\theta}$ from sample allele frequencies. They vary with the assumptions made and the accuracy desired, but the estimates are very close to one another (Weir and Cockerham 1984; Nei 1987; Chakraborty and Danker-Hopfe 1991).

TAKING POPULATION STRUCTURE INTO ACCOUNT

In the early days of DNA population analysis, there appeared to be a clear excess of homozygotes and a deficiency of heterozygotes (Lander 1989; Cohen 1990). The excess was so large as to suggest a high degree of population stratification; Lander described it as "spectacular deviations from Hardy-Weinberg equilibrium." The large deviations, however, turned out to be an artifact, a limitation of the laboratory method (Devlin et al. 1990). As discussed in Chapter 2, a single VNTR band does not necessarily indicate a homozygous person. It might arise because a second band obscured for some reason. When that was taken into account, the excess homozygosity disappeared, and a number of studies have since confirmed that the database populations are very close to HW proportions (e.g., Chakraborty 1991; Chakraborty et al. 1992; Devlin et al. 1992; Risch and Devlin 1992; Weir 1992b,c). It is also illustrated by our numerical examples. Yet, the US population is not *exactly* in HW proportions. In a large-enough sample, the departure from HW could surely be demonstrated. As emphasized before (NRC 1992), the power of standard methods to detect a statistically significant deviation is very small; very large samples are required. But there are stronger methods that test the level of heterozygosity per se, and we have used one earlier (See Footnote 2).

To restate: Our approach is not to assume HW proportions, but to use procedures that take deviations from HW into account. To do that, we return to discussions of population structure as measured by $\bar{\theta}$.

If we assume the population to be subdivided, there are two options. One is to use $\bar{\theta}$ empirically. The second is to estimate neither $\bar{\theta}$ nor the individual values of θ_{ij}, but to take advantage of the fact that for practical purposes they can be assumed to be positive.

The first option is to measure $\bar{\theta}$ empirically and substitute it for θ_{ij} in Equations 4.4. For US white, black, and Hispanic populations in the FBI databases, the value of $\bar{\theta}$ is usually less than 0.01—often considerably less (Weir 1994). We illustrated that for D2S44 earlier in this chapter. In particular, the value for whites is estimated (from data obtained from Lifecodes, a commercial DNA laboratory) as 0.002, for blacks 0.007, and for Hispanics 0.009 (Roeder et al. 1995). So deviations of individual subpopulations from HW are likely to be minor.

However, for VNTRs we recommend that instead of estimating θ_{ij} and applying Equations 4.4, no adjustment be made for heterozygotes and that the more conservative "2p rule" be used for homozygotes. This rule is explained and justified as follows.

We assume only that θ_{ij} is positive for all pairs of alleles. We know that for heterozygotes the HW calculation is generally an overestimate, because from Equation 4.4b the true value includes $(1 - \theta_{ij})$. The assumption of HW proportions always gives overestimates of heterozygotes when $\theta_{ij} > 0$. Therefore, even if we do not know the actual value of each θ_{ij}, we can obtain conservative estimates of match probabilities for all heterozygotes by assuming HW proportions. Negative estimates of θ_{ij} are observed for some data, but these are usually very close to zero and are almost certainly the consequence of sampling errors. In any case, they are usually so small (and thus $1 - \theta_{ij}$ is so close to one) as to have little effect on the calculations.

That is not the case with homozygotes, as is clear from Equation 4.4a, because with small allele frequencies, a small value of θ_{ii} can introduce a large change in the genotype frequency. However, we can obtain conservative estimates of match probabilities for homozygotes by using the 2p rule. Single bands can be from either homozygotes or heterozygotes in which the second allele has been missed. It has been suggested that a single band at allele A_i be assigned a frequency of $2p_i$ (Budowle, Giusti, et al. 1991; Chakraborty et al. 1992; NRC 1992). That has been criticized for being too conservative because it includes in the frequency estimate several heterozygotes that can usually be ruled out. But an exact correction is not feasible in most cases, because the nature of the missing band is uncertain.

We can make a virtue of the suggested procedure. It can be shown[9] that if $2p_i$ is assigned to the frequency of a single band at the position of allele A_i, then this simple formula gives an estimate that is necessarily larger than the true frequency. The upper bound always holds, but it is necessary only if some single bands represent heterozygotes. We emphasize that the 2p rule is intended only for loci, such as VNTRs, in which alleles are rare and single bands may be ambiguous.

---

[9]Let X and Y stand for the maternal and paternal alleles at the A locus. A single band at the position of allele A_i can be either an A_iA_i homozygote or a heterozygote with one of the alleles being A_i. Thus, we want the probability that at least one allele is A_i:

$$P(X = A_i \text{ or } Y = A_i) = P(X = A_i) + P(Y = A_i) - P(X = A_i \text{ and } Y = A_i)$$
$$= 2p_i - P_{ii} \leq 2p_i.$$

For an alternative proof, using standard population genetics methods, note that the probability on the left-hand side of the first equation is equal to

$$P_{ii} + \sum_{j;j \neq i} P_{ij} = 2\left(P_{ii} + \frac{1}{2}\sum_{j;j \neq i} P_{ij}\right) - P_{ii} = 2p_i - P_{ii} \leq 2p_i,$$

as above. Clearly, the rule is very conservative because the summation includes a large number of heterozygotes that would be detected as double bands.

We arrive at a simple procedure for obtaining a conservative estimate, that is, one that generally underestimates the weight of the evidence against a defendant: *Assign the frequency $2p_i$ to each single band and $2p_ip_j$ to each double band.* In arriving at this important conclusion we have made only one assumption: that θ_{ij} ($i \neq j$) is positive. Then the HW rule is conservative, because in a structured population, heterozygote frequencies are overestimated and, with this adjustment, so are homozygote frequencies.

Empirical data show that with VNTRs departures from HW proportions are small enough for the HW assumption to be sufficiently accurate for forensic purposes. For example, a θ-value of 0.01, larger than most estimates, would lead to an error in genotype estimates of about 1%. Nevertheless, to be conservative, we recommend that the HW principle, with the value $2p_i$ for a single band at allele A_i, be used.

MULTIPLE LOCI AND LINKAGE EQUILIBRIUM

With random mating (and in the absence of selection), the population approaches a state in which the frequency of a multilocus genotype is the product of the genotype frequencies at the separate loci. When the population has arrived at such a state, it is said to be in *linkage equilibrium (LE)*. That is a misnomer, in that the principle applies also to loci that are unlinked, as on nonhomologous chromosomes, but we shall adhere to this time-honored convention.

There is, however, an important difference between HW proportions and LE. Whereas, as mentioned earlier, HW proportions are attained in a single generation of random mating, LE is attained only gradually. For pairs of unlinked loci, the departure from LE is halved each generation. Thus, the departure from LE is reduced to 1/2, 1/4, 1/8, . . . of its original value in successive generations. For sets of three or more unlinked loci, the asymptotic rate of approach to LE is still 50% per generation (Nagylaki 1993, p 634 and references therein), so a few generations of random mating bring the population very close to LE, but it does not happen in a single generation.

Loci need not be on nonhomologous chromosomes to attain LE, although loci on the same chromosome approach LE more slowly than those on different chromosomes. For a pair of loci, the departure from LE is reduced to $(1-r)$, $(1-r)^2$, $(1-r)^3$, . . . of its initial value in successive generations, where r is the rate of recombination between the two loci. For example, D1S80 and D1S7 are both in the same chromosome arm, yet they do not exhibit a statistically significant departure from LE between them (Budowle, Baechtel, et al. 1995). Most forensic applications, however, use loci that are on nonhomologous chromosomes (for which r = 0.5).

The consequence of the gradual approach to equilibrium is that allele combinations that were together in an ancestral population might carry over into contemporary descendants. The mixing process that takes place because of migration and intermarriage generally reduces deviations from linkage equilibrium more slowly than it does deviations from HW proportions.[10]

Another important difference between HW and LE is that whereas a population broken into subgroups has a systematic bias in favor of homozygosity, departures from LE increase some associations and decrease others in about equal degrees. Although there might be linkage disequilibrium, we would expect some canceling of opposite effects.[11] The important point, however, is not the canceling but the small amount of linkage disequilibrium (see below). In this case, multiplying together the frequencies at the several loci will yield roughly the correct answer. An estimated frequency of a composite genotype based on the product of conservative estimates at the several loci is expected to be conservative for the multilocus genotypes.

How Much Departure from LE is Expected?

The main cause of linkage disequilibrium for forensic markers is incomplete mixing of different ancestral populations. We can get an idea of the extent of this in the US white population by asking what would happen in a mixed population derived from two different European countries. There are abundant VNTR data from Switzerland and Spain, so we shall use them for illustration (FBI 1993b).

We shall illustrate this with a particular pair of alleles, one at each of two loci. In each European population, let p_{16} stand for the frequency of bin 16 at locus D10S28, q_{13} for that of bin 13 at locus D2S44, and P for that of the 16-13 gamete. In each European population, under the assumption of LE, the proportion of gametes with alleles 16 and 13 is $p_{16}q_{13} = P$. In the first-generation mixed population, under the assumption of an equal number of migrants from each parent population, the values of p_{16}, q_{13}, and P will be the average of the corresponding parental values, $\bar{p}_{16}$, $\bar{q}_{13}$, and $\bar{P}$. The linkage disequilibrium, the difference between $\bar{P}$ and $\bar{p}_{16}\bar{q}_{13}$, is halved each generation, and finally $\bar{P} = \bar{p}_{16}\bar{q}_{13}$. Although P changes each generation, $\bar{p}_{16}\bar{q}_{13}$ does not, since the allele frequencies remain constant. The numerical values are shown in Table 4.6.

The initial linkage disequilibrium is such that $\bar{P}$ is about 4% greater than its value at LE, but this is reduced to less than 1% by the third generation. These alleles are typical of those in the data set. A more extreme difference is found between bin 25 in D10S38 and Bin 20 in D2S44. In this case, the initial value of $\bar{P}$ is about 25% less than expected, and the difference is reduced to about 3%

---

[10]With partial mixing, the rate of approach to HW depends on the rate of mixing; for LE, it depends on both the mixing and crossover rates (Nei and Li 1973). For loose linkage, the two rates might be about the same.

[11]With two or more loci and linkage, multiple homozygotes might be slightly increased in frequency (Haldane 1949). However, the increase is very slight.

TABLE 4.6   The Approach to LE in a Mixed Population[a]

	p_{16}	q_{13}	$p_{16}q_{13}$	P	Difference[b]
Swiss	0.030	0.073	0.00219	0.00219	0
Spanish	0.051	0.098	0.00500	0.00500	0
Generation	$\bar{p}_{16}$	$\bar{q}_{13}$	$\bar{p}_{16}\,\bar{q}_{13}$	$\bar{P}$	Difference
1	0.0405	0.0855	0.00346	0.00360	0.000140
2	.	.	.	0.00353	0.000070
3	.	.	.	0.00350	0.000035
4	.	.	.	0.00348	0.000018
5	.	.	.	0.00347	0.000009
Equilibrium	0.0405	0.0855	0.00346	0.00346	0

[a]The population starts with an equal mixture of persons from Spain and Switzerland and mates at random thereafter. The fraction p_{16} is the frequency of bin 16 at locus D10S28 and q_{13} is that of bin 13 at locus D2S44. Data from FBI (1993b, p 467, 468, 526, 527).
[b]Difference = $P - p_{16}q_{13}$.

by the fourth generation. Four is probably not far from the average number of generations since ancestral migration from Europe.

Many more examples could be chosen, but the general conclusion is that departures from LE are not likely to be large, a few percent at most. The cause of uncertainty in using population averages as a substitute for local data is mainly allele-frequency differences between subpopulations, not departures from HW and LE in each subpopulation.

What Do the VNTR Data Show?

Several authors report agreement with LE or only slight departures from it (Chakraborty and Kidd 1991; Weir 1992a,b, 1993b; Chakraborty 1993). An early study of multiple loci (Risch and Devlin 1992) made use of databases from the FBI and Lifecodes. Risch and Devlin calculated the expected proportion of two-locus matches as the product of the match probabilities at the component loci. From 2,701,834 pairs of profiles in the FBI data involving blacks, whites, eastern Hispanics, and western Hispanics, they calculated an expected total of 95.3 two-locus matches, whereas 104 were observed—not a statistically significant difference.[12] Only one three-locus match was found among 7,628,360 pairs of

[12]The number 2,701,834 was obtained as follows. In the black database, there were 342 persons in whom alleles at the D1 and D2 loci were recorded; the number of pairs is $(342)(341)/2 = 58,311$. There were 350 in whom D1 and D4 were recorded, yielding $(350)(349)/2 = 61,075$. Continuing through five loci within each of the four groups, the totals are 2,701,834 and 104 two-locus matches, for a rate of 3.8×10^{-5}. When persons from different groups were chosen, there were 7,064,266

profiles; curiously, it was between a white and an eastern Hispanic. There were no four- or five-locus matches (see also Herrin 1993).

If there is no important departure from independence for two loci, it is unlikely that there will be any for larger numbers of loci but let us nonetheless look at it empirically. To test beyond two loci, it is necessary to use a system in which matches are much more frequent. Lifecodes uses a different enzyme (Pst I) that produces larger fragments, which leads to higher allele frequencies. That made possible a test of three-locus matches in the white population. Whereas 404 were expected, 416 were observed (Risch and Devlin 1992). We conclude that in the large databases of the major races, the populations are quite close to HW and LE.[13]

That assertion has been questioned by some geneticists. The questions have often not been accompanied by data, but in one exception, a paper that has been frequently quoted in the literature and in court cases, Krane et al. (1992) reported a statistically significant difference in allele frequency between persons of Finnish and Italian ancestry. Subsequent analysis has removed much, but not all, of the discrepancy.[14]

Geisser and Johnson (1992, 1993) analyzed their data in a way that is different from the usual one, dividing the alleles into quantiles of equal frequency. Their analysis showed statistically significant departures from random proportions. Others fail to find this from comparable data sets (Devlin and Risch 1992; Weir 1993b). The cause of this difference might be the identification of single bands

---

pairs and 176 matches, for a rate of 2.5×10^{-5}. As expected, the matching frequency is higher within groups, but it is not much higher; the allele frequencies do not differ greatly, even between groups. As has often been emphasized by population geneticists, most of the variability is between persons within groups, not between groups.

[13]It has been suggested more than once (e.g., Sullivan 1992) that the FBI sample has been edited and that five-locus matches have been removed. The explanation lies in the inadvertent inclusion of the same person in more than one sample. Almost all such cases were accounted for either by examination of the record or by testing additional loci. Furthermore, the fact that there was only one three-locus match and no four-locus match argues against the reality of any seeming five-locus matches. In a larger study of the TWGDAM database (see below), there were no five-locus matches and only two four-locus matches when six loci were compared. Another example that has been mentioned as evidence of multilocus matches is a highly inbred group, the Karitiana, in the Amazon. See Kidd et al. (1993) for a discussion of the lack of relevance of this example to populations in the United States.

[14]Part of the difference lay in simple errors in transcribing data, and another part is attributable to resampling the same persons from small populations (Devlin, Krontiris, et al. 1993). Krane et al. (1992) also emphasized a greater frequency of three-locus matches than that given by the FBI data. But that is to be expected, as it was in the Lifecodes data set; so, although there remains evidence of substructure, the amount is considerably smaller than originally reported. A later study of Finnish and Italian populations showed no such differences (Budowle, Monson, and Giusti 1994), and agreed with data from other populations in various parts of the world (Herrin 1993). But we should note that there are differences among subgroups that would be statistically significant in large samples, but which might be too small to be important.

with homozygotes, and we are persuaded by the careful analyses of large data sets by others that the departures are not large enough to invalidate the product rule (with the 2p rule—see below). It has also been argued that there should be a separate database for each region of the United States. The failure to find important departures make that less important than it would have seemed before the large amounts of data were acquired. Unless local variability is much larger than the data indicate, the loss of information from statistical uncertainties in small samples is likely to outweigh any gain from having local databases.

Regardless of whether the population is exactly in LE, the rarity of multilocus matches is evident even in large data bases. As mentioned earlier, Risch and Devlin (1992) found no four- or five-locus matches among 7,628,360 pairs of profiles. The much larger composite database recorded by TWGDAM (Chakraborty, personal communication) comprises 7,201 whites, 4,378 blacks, and 1,243 Hispanics. Among 58 million pairwise comparisons with four, five, or six loci within racial groups, two matches were found for four loci and none for five or six. The matching pairs did not match for the other two loci tested, so this is not a case of DNA from the same person appearing twice in the database. These pairs were necessarily run on different gels, so the precision may have been less than if they had been run on the same gel, and there might have been close relatives in the databases. Nevertheless, the general conclusion is that four-locus matches are extremely rare and five- and six-locus matches have not been seen in these very large databases.

Finally, we can examine conformity to LE in this very large data set accumulated by TWGDAM (Chakraborty, personal communication). The numbers, especially in the white population, are large enough to provide a sensitive test for departure from LE. The data are shown in Table 4.7. The expected number of two- and three-locus matches were calculated from the observed proportion of single-locus matches, assuming LE. As can be seen, when the numbers are large enough for statistical errors to be small, the departures are very small.

TABLE 4.7   Observed and Expected Numbers of 2-and 3-Locus Matches in the TWGDAM Data Set.[a]

	Two Loci		Three Loci	
	Expected	Observed	Expected	Observed
White	33,013	33,131	321	291
Black	5,137	5,246	35	39
Hispanic	1,568	1,609	18	25
Indian	1,964	2,320	32	66
East Asian	830	864	6	13

[a]The calculations were made from data supplied by R. Chakraborty.

The deviation from expected is 0.4% in whites and 2.1% in blacks. These results reinforce the conclusions of Risch and Devlin that VNTR loci are very close to LE. Only in the American Indian population is there an appreciable departure from randomness. That is expected because of the heterogeneous tribal structure.

With LE, we can proceed as follows. If the proportions of alleles A_i and A_j at the A locus are p_i and p_j and the proportions of B_h and B_k at the B locus are q_h and q_k, the proportion of the composite genotype $A_iA_j B_hB_k$ is $(2p_ip_j)(2q_hq_k)$ and of $A_iA_j B_kB_k$ is $(2p_ip_j)(q_k{}^2)$, or $(2p_ip_j)(2q_k)$ with the 2p rule, and so on for more than two loci.

Table 4.4 gives examples of VNTR allele (bin) frequencies (Budowle et al. 1991). If A stands for locus D2S44 and B for D17S79 and subscripted bin numbers designate alleles, the probability of genotype $A_7A_{11} B_7B_{12}$ is $[2(0.046)(0.083)][2(0.224)(0.032)] = 0.00011$, or 1/9,135. If the A locus had a single band at A_7, the probability would be calculated conservatively with the 2p rule as $[2(0.046)][2(0.224)(0.032)] = 0.00132$, or 1/758. It is not surprising that, even with the 2p rule, the calculated probabilities become very small when four or five loci are tested.

Recently, more VNTR loci have been added. The FBI now has a total of seven and some states use eight. If, at each locus, every allele frequency in the profile equaled 0.1 and eight loci were heterozygous, the probability of the profile would be $[2(0.1)(0.1)]^8 = 2.6 \times 10^{-14}$, about equal to the reciprocal of 7,700 times the world population. If the population consisted of cousins, with $F = 1/16$, the probability (see Equation 4.8b) would be 6.6×10^{-12}, about the reciprocal of 30 times the world population.

Calculations like those, assuming HW within each locus and LE between loci, illustrate what is called the *product rule* (NRC 1992). As just stated, when the 2p rule is used for a single band at locus A_i and $2p_ip_j$ for a double band at alleles A_i and A_j, the calculation is conservative (that is, it generally overestimates the true probability) within loci. Because there is no systematic effect of population structure on the direction of departure from LE and the empirical data show only small departures, we believe it reasonable to regard the product rule with the 2p rule as conservative.

Here is an illustration. Consider the white population frequencies in Table 4.8. Suppose that we have an evidence genotype $A_6 - B_8B_{14} C_{10}C_{13} D_9D_{16}$, the dash indicating a single band at allele A_6. The calculation is

$[2(0.035)][2(0.029)(0.068)][2(0.072)(0.131)][2(0.047)(0.065)] = 3.182 \times 10^{-8} \approx 1/31$ million.

With four or more loci, match probabilities for VNTR loci are usually quite small, as this example illustrates.

How much do racial groups differ? Table 4.8 gives bin frequencies for white, black, and Hispanic populations in the United States for four VNTR loci. Suppose that we have an evidence genotype as above. The probability that a randomly

TABLE 4.8   Bin (Allele) Frequencies of Two VNTR Alleles for Four Loci in Three US Populations[a]

Locus	Bin	White	Black	Hispanic
A. D2S44	6	0.035	0.092	0.105
	11	0.083	0.047	0.018
Number (2N)		1,584	950	600
B. D1S7	8	0.029	0.035	0.031
	14	0.068	0.063	0.056
Number (2N)		1,190	718	610
C. D4S139	10	0.072	0.066	0.106
	13	0.131	0.103	0.101
Number (2N)		1,188	896	622
D. D10S28	9	0.047	0.076	0.046
	16	0.065	0.036	0.059
Number (2N)		858	576	460

[a]The bins are designated by number (see Table 4.3). N is the number of persons, and 2N is the number of genes in the database. Data from Budowle et al. (1991). The Hispanic sample is from the southeastern United States.

chosen person from the white population matches this genotype is one in 31 million, in the black population one in 17 million, and in the Hispanic population one in 12 million. The three estimates are within about a factor of 3. Of course, other examples might differ more or less than this one.

We emphasize that, although the product rule with the 2p rule provides a good, if conservative, average estimate, there is uncertainty about individual calculations. That can arise from uncertainties about allele frequencies in the database and from the inappropriateness of the product rule in individual cases. We need some estimate of how far off the calculations in a given case might be. Although small amounts of linkage disequilibrium do not introduce an important systematic bias, they can increase the variability, and therefore the uncertainty, of the estimate. More importantly, however, allele frequencies can differ among subpopulations; although these largely cancel out in the average, the calculations might be inaccurate for a particular person who belongs to a subgroup with frequencies differing from the population average.

Our approach to dealing with such uncertainty is to look at empirical data, as we do in Chapter 5. But, to anticipate the results of the analysis in Chapter 5, the profile frequencies calculated from adequate databases (at least several hundred persons) by our procedures are, we believe, correct within a factor of about 10-fold in either direction.

RELATIVES

It is possible that one or more near-relatives of a suspect are included in the pool of possible perpetrators. That has been discussed by several writers (Lempert 1991, 1993; Evett 1992; Balding and Donnelly 1994a; Balding, Donnelly, and Nichols 1994). The most likely possibility of a relative unknown to the suspect is a paternal half-sibling—a person with the same father and a different mother. Because one or a few relatives in a large population will have only a very slight effect on match probability, we believe that the importance of unknown relatives has been exaggerated. However, there might be other, good reasons to suspect a relative, known or unknown.

If there is evidence against one or more relatives of a suspect, the DNA profiles of such relatives should be obtained whenever feasible. Furthermore, when the pool of possible suspects includes known relatives, determining their profiles might well eliminate them from consideration.

If a suspected relative cannot be profiled, we would want to know the conditional probability that the relative has a particular genotype, given that the suspect is of this type (Weir and Hill 1993). For noninbred unilineal relatives (relatives who have at most one gene identical by descent at a locus), the formulae can be expressed in terms of the kinship coefficient, F. They are as follows:

Genotype of suspect	Probability of same genotype in a relative	
Homozygote: A_iA_i	$p_i^2 + 4p_i(1 - p_i)F,$	(4.8a)
Heterozygote: A_iA_j	$2p_ip_j + 2(p_i + p_j - 4p_ip_j)F.$	(4.8b)

For parent and offspring, $F = 1/4$; for half-siblings, $1/8$; for uncle and nephew, $1/8$; for first cousins, $1/16$. Other values are easily calculated from Wright's (1951) algorithm.

Full siblings, being bilineal rather than unilineal, require different formulae:

$$A_iA_i: \quad (1 + 2p_i + p_i^2)/4, \tag{4.9a}$$
$$A_iA_j: \quad (1 + p_i + p_j + 2p_ip_j)/4. \tag{4.9b}$$

A few other bilineal relatives occur, such as double first cousins, but they are not common. Equations 4.8 and 4.9 depend on the assumption that the population is in HW proportions.

Since VNTR and other forensic loci are unlinked and appear to be close to LE, the conditional probability of a multilocus genotype in a relative is the product of the pertinent single-locus conditional probabilities.

PERSONS FROM THE SAME SUBPOPULATION

In the great majority of cases, very little is known about the person who left the DNA evidence, and the procedures so far discussed are appropriate. It might be known that the DNA came from a white person, in which case the white database is appropriate. If the race is not known or if the population is of racially mixed ancestry, the calculations can be made with each of the appropriate databases and these presented to the court. Alternatively, if a single number is preferred, one might present the calculations for the major racial group that gives the largest probability of a match. Similar procedures can be used for persons of mixed ancestry.

If it is known that the contributor of the evidence DNA and the suspect are from the same subpopulation and there are data for that subpopulation, this is clearly the set of frequencies to use to obtain the most accurate estimate of the genotype frequency in the set of possible perpetrators of the crime. Of course, the database should be large enough to be statistically reliable (at least several hundred persons), and rare alleles should be rebinned (see Chapter 5) so that no allele has a frequency less than five. The product rule is appropriate, in that departures from random mating within a subgroup are not likely to be important (and, as mentioned above, this is supported empirically). The use of the 2p rule makes the product rule conservative.

Some have argued that even if there is no direct evidence, it should be assumed for calculation purposes that the person contributing the evidence and the suspect are from the same subgroup (Balding and Nichols 1994). Even though it is not known to which subpopulation both persons belong, Balding and Nichols assume that the two are likely to be more similar than if they were chosen randomly from the population at large. In our view, that is unnecessarily conservative, and we prefer to make this assumption only when there is good reason to think it appropriate—for example, if the suspect and all the possible perpetrators are from the same small, isolated town. Most of the time, we believe, the subgroup of the suspect is irrelevant.

To continue with the assumption that the person contributing the evidence and the suspect are from the same subgroup, an appropriate procedure is to write the conditional probability of the suspect genotype, given that of the perpetrator. As before, we measure the degree of population subdivision by $\bar{\theta}$, although a single parameter $\bar{\theta}$ is not sufficient to describe the situation exactly. A number of formulae have been proposed to deal with this (Morton 1992; Crow and Denniston 1993; Balding and Nichols 1994, 1995; Roeder 1994; Weir 1994). They depend on different assumptions and methods of derivation but agree very closely for realistic values of $\bar{\theta}$ and p.[15] The simplest of the more accurate formulae is due to Balding and Nichols (1994, 1995):

$$\text{Homozygote: } P(A_iA_i|A_iA_i) = \frac{[2\bar{\theta} + (1-\bar{\theta})p_i][3\bar{\theta} + (1-\bar{\theta})p_i]}{(1+\bar{\theta})(1+2\bar{\theta})}, \quad (4.10a)$$

---

[15]Deriving a formula for these conditional probabilities requires some assumption about the population structure. Some models that have been used are a pure random-drift model, a mutation-drift, infinite-allele model, or a mathematically identical migration-drift infinite-allele model; or

$$\text{Heterozygote: } P(A_iA_j|A_iA_j) = \frac{2[\bar{\theta}+(1-\bar{\theta})p_i][\bar{\theta}+(1-\bar{\theta})p_j]}{(1+\bar{\theta})(1+2\bar{\theta})}. \quad (4.10b)$$

Nothing in population-genetics theory tells us that θ_{ij} should be independent of genotype. In fact, there is likely to be a different θ_{ij} for each pair of alleles A_i and A_j. Since individual genotypes are usually rare, these values are inaccurately measured and ordinarily unknown. The best procedure is to use a conservative value of $\bar{\theta}$ in Equations 4.10, knowing that the true individual values are likely to be smaller. Balding and Nichols (1994) extend Equations 4.10 to account for undetected bands. They also give an upper limit for homozygotes, analogous to the 2p rule. Their upper bound on the conditional probability is $2(\bar{\theta} + (1-\bar{\theta})p_i)$. We believe, however, that because Equation 4.10a is already conservative, this rule is usually unnecessary.

The value of $\bar{\theta}$ has been estimated for several populations. As mentioned above, typical values for white and black populations are less than 0.01, usually about 0.002. Values for Hispanics are slightly higher, as expected because of the greater heterogeneity of this group, defined as it is mainly by linguistic criteria.

Table 4.9 gives numerical examples of calculations for three racial groups, using the data of Table 4.8. Two alternative assumptions are made: that the evidence profile is heterozygous (there are two clear bands) at all four loci, and that locus A has a single band at allele A_6. In this example, the three racial groups are very similar; if all are heterozygous or if the 2p rule is used for homozygotes, they are within a factor of 3. That will not always be true. If one locus is single-banded, the 2p rule makes a substantial difference in the calculation. With four multiallelic loci, such as VNTRs, most four-locus profiles will be heterozygous at all loci. (For example, if the heterozygosity per locus is 0.93, as it is for D2S44, the probability that all four loci will be heterozygous is about 0.75.)

If all loci are heterozygous, then assuming that the evidence DNA and the DNA from the suspect came from the same subpopulation, using Equations 4.10 has a fairly small effect on the calculations when $\bar{\theta} = 0.01$. However, using a value of $\bar{\theta} = 0.03$ decreases the likelihood ratio (increases the match probability—see Chapter 5) by a factor of 10. If the A locus is homozygous, then Equation 4.1a with the 2p rule is more conservative than Equation 4.10a with $\bar{\theta} = 0.01$ and very close to Formula 4.10a with $\bar{\theta} = 0.03$.

---

various statistical assumptions concerning the distribution of allele frequencies among the subpopulations. A more appropriate model would be a stepwise-mutation theory because VNTR lengths tend to change by small steps, but that has not been worked out. Even that would not be completely satisfactory unless one also takes migration, which may be more important than mutation, into account. When $\bar{\theta}$ is small (< 0.02), the formulae derived from different models agree closely. Although the specific models are highly idealized, when different assumptions lead to similar results, it increases our confidence in the final formulae. The formulae given are from Balding and Nichols (1994), and were chosen because they are both simple to evaluate and accurate.

TABLE 4.9   Likelihood Ratio (Reciprocal of Match Probability) for Four-Locus Profiles in Three Populations Calculated by Various Formulae[a]

	White	Black	Hispanic
Equations 4.1			
All loci heterozygous	3.79×10^8	3.52×10^8	6.56×10^8
A-locus homozygous	1.80×10^9	3.60×10^8	2.25×10^8
A-locus single band, 2p rule	3.14×10^7	1.66×10^7	1.18×10^7
Equations 4.10, $\bar{\theta} = 0.01$			
All loci heterozygous	1.20×10^8	1.16×10^8	1.74×10^8
A-locus homozygous	2.80×10^8	9.87×10^7	6.63×10^7
Equations 4.10, $\bar{\theta} = 0.03$			
All loci heterozygous	2.04×10^7	2.06×10^7	2.53×10^7
A locus homozygous	2.48×10^7	1.39×10^7	1.02×10^7

	All Races
Interim Ceiling Principle	
All loci heterozygous	2.68×10^6
A-locus single-band, 2p rule	2.68×10^5

[a]The data are from Table 4.8. The evidence profile is either (1) all loci heterozygous, $A_6A_{11} B_8B_{14}$ $C_{10}C_{13} D_9D_{16}$, or (2) A-locus single-banded, $A_6 -$. All calculations use the product rule.

For urban populations, 0.01 is a conservative value. A higher value—say, 0.03—could be used for isolated villages.[16]

The table also gives calculations based on the interim ceiling principle (using 1.645 instead of the value 1.96 cited in NRC 1992—see Chapter 5). As will be explained in Chapter 5, we believe that the ceiling principles are unnecessary. We give the calculation for illustration only.

PCR-BASED SYSTEMS

As described in Chapter 2, other systems are coming into greater use. Most of them are based on PCR, require much smaller amounts of DNA, and have the additional advantage that the exact allele can usually be determined, so the

---

[16]Empirical estimates of $\bar{\theta}$, essentially the same as F_{ST} and G_{ST}, are found throughout the population-genetics literature. An extensive compilation is given by Cavalli-Sforza et al. (1994). The values in the compilation are sometimes considerably higher than the values that we use. There are two reasons: The Cavalli-Sforza comparisons are often between major groups, and many of the comparisons are for blood groups and similar polymorphisms, which have much lower mutation rates than VNTRs and are often subject to selection. Selection can differ in different populations; for example, selection for malaria-resistance genes is strong in hot, wet areas. We regard the empirical estimates of $\bar{\theta}$ from VNTRs, made either from comparison of homozygote and heterozygote frequencies (when the interpretation of single bands is not a substantial problem) or directly by comparisons among groups, as being a much better guide for forensic calculations.

complications of matching and binning are eliminated. That is true for mitochondrial DNA, DQA, and other markers such as STRs.

The newer systems have not had the large amount of population study that VNTRs have had. The databases are smaller, but the studies that have been done show the same agreement with HW and LE that VNTRs do (Herrin et al. 1994; Budowle, Baechtel, et al. 1995; Budowle, Lindsay, et al. 1995). STRs and some of the other loci share the property of VNTRs of not producing a protein product or having any known selectable function. Their chromosomal positions are known, and they can be chosen so that no two are linked. It should be relatively easy to get more population data, because it is not necessary to find the people; DNA samples for large populations already exist.

The previously mentioned advantages of STRs and other new methods (exact genotype determination, fast turnaround, lower cost, and small DNA-sample requirements) are such that the use of these methods will continue to increase. We also expect that population data will continue to accumulate and that tests, particularly of HW and LE, will continue to be carried out; and thus, the new methods will soon be on the same solid footing as VNTRs. Meanwhile, the similarity of some of these loci to VNTR loci and results of studies already done offer evidence that the methods given here will provide to the degree of accuracy required for forensic use.

A locus that is being increasingly used is D1S80. It is also a length variant, but unlike VNTRs, the size of the DNA fragment is small enough to permit PCR analysis. The locus consists of 16-base units, each of which is repeated from 14 to 41 times. It has been validated, both for robustness to environmental insults and for agreement with HW proportions (Sajantila et al. 1992; Budowle, Baechtel, et al. 1995; Cosso and Reynolds 1995).

STR loci appear to be particularly appropriate for forensic use. Like VNTRs, they can be chosen to be in noncoding regions and therefore can be expected to be selectively neutral. Also, they have many alleles, and there are potentially a very large number of loci. Unlike VNTRs, they can be amplified with PCR, and the individual alleles are identifiable.

Table 4.10 compares VNTR loci with two PCR-based systems, STR and Polymarker.[17] The total gene diversity is the proportion of heterozygotes that would exist if the entire population were in random-mating proportions. In the table, the gene diversity within subpopulations is given as a fraction of this total

---

[17]The six STR loci represent seven populations from three races, grouped as follows (subgroups within races are in parentheses: east Asians (Chinese, Japanese, Houston Asians), whites (German, Houston), and blacks (Nigeria, Houston). The Polymarker data come from 12 populations from five races: Eskimos (Barrow, Bethel), whites (two US samples, Swiss), blacks (two US samples), Hispanics (three US samples), and east Asians (Chinese, Japanese). Polymarker designations are: DQA (part of the HLA region); LDLR (low density lipoprotein receptor); GYPA (glycophorin A, the MN blood group), HBGG (hemoglobin G gamma globin), D7S8 (a marker of unknown function on chromosome seven), and GC (group specific component).

TABLE 4.10   Comparison of VNTR, STR, and Polymarker Systems[a]

Locus	No. of Alleles	Repeat Size	Gene Diversity Total	Proportion (a)	(b)	(c)
VNTR loci	≤ 31 bins					
D1S7		9	0.9470	0.995	0.005	0.001
D2S44		31	0.9342	0.985	0.007	0.009
D4S139		32	0.9103	0.989	0.005	0.006
D10S28		33	0.9489	0.990	0.005	0.005
D17S79		38	0.8366	0.971	0.011	0.018
Mean			0.9154	0.986	0.006	0.008
STR loci						
CSF1R	10	4	0.751	0.987	0.005	0.008
TH01	8	4	0.781	0.905	0.011	0.084
PLA2A	9	3	0.814	0.945	0.004	0.051
F13A1	14	4	0.798	0.902	0.006	0.092
CYP19	10	4	0.723	0.947	0.007	0.046
LPL	7	4	0.656	0.956	0.006	0.038
Mean			0.708	0.939	0.007	0.054
Polymarker loci plus DQA						
DQA1	6		0.788	0.948	0.009	0.043
LDLR	2		0.483	0.914	0.004	0.082
GYPA	2		0.478	0.971	0.012	0.017
HBGG	3		0.539	0.876	0.003	0.121
D7S8	2		0.475	0.995	0.002	0.003
GC	3		0.654	0.909	0.003	0.088
Mean			0.571	0.934	0.006	0.060

[a](a) Proportion of gene diversity accounted for by between-individual variability within subpopulations; (b) proportion within races between subpopulations; (c) proportion between races (Chakraborty, Jin, et al. 1995).

(a), as are the increments added by subpopulation differences (b) and racial differences (c). As these figures emphasize, for VNTRs, almost all the variability is between individuals within subgroups. Although these proportions, based on limited data sets, suggest that (b) and (c) are approximately the same, in general the divergence between races is larger than that between subgroups within a race (Latter 1980; Chakraborty and Kidd 1991; Devlin and Risch 1992; Devlin, Risch and Roeder 1993, 1994).

The population genetics of the Polymarker loci make these loci less advantageous than VNTRs, for three reasons. First, the number of alleles is small, and that is reflected in the lower gene diversity; several more loci are required than for VNTRs. Second, the variability between races is greater. That is particularly true for the loci LDLR, HBGG, and GC, which are all associated with functional genes (Chapter 2). Third, Polymarker loci have lower mutation rates and are less likely to be selectively neutral than VNTRs and STRs. These factors might cause the differences between groups.

STRs are intermediate in diversity between VNTRs and Polymarkers, as expected given that they have an intermediate number of alleles. The allocation of gene diversity to individual versus group and subgroup differences is also intermediate. Additional data from different STRs in different racial populations are in substantial agreement with the findings presented in the table (e.g., Bever and Creacy 1995; Meyer et al. 1995). An extensive study of blacks, whites, and Hispanics in Houston involving 12 STR loci found a mean heterozygosity (diversity) of about 75%, and 97.6% of the genetic diversity was within racial groups (Edwards et al. 1992; Hammond et al. 1994), in good agreement with the data in Table 4.10.

Compared with VNTRs, STRs have less exclusion power per locus, and Polymarker loci have less than STRs. The power of exclusion depends strongly on the heterozygosity (see footnote 4). Assuming HW proportions and LE and using the data in Table 4.10, the probability that two randomly selected individuals would have the same profile is about 10^{-10} for the five VNTR loci, about 10^{-6} for the six STR loci (using the 12 STRs mentioned in the paragraph above would lower the probability to about 10^{-12}), and about 10^{-4} for the six Polymarker loci.

Whereas the total database for VNTRs now numbers in the tens of thousands, the number for the newer systems is still in the hundreds, but the numbers are increasing rapidly, and the studies are being extended to different populations.

It is quite proper to combine different systems (e.g., VNTRs and STRs) in the product rule, provided, of course, that the loci are close to LE.

What do we conclude about PCR-based systems? We believe that they are ready to be used along with VNTRs. Newer data (Chakraborty et al. 1995; Gill and Evett 1995; Promega 1995; Evett, Gill et al. 1996) show low values of $\bar{\theta}$, comparable to those for VNTRs. Within the limitations of the data, there is good agreement with HW and LE. Graphs such as those in Figures 5.3 and 5.4 show about the same degree of uncertainty as VNTRs. Most STRs are at neutral loci. PCR-based systems have fewer alleles and hence higher allele frequencies than VNTRs. This means that the value of $\bar{\theta}$ has less influence (see Equation 4.4a). Yet, mutation rates for PCR loci are generally lower than those for VNTRs, and this might lead one to expect greater values of $\bar{\theta}$.

We conclude that PCR-based systems should be used. A value of 0.01 for $\bar{\theta}$ would be appropriate. However, in view of the greater uncertainty of PCR-based markers because of less extensive data than for VNTRs, a more conservative value of 0.03 may be chosen.

A Conservative Rule for PCR Loci

For VNTRs, we used the 2p rule and showed that it was conservative for populations in which the values of θ_{ij} are positive. The rule was originally introduced to adjust for uncertainty as to whether a single band is a homozygote or heterozygote. That problem does not arise with loci at which there is no ambiguity about allele identification. Is there a conservative adjustment for subdivided populations for such loci that corresponds to the 2p rule? It is simple to choose one:[18] Assign to each homozygote a frequency p_i (rather than p_i^2). This, however, is unnecessarily conservative.[19]

A more accurate but still conservative procedure, and one that we recommend, is to use Equation 4.4a with a conservative value of $\bar{\theta}$. Since observed values of $\bar{\theta}$ are usually less than 0.01, this value would be appropriate. (In view of the greater uncertainty of PCR calculations because of less extensive population data than for VNTRs, a more conservative value of 0.03 might be chosen.) For small, isolated populations, a value of 0.03 is appropriate. This value is intermediate between those that would be found in populations of first- and of second-cousin matings and is a reasonable upper limit for what might be expected.

The 2p rule for VNTRs was introduced because single bands may actually come from heterozygotes. If the techniques are or become good enough that this ambiguity does not exist, then VNTRs should be treated like the PCR-based systems, and the procedure of the previous paragraph should be applied. Conversely, even in PCR-based systems, it may be desirable to use the 2p rule if there is uncertainty caused by null alleles. In a well-characterized system, the frequency of null alleles can often be estimated, and a more accurate correction can then be applied.

DEVELOPMENT OF NEW SYSTEMS

PCR-based systems have several advantages, the most important being that they can be used when source material is sparse or degraded and a second being that there need not be uncertainties of measurement. But there are also

---

[18]Here are two proofs in the style and notation of Footnote 9. First, we have

$$P_{ii} = P(X = A_i \text{ and } Y = A_i) \leq P(X = A_i) = p_i.$$

Second, note that

$$p_i = P_{ii} + \frac{1}{2} \sum_{j:j \neq i} P_{ij} \geq P_{ii}.$$

as above.

[19]The error involved in assuming HW ratios and ignoring subpopulations makes little difference for heterozygotes. From Equation 4.4b, we see that the frequency is overestimated by a factor $1/(1 - \theta)$, or approximately $1 + \theta$ when θ is small. Furthermore, the error is in the desired direction of conservatism. In contrast, from Equation 4.4a it is seen that the error for homozygotes can be considerable, and in the wrong direction. For example, if $p_i = 0.03$ and $\theta = 0.03$, assuming HW gives an estimate of 0.0009, whereas Equation 4.4a gives 0.0018, a two-fold error. But note that this "p rule" is excessively conservative in assigning a value of 0.03 instead of 0.0018, a 17-fold difference—too conservative, we believe.

disadvantages. VNTRs have many alleles, none of which is at a high frequency. Presumably, the high mutation rate accounts for that and for the small differences in frequencies among subgroups.[20] The VNTRs used for forensics also occur at loci that have no function and therefore are probably not affected by natural selection. Some of the loci used in PCR-based systems have only a small number of alleles, and the loci are at functional genes, which means that there is less assurance of HW and LE. Many more loci are required to produce the same probability levels than are required for VNTRs.

Yet, the statistical uncertainties with VNTRs (discussed in more detail in Chapter 5) make it desirable to bring new loci into the system. The extensive activity in mapping human genes is leading to the rapid discovery of many more possible markers, some of which are expected to have the kinds of properties that are desirable for forensic use: high mutation rate, multiple alleles, lack of function (which increases the probability of neutrality), speed of analysis, low cost, and unambiguous identification of alleles. We encourage the development and validation of such systems.

INADEQUATE DATABASES

There are situations in which the database is inadequate. The population of possible suspects might be so structured that no reasonable average allele frequency can be determined, or there might be no basis for estimating $\bar{\theta}$. Such a situation may be found among some American Indian tribes, Inuits, or isolated immigrant groups. As databases become more extensive and varied, such gaps should be filled.

If an inadequate database is encountered, one procedure is to use allele frequencies from other groups. These should be groups for which the databases are large enough to be reliable, and they should be as closely related to the group in question as possible. We emphasize that they be closely related to discourage the use of a population, possibly unrelated, solely because it has a set of frequencies favorable to the position being argued. For the same reason, we believe that the number of groups examined should be limited. The calculations based on each of the groups, or some sort of average—or if the desire is for the most conservative estimate, the one that is most favorable to the defendant—can be presented to the court.

---

[20]VNTR systems have a high mutation rate, and mutations usually consist of small changes in the length of the VNTR segment. These two factors are largely responsible for the large number of alleles, none of which is very common, in VNTR systems. The resulting high diversity between individuals and small diversity between groups make VNTRs particularly useful as forensic evidence. Although the mutation rates for STRs are not as high as those for VNTRs, the rates are still much higher for STRs than for classical loci. A high mutation rate is desirable for forensic identification (although not for paternity testing).

CONCLUSIONS AND RECOMMENDATIONS

Sufficient data now exist for various groups and subgroups within the United States that analysts should present the best estimates for profile frequencies. For VNTRs, using the 2p rule for single bands and HW for double bands is generally conservative for an individual locus. For multiple loci, departures from LE are not great enough to cause errors comparable to those from uncertainty of allele frequencies estimated from databases.

With appropriate consideration of the data, the principles in this report can be applied to PCR-based systems. For those in which exact genotypes can be determined, the 2p rule should not be used. A conservative estimate is given by using the HW relation for heterozygotes and a conservative value of $\bar{\theta}$ in place of θ_{ii} in Equation 4.4a for homozygotes.

Recommendation 4.1: In general, the calculation of a profile frequency should be made with the product rule. If the race of the person who left the evidence-sample DNA is known, the database for the person's race should be used; if the race is not known, calculations for all racial groups to which possible suspects belong should be made. For systems such as VNTRs, in which a heterozygous locus can be mistaken for a homozygous one, if an upper bound on the genotypic frequency at an apparently homozygous locus (single band) is desired, then twice the allele (bin) frequency, 2p, should be used instead of p^2. For systems in which exact genotypes can be determined, $p^2 + p(1-p)\bar{\theta}$ should be used for the frequency at such a locus instead of p^2. A conservative value of $\bar{\theta}$ for the US population is 0.01; for some small, isolated populations, a value of 0.03 may be more appropriate. For both kinds of systems, $2p_ip_j$ should be used for heterozygotes.

A more conservative value of $\bar{\theta} = 0.03$ might be chosen for PCR-based systems in view of the greater uncertainty of calculations for such systems because of less extensive and less varied population data than for VNTRs.

Evidence DNA and Suspect from the Same Subgroup

Sometimes there is evidence that the suspect and other possible sources of the sample belong to the same subgroup. That can happen, e.g., if they are all members of an isolated village. In this case, a modification of the procedure is desirable.

Recommendation 4.2: If the particular subpopulation from which the evidence sample came is known, the allele frequencies for the specific subgroup should be used as described in Recommendation 4.1. If allele frequencies for the subgroup are not available, although data for the full population are, then the calculations should use the population-structure Equations 4.10 for each locus, and the resulting values should then be multiplied.

Insufficient Data

For some groups—and several American Indian and Inuit tribes are in this category—there are insufficient data to estimate frequencies reliably, and even the overall average might be unreliable. In this case, data from other, related groups provide the best information. The groups chosen should be the most closely related for which adequate databases exist. These might be chosen because of geographical proximity, or a physical anthropologist might be consulted. There should be a limit on the number of such subgroups analyzed to prevent inclusion of more remote groups less relevant to the case.

Recommendation 4.3: If the person who contributed the evidence sample is from a group or tribe for which no adequate database exists, data from several other groups or tribes thought to be closely related to it should be used. The profile frequency should be calculated as described in Recommendation 4.1 for each group or tribe.

Dealing with Relatives

In some instances, there is evidence that one or more relatives of the suspect are possible perpetrators.

Recommendation 4.4: If the possible contributors of the evidence sample include relatives of the suspect, DNA profiles of those relatives should be obtained. If these profiles cannot be obtained, the probability of finding the evidentiary profile in those relatives should be calculated with Formulae 4.8 or 4.9.

APPENDIX 4A

Here, we derive the relation (Equation 4.5) between the average $\bar{\theta}$ of the parameters θ_{ij} and Wright's (1951) fixation index, F_{IT} (Nei 1977, 1987, p 159-164; Chakraborty and Danker-Hopfe 1991; Chakraborty 1993). We begin with an arbitrary mating pattern; in particular, we do not assume that random mating occurs within subpopulations, or even that distinct subpopulations occur. Later, we posit distinct subpopulations and random mating in each of them.

The homozygosity, f_0, and heterozygosity, h_0, in the substructured population are

$$f_0 = \sum_i P_{ii}, \qquad h_0 = 1 - f_0 = \sum_{i,j:i<j} P_{ij},$$

where P_{ij} is the frequency of genotype A_iA_j. If the entire population mated at random, these quantities would become

$$f_T = \sum_i p_i^2, \qquad h_T = 1 - f_T,$$

where the allele frequencies p_i satisfy

$$\sum_i p_i = 1.$$

We can rewrite h_T as

$$h_T = \sum_i p_i(1 - p_i) = \sum_{i,j:i<j} 2p_ip_j.$$

First, we express the homozygote parameters θ_{ii} in terms of the heterozygote parameters θ_{ij} ($i \neq j$). Substituting Equations 4.4 into the equation

$$p_i = P_{ii} + \frac{1}{2} \sum_{j:j\neq i} P_{ij}$$

and noting that $p_i \neq 0$ leads to

$$(1 - p_i)\theta_{ii} = \sum_{j:j\neq i} p_j\theta_{ij}.$$

Multiplying that by p_i and summing over i enables us to define the mean

$$\bar{\theta} = \frac{1}{h_T} \sum_i p_i(1 - p_i)\theta_{ii} = \frac{1}{h_T} \sum_{i,j:i<j} 2p_ip_j\theta_{ij}.$$

Thus, the weighted means of the homozygote and heterozygote parameters are equal.

We insert Equation 4.4b to deduce that

$$\bar{\theta} = \frac{1}{h_T} \sum_{i,j:i<j} (2p_ip_j - P_{ij}) = \frac{h_T - h_0}{h_T} = F_{IT}.$$

If the subpopulations are distinct and mating is random in each subpopulation, then $F_{IT} = F_{ST}$, and hence $\bar{\theta} = F_{ST}$.

5

Statistical Issues

In Chapter 4, we presented ways to estimate the frequencies of genotypes and profiles in the population. In this chapter, we consider how to interpret frequencies as probabilities and likelihood ratios and how to make adjustments when a suspect is found through a database search. We also discuss the degree of uncertainty of such estimates according to statistical theory and empirical tests that use different databases. Finally, we ask how many loci would be needed to establish a profile as unique. The chapter includes a discussion of the statistics of matching and binning of VNTRs.[1]

Two major issues regarding uncertainty must be addressed in the statistical evaluation of DNA evidence. One is associated with the characteristics of a database, such as its size and whether it is representative of the appropriate population. The other might be called the subpopulation problem. In the first instance, inferences based on values in a database might be uncertain because the database is not compiled from a sample of the most relevant population or the sample is not representative. If the database is small, the values derived from it can be uncertain even if it is compiled from a scientifically drawn sample; this can be addressed by providing confidence intervals on the estimates. The second issue, the subpopulation problem, is broader than the first. Although the formulae might provide good estimates of the match probability for the average member of the population, they might not be appropriate for a member of an unusual

---

[1]Some references for general background that are pertinent to this chapter or parts of it are Aldous (1989), Finkelstein and Levin (1990), Aitken and Stoney (1991), Aitken (1995).

subgroup. Our approach is empirical: we compare different subpopulations and also, to mimic a worst case scenario, perform sample calculations deliberately using an inappropriate database.

DATA SOURCES

A simple random sample of a given size from a population is one chosen so that each possible sample has an equal chance of being selected. Ideally, the reference data set from which genotype frequencies are calculated would be a simple random sample or a stratified or otherwise scientifically structured random sample from the relevant population. Several conditions make the actual situation less than ideal. One is a lack of agreement as to what the relevant population is (should it be the whole population or only young males? should it be local or national?) and the consequent need to consider several possibilities. A second is that we are forced to rely on convenience samples, chosen not at random but because of availability or cost. It is difficult, expensive, and impractical to arrange a statistically valid random-sampling scheme. The saving point is that the features in which we are interested are believed theoretically and found empirically to be essentially uncorrelated with the means by which samples are chosen. Comparison of estimated profile frequencies from different data sets shows relative insensitivity to the source of the data, as we document later in the chapter. Furthermore, the VNTRs and STRs used in forensic analysis are usually not associated with any known function and therefore should not be correlated with occupation or behavior. So those convenience samples are effectively random.

The convenience samples from which the databases are derived come from various sources. Some data come from blood banks. Some come from genetic-counseling and disease-screening centers. Others come from mothers and putative fathers in paternity tests. The data summarized in FBI (1993b), which we have used in previous chapters and will again in this chapter, are from a variety of sources around the world, from blood banks, paternity-testing centers, molecular-biology and human-genetics laboratories, hospitals and clinics, law-enforcement officers, and criminal records.

As mentioned previously, most markers used for DNA analysis, VNTRs and STRs in particular, are from regions of DNA that have no known function. They are not related in any obvious way to gene-determined traits[2], and there is no reason to suspect that persons who contribute to blood banks or who have been

---

[2]Some loci used in PCR-based typing are associated with genes. It is important to determine if a particular forensic allele is associated with a disease state and hence subject to selection. A forensic marker might happen to be closely linked to an important gene, such as one causing some observable trait, and could conceivably be in strong linkage disequilibrium. As the number of mapped genes increases, this will become increasingly common. But for that to affect the reliability of a database, the trait would have to appear disproportionately in the populations that contribute to the database.

involved in paternity suits or criminal proceedings differ from a random sample of the population with respect to DNA markers. In addition, there is empirical evidence to the contrary: If we compare samples chosen in different ways, the results from calculations made from the different databases are quite similar

Although most of the data that we are concerned with are from persons in the United States, there are increasing numbers from elsewhere in the world, and these can be used for comparison. The 1993 FBI compendium includes samples from whites in the United States (Arizona, California, Florida, Georgia, Illinois, Kentucky, Maryland, Michigan, Minnesota, Missouri, Nevada, North Carolina, Oregon, South Carolina, Vermont, Virginia, and Washington), France, Israel, Spain, Switzerland, Denmark, England, Germany, Finland, Italy, and Tasmania. Data on blacks come from the United States (California, Florida, Georgia, Kentucky, Maryland, Michigan, Minnesota, Nevada, North Carolina, Oregon, South Carolina, Virginia, and Washington), Haiti, Togo, and England. Data on Hispanics come from several states in the United States. The FBI places data from eastern and western US Hispanics into separate databases because of the somewhat different origins of these populations.

American Indians present a special difficulty because they have more population subdivision, as demonstrated by higher values of $\bar{\theta}$ (see Chapter 4), than populations of whites, blacks, or Hispanics. The data are increasing rapidly, and substantial numbers are available from Arizona, Minnesota, North Carolina, Oregon, Ontario, and Saskatchewan, as well as from particular tribes (Sioux, Navaho).

MATCH PROBABILITY AND LIKELIHOOD RATIO

Suppose that a DNA sample from a crime scene and one from a suspect are compared, and the two profiles match at every locus tested. Either the suspect left the DNA or someone else did. We want to evaluate the probability of finding this profile in the "someone else" case. That person is assumed to be a random member of the population of possible suspects. So we calculate the frequency of the profile in the most relevant population or populations. The frequency can be called the random-match probability, and it can be regarded as an estimate of the answer to the question: What is the probability that a person other than the suspect, randomly selected from the population, will have this profile? The smaller that probability, the greater the likelihood that the two DNA samples came from the same person. Alternatively stated, if the probability is very small, we can say that either the two samples came from the same person or a very unlikely coincidence has occurred. (As in Chapter 4, the calculations in this chapter assume that no error has occurred in the determination of the DNA profiles.)

An alternative is to calculate the likelihood ratio (LR), a measure of the strength of the evidence regarding the hypothesis that the two profiles came from the same source. Suppose we find that the profiles of the person contributing the evidence DNA (E) and of the suspect (S) are both x. We consider two hypotheses: (1) the source of the evidence and the suspect are the same person, (2) the source of the evidence is a randomly selected person unrelated to the suspect. Although there are other possible hypotheses, it is usually sufficient to consider only these two. The likelihood ratio is the probability under hypothesis (1) that the suspect profile and the evidence-sample profile will both be x, divided by the corresponding probability under hypothesis (2). The greater the likelihood ratio, the stronger is the evidence in favor of the hypothesis corresponding to the numerator, that the source of the evidence-sample DNA and the suspect are the same person.

To write that symbolically, we let Pr_1 and Pr_2 indicate probabilities calculated under hypotheses 1 and 2. The LR for this simple comparison is

$$LR = \frac{Pr_1(E = x \ \& \ S = x)}{Pr_2(E = x \ \& \ S = x)}. \tag{5.1a}$$

Using a vertical line to indicate conditioning (statements to the left of the vertical line are conditional on statements to the right; for example, $Pr(E = x|S = x)$ is the probability that the evidence sample will have profile x given that the suspect has profile x), we note that

$$Pr(E = x \ \& \ S = x) = Pr(E = x)Pr(S = x|E = x) = Pr(S = x)Pr(E = x|S = x).$$

We can then rewrite Equation 5.1a in two algebraically equivalent forms:

$$LR = \frac{Pr_1(E = x|S = x)}{Pr_2(E = x|S = x)}, \tag{5.1b}$$

$$LR = \frac{Pr_1(S = x|E = x)}{Pr_2(S = x|E = x)}. \tag{5.1c}$$

Unless an error has occurred in the DNA typing, the numerator in Equations 5.1b and 5.1c will always equal one if the profiles match. Suppose that the population frequency of x is $P(x)$, and assume that the persons who contributed E and S, if different, are unrelated (and E and S are therefore statistically independent). Then the denominator is $P(x)$, so

$$LR = 1/P(x). \tag{5.2}$$

Therefore, in the usual case, the likelihood ratio is the reciprocal of the probability of a random match.[3]

The likelihood ratio, then, is a way of summarizing the DNA evidence. If

---

[3]Under some circumstances, such as if the match window is small, the probability of a match between two samples from the same person might be less than 1. In principle, this could change the likelihood ratio (Kaye 1995b); in practice, the possible error is minuscule in comparison with uncertainties in the denominator. The effect of the size of the match window on the probability of a false negative is discussed later in the chapter.

the LR is 1,000, the probability that the profiles are the same is 1,000 times as great if the samples came from the same person as it is if they came from different persons.

In the situation described above and reflected in the notation E and S, we imagine an evidence sample left at the crime scene by the putative perpetrator and a suspect with a matching profile. Although that is conceptually the simplest scenario and is used throughout this report for illustrative purposes, the mathematical formalism is valid more generally. For example, if a suspect is apprehended with blood on his clothes, this blood is the evidence sample to be matched against the genotypic profile of the victim. The LR given above is still valid, although for the most direct interpretation one would use Equation 5.1b, with S denoting the profile of the victim and E the evidence-sample profile.

Mixed Samples

Mixed samples are sometimes found in crime situations—for instance, blood from two or more persons at the scene of a crime, victim and assailant samples on a vaginal swab, and material from multiple sexual assailants. In many cases, one of the contributors—for example, the victim—is known, and the genetic profile of the unknown is readily inferred. In some cases, it might be possible to distinguish the genetic profiles of the contributors to a mixture from differences in intensities of bands in an RFLP pattern or dots in a dot-blot typing; in either case, the analysis is similar to the unmixed case. However, when the contributors to a mixture are not known or cannot otherwise be distinguished, a likelihood-ratio approach offers a clear advantage and is particularly suitable.

Consider a simple case of a VNTR analysis in which, for a particular locus, there are four bands in the lane, known to be contributed by two persons. If the alleles from the two persons are known and correspond to the set of four in the lane, there is usually no problem of interpretation, since two of the bands will match one suspect and the other two bands will match the other. However, two of the bands might match the alleles of only one suspect, and the source of the other two might be unknown. The 1992 report (NRC 1992, p 59) says: "If a suspect's pattern is found within the mixed pattern, the appropriate frequency to assign such a 'match' is the sum of the frequencies of all genotypes that are contained within (i.e., that are a subset of) the mixed pattern." Suppose the four bands correspond to alleles (bins) A_1, A_2, A_3, and A_4, whose frequencies are p_1, p_2, p_3, and p_4. This procedure recommended in the 1992 report would calculate the match probability as

$$2(p_1p_2 + p_1p_3 + p_1p_4 + p_2p_3 + p_2p_4 + p_3p_4),$$

that is, the probability that a randomly selected person would have two alleles from the set of possibilities $\{A_1, A_2, A_3, A_4\}$. As above, the reciprocal of this probability can be interpreted as a likelihood ratio.

That calculation is hard to justify, because it does not make use of some of the information available, namely, the genotype of the suspect. The correct procedure, we believe, was described by Evett et al. (1991). Suppose that the suspect's genotype is A_1A_2. The hypothesis we wish to test is that the samples came from the suspect and one other person. The probability under this hypothesis of finding the profile shown by the evidence sample is $2p_3p_4$, because under this hypothesis it is certain that two of the bands are A_1 and A_2. If the samples came from two randomly selected persons, the probability of any particular pair of profiles, such as A_1A_3 and A_2A_4, is $(2p_1p_3)(2p_2p_4) = 4p_1p_2p_3p_4$. There are six possible pairs of two-band profiles corresponding to the four bands, so the total probability is $24p_1p_2p_3p_4$. The likelihood ratio, analogous to Equations 5.1, is

$$LR = \frac{2p_3p_4}{24p_1p_2p_3p_4} = \frac{1}{12p_1p_2}.$$

This LR, compared with that derived from the recommendation of the 1992 NRC report, is larger when the suspect bands are relatively rare and smaller when the suspect bands are relatively common. The reason is that we have taken account of the information in the genotype of the suspect rather than averaging over the set of possible genotypes consistent with the four-band evidence-sample profile.

There might be fewer than four bands, or multiple suspects might be identified. These and other, more complex cases can be analyzed in a similar manner (Evett et al. 1991). Some cases are treated in Appendix 5A and summarized in Table 5.1.

We have considered only simple cases. With VNTRs, it is possible, though very unlikely, that the four bands were contributed by more than two persons, who either were homozygous or shared rare alleles. With multiple loci, it will usually be evident if the sample was contributed by more than two persons. Calculations taking those possibilities into account could be made if there were reason to believe that more than two persons contributed to the sample.

Mixed samples are often difficult to analyze in systems where several loci are analyzed at once. Mixed samples can also lead to more complicated calculations with DQA, where some alleles are inferred by subtraction. (For example, there is no specific probe for the allele 1.2; the presence or absence of this allele is inferred from the reaction of DNA probes with the product of the combination 1.2, 1.3, and 4, but not with the products of 1.3 and 4 individually.)

The problem is complex, and some forensic experts follow the practice of making several reasonable assumptions and then using the calculation that is most conservative. For a fuller treatment of mixed samples, see Weir et al. (1996).

Bayes's Theorem

The likelihood ratio and the match probability, being reciprocals, contain the same information. The LR, however, has a property that makes it especially useful, provided that prior odds are available on the hypothesis that the two DNA profiles have the same source. (Prior odds are the odds that the two DNA samples came from the same person on the basis of information other than the DNA. Posterior odds are the odds when the DNA information is included in the analysis.) That property can be stated this way:

The posterior odds are the prior odds multiplied by LR.[4]

In everyday words: *Whatever are the odds that the two samples came from the same person in the absence of DNA evidence, the odds when the DNA evidence is included are LR times as great.* That statement is an instance of Bayes's theorem.

For example, if there is reason to think that the prior odds that two DNA samples came from the same person (however this is determined) are 1:2, and the LR is 10,000, the posterior odds are 5,000:1. Many statisticians and forensic scientists prefer to use the likelihood ratio rather than the match probability (Berry 1991a; Berry et al. 1992; Evett et al. 1992; Balding and Nichols 1994; Collins and Morton 1994) because it admits an inferential interpretation that the simple match probability does not. Odds can be converted into a probability by the relation Prob = Odds/(Odds + 1), or Odds = Prob/(1 − Prob). Thus, a likelihood ratio, which is not a probability, can be used to obtain a probability.

Paternity testing

The relation between posterior and prior odds is routinely used in paternity analysis (Walker 1983; AABB 1994). If the putative father is not excluded by blood-group, enzyme, and DNA evidence, a "paternity index" is calculated. The paternity index PI is a likelihood ratio—the probability of the mother-child-father profile combination if the putative father is the true father divided by the probability of this combination if a randomly selected man is the father. Customarily, the calculations make use of a database or databases appropriate to the race(s) of the persons involved.

If the prior odds are 1:1—that is, if the putative father is assumed to be equally likely to be and not to be the true father—the posterior odds are the same as the likelihood ratio; but for other prior odds, that is not the case. Suppose that PI is calculated to be 1,000. If the prior odds (from evidence other than that from DNA) in favor of the putative father's being the true father are judged to be 10:1, the posterior odds are 10 times PI, or 10,000:1. If the prior odds of his being the father are 1:10, the posterior odds are 0.1 times PI, or 100:1.

In routine parentage testing, probabilities are used instead of odds. As men-

---

[4]This supposes that two simple hypotheses are being compared. When more complicated hypotheses are being compared (when the alternative hypothesis consists of different possibilities with different a priori probabilities), a Bayes factor, essentially a weighted LR, plays the role of the LR (Kass and Raftery 1995).

tioned earlier, odds are converted into a probability by the relation Prob = Odds/
(Odds + 1). In this example, the posterior probabilities that the putative father
is the true father are 10,000/10,001 = 0.9999 and 100/101 = 0.9901, for prior
probabilities 10/11 (odds 10:1) and 1/11 (odds 1:10).

If the prior odds are assumed to be 1:1 (making the prior probability 1/2),
the posterior probability is simply PI/(PI + 1). Thus, a paternity index of 1,000
corresponds to a posterior probability of 1,000/1,001, or 0.9990. This posterior
probability is routinely called the "probability of paternity." We emphasize that
it is a true probability of paternity only if the prior probability is 1/2, an assumption
that should be clearly stated. It is sometimes justified on the grounds that it gives
equal weight to the two parties, the mother and the putative father, in a paternity
dispute, although, naturally, this justification has been criticized. A better procedure, used by some laboratories, is to use an empirically determined prior probability or to give several posterior probabilities corresponding to a range of prior
probabilities.

With the high LRs typically found when DNA markers are used (and the
putative father has not been excluded), a wide range of prior probabilities makes
little difference. In our example, where the paternity index is 1,000, the posterior
probabilities for the three prior probabilities, 10/11, 1/2, and 1/11, are 0.9999,
0.9990, and 0.9901. The high LR has made a 100-fold difference in prior odds
largely irrelevant.

Bayes's Theorem in Criminal Cases

What we would like to know and could most easily interpret is the probability
that the suspect contributed the DNA in the evidence sample. To find that
probability, we need to use a prior probability and Bayes's theorem. Despite the
regular use of Bayes's theorem in genetic counseling and in paternity testing, it
has been only rarely used in criminal cases in the United States. The main
difficulty is probably an unwillingness of the courts to ask juries to assign odds
on the basis of non-DNA evidence. It is difficult even for experts to express
complex nonscientific evidence in terms of quantitative odds, and some commentators have regarded assigning prior odds to the probability that the evidence and
suspect DNA came from the same person as a violation of the presumption of
innocence (see Chapter 6). In many cases, however, the prior odds, within a wide
range, are not important to a decision. With a four- or five-locus match, whether
the prior odds are 1:20 or 20:1 will usually have no important effect on the
posterior probability; if the LR is 100 million, multiplying it by 20 or 1/20 is not
likely to change the conclusion. The procedure of presenting posterior probabilities
for a range of assumed prior probabilities has found favor among some legal
scholars. Various approaches for use in the courts are discussed in Chapter 6.

There are two additional reasons for presenting posterior probabilities corresponding to a range of priors. First, a prior probability that might be used with

Bayes's theorem would properly be assessed by jurors, not an expert witness or an officer of the court. A prior probability might reflect subjective assessments of the evidence presented. Such assessments would presumably be done separately by each juror in light of that juror's experience. Second, there is no logical reason that non-DNA evidence has to be presented first. It might be confusing for a juror to hear prior odds assigned by one expert, then hear a likelihood ratio from that expert or another, followed by more non-DNA evidence. It might not be feasible to present the information to a jury in the order most easily incorporated into a Bayesian probability. For all those reasons, we believe it best, if Bayes's theorem is used, to present posterior probabilities (or odds) for a range of priors.

TWO FALLACIES

Two widely recognized fallacies should be avoided (Thompson and Schumann 1987; Balding and Donnelly 1994b). The "prosecutor's fallacy"—also called the fallacy of the transposed conditional—is to confuse two conditional probabilities. Let P equal the probability of a match, given the evidence genotype. The fallacy is to say that P is also the probability that the DNA at the crime scene came from someone other than the defendant. An LR of 1,000 says that the match is 1,000 times as probable if the evidence and the suspect samples that share the same profile are from the same person as it is if the samples are from different persons. It does *not* say that the odds that the suspect contributed the evidence DNA are 1,000:1. To obtain such a probability requires using Bayes's theorem and a prior probability that is assumed or estimated on the basis of non-DNA evidence. As stated earlier, only if that prior probability is 1/2 will the posterior odds equal the LR.

The "defendant's fallacy" is to assume that in a given population, anyone with the same profile as the evidence sample is as likely to have left the sample as the suspect. For example, if 100 persons in a metropolitan area are expected to have the same DNA profile as the evidence sample, it is a fallacy to conclude that the probability that the suspect contributed the sample is only 0.01. The suspect was originally identified by other evidence, and such evidence is very unlikely to exist for the 99 other persons expected to have the same profile. Only if the suspect was found through a search of a DNA database might this kind of reasoning apply, and then only with respect to other contributors to the database, as we now discuss.

SUSPECT IDENTIFIED BY A DNA DATABASE SEARCH

Thus far, we have assumed that the suspect was identified by evidence other than DNA, such as testimony of an eyewitness or circumstantial evidence. In that case, the DNA is tested and the match probability or likelihood ratio is computed for the event that a person selected at random from some population will have the genotypic profile of the evidence sample. There is an important difference between that situation and one in which the suspect is initially identified by searching a database to find a DNA profile matching that left at a crime scene. In the latter case, the calculation of a match probability or LR should take into account the search process.

As the number and size of DNA databanks increase, the identification of suspects by this means will become more common. Already, more than 20 suspects have been identified by searches through databases maintained by various states. The number and sizes of these databases are sure to increase.

To see the logical difference between the two situations described above, observe that if we toss 20 reputedly unbiased coins once each, there is roughly one chance in a million that all 20 will show heads. According to standard statistical logic, the occurrence of this highly unlikely event would be regarded as evidence discrediting the hypothesis that the coins are unbiased. But if we repeat this experiment of 20 tosses a large enough number of times, there will be a high probability that all 20 coins will show heads in at least one experiment. In that case, an event of 20 heads would not be unusual and would not in itself be judged as evidence that the coins are biased. The initial identification of a suspect through a search of a DNA database is analogous to performing the coin-toss experiment many times: A match by chance alone is more likely the larger the number of profiles examined.

There are different ways to take the search process into account. The 1992 NRC report recommends that the markers used to evaluate a match probability be different from those used to identify a suspect initially. In that case, the database search is much like identifying the suspect from non-DNA evidence, and the methods of Chapter 4 apply. However, the procedure might be difficult to implement. To avoid identifying several suspects who must then be investigated, one might need to use a large number of markers in the database search. Then, according to that procedure, those markers could not also be used in further analysis. If the amount of DNA in the evidence sample is too small, following the recommendation in the 1992 report could leave too few additional loci for computing a match probability or LR.

A correction to account for the database search can be made in computing the match probability. Let M_i denote the event that the i-th DNA profile in the database matches the evidence sample. To decide if the database search itself has contributed to obtaining a match (much as the repeated experiments might be held responsible for producing the 20 heads in the example given above), an event of interest is M, that at least one of the database profiles matches the evidence sample. Suppose that we hypothesize that the evidence sample was not left by someone whose DNA profile is in the database (or a close relative of such a person) and find that under this hypothesis P(M) is small. The usual statistical logic then leads to rejection of that hypothesis in favor of the alternative that (one of) the matching profile(s) in the database comes from the person who left the evidence sample.

Under the hypothesis that the person leaving the evidence sample is not represented in the database of N persons, a simple upper bound on the probability of M is given by

$$P(M) \leq \sum_i P(M_i) = NP(M_i). \tag{5.3}$$

The equality in Equation 5.3 holds if the database is homogeneous, that is, if $P(M_i)$ is the same for all profiles in the database (see Appendix 5B).

Equation 5.3 motivates the simple rule sometimes suggested by forensic scientists: multiply the match probability by the size of the database searched (or that part of the database that is relevant—for example, males in a search for a match to a semen sample). Suppose that $P(M_i) = 10^{-6}$ and $N = 1,000$. Then $P(M) \leq 0.001$.

In a computerized database search, the computer output ordinarily lists all profiles in the database that match the evidence-sample profile. It is also possible to search profiles one by one in one or more databases until one or more matches are obtained. If that procedure is followed, the appropriate database for computing the match probability is the complete set of profiles that are actually compared with the evidence sample. Other situations might not be so simple.[5]

VERY SMALL PROBABILITIES

Some commentators have stated that very small probabilities are suspect because they are outside the range of previous experience. They argue that a probability of, say, one in 10 billion is not to be trusted simply because it is so small. However, it is not the magnitude of the number that is at issue but rather the reliability of the assumptions on which the calculation is based. The relevant issues are the reliability of the database and the appropriateness of the population genetics model, and these are the same for large as well as small probabilities.

---

[5]If all potential suspects in a specific crime are asked to submit to DNA profiling, the situation is similar to the database searches described in the text, but it is more difficult to interpret. If all possible suspects are indeed tested (although it would be difficult or even impossible to show that this is the case), a match probability can be computed with the procedures in this chapter. However, the time and expense involved in DNA profiling may lead those doing the testing to terminate the search as soon as a match is obtained. Although the probability of obtaining a random match within the group tested is no different in this case than it would be if the database had been assembled before the suspect(s) had been identified, the obvious motivation of a perpetrator to avoid or delay testing weakens the statistical logic that a small match probability is evidence in favor of the hypothesis that the person who left the evidence sample and the person providing the matching sample are the same. If such a procedure for generating a DNA database is used, testing should continue through the whole database.

Nevertheless, we need to distinguish between relative and absolute errors. Small relative errors will have little impact on estimation of small probabilities, but small absolute errors can be disastrous. To a considerable extent, uncertainties in θ_{ij} for application to heterozygote probabilities lead to relative errors, and hence have small impact (see Equations 4.4). Uncertainties in θ_{ii} for application to homozygote probabilities lead to absolute errors, and hence can have much more misleading consequences when the probabilities are small. The procedures we have recommended in Chapter 4 take this into account.

Some experts seek to avoid arguments about small probabilities in court by reporting threshold values instead of estimates. A calculated match probability of 10^{-10} might be presented simply as less than one in a million. For example, the Kentucky State Police Forensic Laboratory states any probability less than the reciprocal of the number of people living in the United States as simply less than 1/N, where N is the US population size. Since that practice entails a loss of information, we do not recommend it. However, if a threshold practice is followed, all necessary adjustments to the probability should already have been made before the threshold value is reported. Suppose that the probability, P, of a profile is 10^{-10}, and N, the size of the database searched, is 1,000, so that $NP = 10^{-7}$. Suppose further that the empirically estimated uncertainty is a factor of 10 (see section on individual variability and empirical comparisons in this chapter), so a conservative estimate is 10^{-6}. It would then be legitimate to report that the match probability is less than one in a million.

UNIQUENESS

There has been much discussion of when it might be possible to use DNA typing to identify each person in a population uniquely. The 1992 NRC report says: "Regardless of the calculated frequency, an expert should—given . . . the relatively small number of loci used and the available population data—avoid assertions in court that a particular genotype is unique in the population" (NRC 1992, p 92). In a recent decision (State v Buckner, 125 Wash. 2d 915, 890 p.2d 460, 1995), the calculated probability of a match between suspect and evidence DNA was one in 19 billion. Since the denominator is more than three times the population of the earth, should this genotype be regarded as unique? The court held as improper any testimony that the profile was unique. Yet, as the number of available DNA markers increases, even smaller probabilities will be introduced with growing frequency. How small must they be before a profile can be considered unique?

The match probability computed in forensic analysis refers to a particular evidentiary profile. That profile might be said to be unique if it is so rare that it becomes unreasonable to suppose that a second person in the population might have the same profile. More precisely, suppose that a given genetic profile, G, occurs with probability P_G and has been observed exactly once, namely, in the evidence sample. In a population of N unrelated persons, the probability, before a suspect has been profiled, that at least one G occurs among the N − 1 unobserved profiles is

$$1 - (1 - P_G)^{N-1} \doteq NP_G. \tag{5.4}$$

Therefore, one might say that a given profile is unique in a given population if P_G is small compared with the reciprocal of the population size. More specifically, the probability that the profile is not unique is less than P_G times N. Suppose that the profile probability, P_G, is one in ten billion. Then, for the US population of about 250 million, the product is 1/40. It could be argued that if the probability of finding another person with this profile is such a small fraction, probably no other person in the United States has it. Clearly, if the fraction is very small, the profile is almost certainly unique. But we leave it to the courts to decide just how small this fraction should be in order to declare a profile to be unique.

Another approach to the question of uniqueness appears not to have been considered in the scientific literature. This approach considers the uniqueness of all profiles in the population simultaneously. It is much more stringent than the requirement that a given profile be so rare that it can reasonably be judged unique. Consider a population of N unrelated persons, and assume that the population is in HW and LE proportions. Let M denote the number of pairwise matches in the population when K loci are typed, and f_L be the mean homozygosity (see Chapter 4) at locus L. We interpret unique identification to mean that $P\{M \geq 1\} \leq 0.01$, or some other chosen small number. An approximate upper bound for the probability is

$$1 - \exp(-N^2 2^{K-1} f^{2K}) \leq N^2 2^{K-1} f^{2K}, \tag{5.5}$$

where $f = (\Pi_L f_L)^{1/K}$, the geometric mean of the homozygosities at the different loci (see Appendix 5C for derivation and discussion). The sharper approximate upper bound derived in Appendix 5C is shown in Figure 5.1.

Thus, the parameters governing the probability that at least one match will occur are the population size, the number of loci, and the geometric mean of the homozygosities. For example, if testing is done at 10 loci with geometric mean homozygosity of 0.05 and N is the world population size, which we take as about 5 billion, the probability of finding at least one pair of persons with the same profile is at most about 0.0001, which meets the illustrative criterion of 0.01 or less that was given above. The minimum probability that each person's profile is unique is about 0.9999 in this case. If we assume that the geometric-mean homozygosity is 0.1 rather than 0.05, then 13 loci are needed to give an upper bound on the probability of about 0.001.

At the VNTR locus D2S44, the homozygosity in US whites is 0.074 (Table 4.5). In the example above, the upper bound would be about 0.003 for 11 loci with that homozygosity. Most of the markers used in PCR-based systems have higher homozygosities than those illustrated above; for example, D1S80 has an

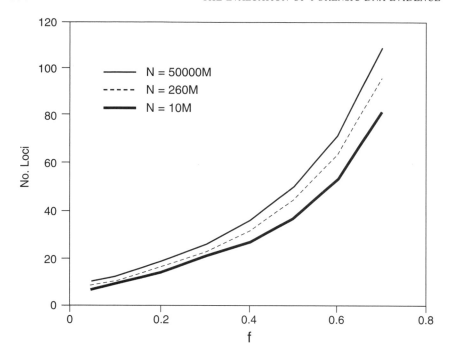

FIGURE 5.1   The number of loci required to assure with a probability of at least about 0.99 that no two persons in a randomly mating population share a profile. Then N is the population number and f is the geometric mean homozygosity. M = 1,000,000.

average homozygosity in the white population of about 0.20 (Budowle, Baechtel, et al. 1995). About 20 such loci would be required to meet the criterion used for illustrative purposes in the above discussion.

In some cases, the population of interest might be limited to a particular geographic area. For an area with a population of one million, six loci with geometric-mean homozygosities of 0.05 would yield an approximate upper bound of 0.008.

We have discussed two different approaches to the question of uniqueness. Our first approach was to ask for the probability that a given profile is unique. The second and more complicated one asks for the probability that no two profiles are identical. The first question is likely to be asked much more often in a forensic setting.

The number of loci and the degree of heterozygosity per locus that are needed to meet the criteria illustrated above do not seem beyond the reach of forensic science, so unique typing (except for identical twins) may not be far off. How relatives affect determinations of uniqueness will require further analysis, and how the courts will react remains to be seen (see Chapter 6).

STATISTICAL ASPECTS OF VNTR ANALYSIS

VNTR alleles differ from one another by discrete steps, but because of measurement uncertainty and the fact that the repeat units are not always the same size, the data are essentially continuous. Therefore, the most accurate statistical model for the interpretation of VNTR analysis would be based on a continuous distribution. Consequently, methods using a continuous distribution and likelihood-ratio theory have been advocated (Berry 1991a; Buckleton et al. 1991; Berry et al. 1992; Evett et al. 1992; Devlin, Risch, and Roeder 1992; Roeder 1994; Roeder et al. 1995). If models for measurement uncertainty become available that are appropriate for the wide range of laboratories performing DNA analyses and if those analyses are suitably robust with respect to departures from the models, we would then recommend such methods. Indeed, barring the development of analytical procedures that render statistical analyses unnecessary, we expect that any problems in the construction of such models will be overcome, and we encourage research on those models.

An analysis based on a continuous distribution would proceed under the hypotheses that the DNA from the evidence sample and from the suspect came from the same person and that they came from different persons. One would seek the relative likelihoods that, with a suitable measure of distance, the bands would be as similar to one another as was observed. At present, however, most presentations of DNA evidence use some form of grouping of alleles. Grouping reduces statistical power but facilitates computation and exposition. A likelihood analysis based on grouping uses an appropriate distance-criterion to calculate the probability that the bands match. That criterion is discussed below.

Determining a Match

According to standard procedure, a match is declared in two stages. Usually the bands in the two lanes to be compared will be in very similar positions or in clearly different positions. If they appear to the analyst to be in similar positions, a visual match is declared. This declaration must then be confirmed by measurement; otherwise, the result of the test is declared to be either an exclusion (no match) or inconclusive. A poor-quality autorad, for example, might result in an inconclusive test. The visual match is a preliminary screen to eliminate obvious mismatches from further study. It excludes some autorads that might pass the measurement criterion as matches if the analyst took into account the correlation of measurement errors (in particular, band-shifting, in which the bands in one lane are shifted relative to those in another), but ordinarily it does not otherwise substitute the analyst's judgment for objective criteria. It would be desirable to develop a way to incorporate any correlation of measurement uncertainty in the objective criterion.

The measurement-confirmation step in the above procedure is based on the size of the band as determined by the molecular-weight standards on the same autorad. The recorded size of this band is, however, subject to measurement uncertainty. Studies at the FBI and the National Institute of Standards and Technology (NIST) have shown that the measurement uncertainty is roughly proportional to the molecular weight (band size is usually measured in units of number of nucleotide pairs rather than in daltons). For example, in the systems published by the FBI and widely used in FBI and other laboratories, the standard deviation of repeated measurements of DNA from the same person is about 1% (Budowle, Giusti, et al. 1991; Mudd et al. 1994). An amount determined by the precision of the measurement is added to and subtracted from the band size, and that determines an "uncertainty window", $X \pm \alpha X$, where X is the measurement of the band size and α is the uncertainty value. The uncertainty window is usually taken to be $\pm$ 2.5% of the molecular weight (about 2.5 standard deviations), so that $\alpha = 0.025$ in this case. This procedure is followed for both the DNA from the evidence sample and that from the suspect. If these two uncertainty windows do not overlap, there is either no match or the result is inconclusive (Figure 5.2a). If the windows overlap, a match is declared (Figure 5.2b). FBI studies (Budowle, Baechtel, et al. 1990; Budowle, Giusti, et al. 1991) report that in 200 within-individual test-band comparisons involving 111 persons, no bands failed to match by this criterion, although Weir and Gaut (1993) report that a slightly larger uncertainty window ($\pm$ 2.8%) was required to obtain the same result for a sample from another laboratory.

The NIST studies (Mudd et al. 1994) provide support for the values found by the FBI. Using measurements obtained by many laboratories over several years, Mudd et al. derived an approximate formula for the standard deviation, σ, of a measurement in base pairs (bp):

$$\sigma = 10.4 \times 10^{(bp/8300)}. \qquad (5.6)$$

Expressed as percentages, the values of σ are between 0.79 and 0.92 for VNTRs between 2,000 and 6,000 bp.[6]

The probability of a match between two replicate determinations from the same person increases rapidly with the value of α and is very close to 1 for $\alpha = 0.025$ (Budowle, Baechtel, et al. 1990; Budowle, Giusti, et al. 1991; Evett, Scranage, and Pinchin 1993) The match window should not be set so small that true matches are missed. At the same time, the window should not be so wide that bands that are clearly different will be declared to match. The 2.5% value used by the FBI, although selected to prevent erroneous nonmatches, nonetheless

---

[6]In the NIST study, 22 labs were sent duplicate pieces of cloth with blood stains on them. The equation is the least-squares fit for the standard deviation of the values obtained by different laboratories. Differences among analysts within a laboratory and differences between laboratories contributed about equally to the total variance. Notice that if the number of base pairs exceeds 6,732, the standard deviation is greater than 1%.

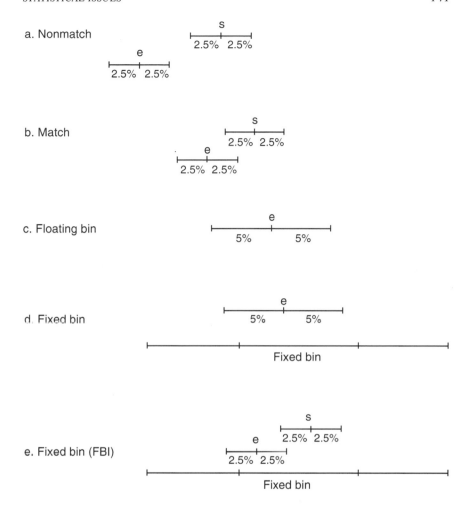

FIGURE 5.2   An illustration of the matching procedure and the bin assignment with floating and fixed bins.

seems to deal reasonably well with erroneous matches, too. Bands from the same person are usually very close, within about 1%; those from nonmatching persons are usually far apart. The possibility of coincidental matches for all bands in a multilocus analysis is extremely remote, as the very small match probabilities associated with such a profile indicate (see Chapter 4 for details). The size of the match window should be defined in the laboratory protocol, and not vary from case to case. We believe that technological improvements in laboratory methods should permit the cautious reduction of the match window, as the size of the standard deviation of the measurement declines.

The 1992 NRC report recommended that all determinations of matches and bin-allocations be done by objective measurements, following the rules described above (with variations for different laboratories with different systems). The report explicitly stated that visual matches should not be permitted. That is too restrictive, as long as the visual inspection is employed only as a screen. But the use of visual inspection other than as a screen before objective measurement would potentially undermine the basis of the quantitative estimation of the likelihood of a match and should usually be avoided.

An experienced forensic scientist can often use visual screening to recognize band-shifting and other phenomena. For example, degraded DNA sometimes migrates farther on a gel than better-quality DNA (Budowle, Baechtel, and Adams 1991), and an experienced analyst can notice whether two bands from a heterozygote are shifted in the same or in the opposite direction from the bands in another lane containing the DNA being compared. If the bands in the two lanes shift a small distance in the same direction, that might indicate a match with band-shifting. If they shift in opposite directions, that is probably not a match, but a simple match rule or simple computer program might declare it as a match. However, a sophisticated computer program might eventually replace visual matching. As was stated in Chapter 3, if for any reason the analyst by visual inspection overrides the conclusion from the measurements, that should be clearly stated and reasons given.

Binning

Once a match has been declared and confirmed by measurement, it is necessary to estimate the probability of a match on the assumption that the suspect sample and the evidence sample are not from the same source in order to calculate the match probability or likelihood ratio.

Floating bins

One accurate, unambiguous method is to use *floating bins* (Balazs et al. 1989). Let e and s be the measurements of the DNA bands from the evidence sample and from the suspect. Figures 5.2a and b show that for a match to be declared, the upper end of each uncertainty window must be above the lower end of the other. Therefore, all bands from the DNA of the suspect that satisfy the inequalities $(1 + \alpha)e > (1 - \alpha)s$ and $(1 + \alpha)s > (1 - \alpha)e$ would be declared a match. Thus, all such bands within the interval (called the match window)

$$\left(\frac{1 - \alpha}{1 + \alpha}\right)e \leq s \leq \left(\frac{1 + \alpha}{1 - \alpha}\right)e \qquad (5.7a)$$

(Weir and Gaut 1993) would have been declared a match, so the analysis must use the frequency (or proportion) of all such bands in the pertinent database. For $\alpha \ll 1$, Equation 5.7a is very close to

$$(1 - 2\alpha)e \le s \le (1 + 2\alpha)e. \qquad (5.7b)$$

For $\alpha = 0.025$, Equation 5.7b is sufficiently accurate.

Equation 5.7b determines the approximate floating bin $e \pm 2\alpha e$, or $e \pm 0.05e$ when $\alpha = 0.025$ (Figure 5.2c). The frequency of that bin is the total proportion of alleles in the database that are within the limits given by Equation 5.7b. With that approach, the floating bin is always the same as the match window. Using a floating bin different from the match window is incorrect; a smaller bin (such as $\pm 2.5\%$ instead of $\pm 5\%$) will underestimate the match probability; a larger bin will overestimate it.

Fixed bins

Most forensic laboratories have adopted *fixed bins*, perhaps because of the presumed difficulties of employing floating bins on a wide scale, particularly the necessity of searching the whole database for each calculation (Budowle, Giusti et al. 1991). With current computer-search speeds, these difficulties should be negligible, and the use of floating-bin procedures is statistically preferable because they directly and unambiguously address the central question of estimating the probability of a match. The FBI data set of individual profiles is available on a floppy disk, so laboratories can easily use the FBI database with floating bins.

In the fixed-bin procedures currently employed by many forensic laboratories, alleles of similar size are placed into fixed bins determined by comparing the positions of the evidence bands with bands in a control lane (Figure 5.2d). For example, the alleles at locus D2S44 are grouped into 31 bins for a given database, then adjacent bins with frequencies of fewer than five persons are combined ("rebinned") to produce a grouped frequency distribution for that locus (see Table 4.4) With fixed bins, some statistical power is lost, but there are computational and expository gains.

If the match window is entirely within a bin, the frequency used is that of the bin. When the match window overlaps two or more bins, some method of estimating the frequency is required.

One must distinguish between two uses of fixed bins. Some experts might use them to derive an upper bound to the floating-bin match probability, whereas others might use them to approximate that probability. Distinguishing these two uses is essential whenever the match window around the evidence-sample band, e, specified by Equation 5.7b and usually about 10% wide, overlaps two or more fixed bins. Although bin widths also average about 10%, they vary considerably and some are considerably smaller. To calculate an upper bound, an analyst must add the frequencies of all fixed bins overlapped by the match window, as recommended by the 1992 NRC report. Thus, fixed bins, when used with the criteria described in NRC (1992), yield a more conservative estimate than floating bins. To approximate the floating-bin match probability, we recommend using the fixed bin with the largest frequency among those overlapped by the match window. That approach is based on the observations that both floating and fixed bins are about 10% wide and that bands generally do not cluster around fixed-bin boundaries (Budowle, Giusti et al. 1991; Chakraborty, Jin et al. 1993; Monson and Budowle 1993). The reasons for recommending the procedure are explained below (see also Figure 5.2d).

The FBI and many police agencies follow an approximating procedure that is, on the average, less conservative than the one we recommend (Budowle, Giusti et al. 1991). They use the fixed bin with the largest frequency among those overlapped by the union of the $\pm$ 2.5% (5% wide) evidence-sample and suspect-sample windows (Figure 5.2e). However, those windows are each only about one half the width of the match window, so their union could be of any size ranging from about half that of the match window to about equal to that of the match window, depending on the relative positions of e and s. In the extreme case where the evidence-sample and suspect-sample windows barely overlap, three-fourths of this union is included in the match window; otherwise the fraction included is greater. Thus, for every match, at least about three-fourths, but usually most or all of this union is included in the match window. One, two, or more bins might be overlapped.

Monson and Budowle (1993) showed that using the fixed bin with the largest frequency among those overlapped by the $\pm$ 2.5% evidence-sample window adequately approximates and is usually more conservative than the match probability calculated from the $\pm$ 5% floating bin. Either of the fixed-bin procedures described in the last two paragraphs is more conservative than that of Monson and Budowle (1993), because a larger interval (the $\pm$ 5% match window in the first method and the union of the $\pm$ 2.5% evidence-sample and suspect-sample windows in the second) might overlap a bin with a higher frequency than does the $\pm$ 2.5% evidence-sample window.

We conclude that both the procedure we recommend and that employed by the FBI provide adequate and usually conservative approximations to the correct floating-bin frequency. As Equations 5.7 demonstrate, the match probability depends on e; thus, for this computation the suspect window is irrelevant. The procedure we have recommended is therefore more logical and, on the average, more conservative than that used by the FBI. It is more conservative because a window that is 10% wide might overlap more bins than one that is 5% to 10% wide. Although adding the frequencies of the fixed bins overlapped by the match window is the only procedure that is always conservative, in our view it is excessively cautious (Monson and Budowle 1993) and will usually produce less accurate estimates than our recommendation to take the largest of the overlapped bins. Adding bins would approximately double the best fixed-bin estimate of the match probability for each allele where the match window overlaps two bins.

Box 5.1. Calculating Uncertainty Windows: A Numerical Example

Table 4.4 shows the bin sizes for two VNTR loci, D2S44 and D17S79. For locus D17S79, suppose that the evidence-sample band size, e, is measured as 1,200 base pairs (bp). 2.5% of that is 30 bp. The lower limit of the uncertainty window is $1,200 - (0.025)(1,200) = 1,170$ bp. The upper limit is $1,200 + (0.025)(1,200) = 1,230$ bp. The suspect-sample band size, s, is 1,625 bp. The same calculation as above gives a range of 1,584 to 1,666 bp for the uncertainty-window of the sample from the suspect. Since the lower limit of the window for that sample, 1,584 bp, is greater than the upper limit of the window for the evidence sample, 1,230 bp, the bands do not match. Of course, in this case a nonmatch would have been declared visually, and the calculations would be unnecessary.

For locus D2S44, suppose that the size of the evidence-sample band is 2,747 bp; the lower and upper ends of the $\pm$ 2.5% uncertainty window are then 2,678 and 2,816 bp. Suppose further that the corresponding values for the suspect sample are 2,832, 2,761, and 2,903 bp. Those windows overlap, so a match would be declared.

The $\pm$ 2.5% evidence-sample window overlaps bins 15 and 16. The approximate match window (from Equation 5.7b), with width 10%, is from 2,610 to 2,884 bp and overlaps bins 15 (freq. = 0.041), 16 (0.040), and 17 (0.086). The bin with the largest frequency among those overlapped by the match window is 17, so our suggested approximate frequency is 0.086.

The FBI would use the bin with the largest frequency among those overlapped by the union of the evidence-sample and suspect-sample uncertainty windows, 2,678 to 2,903 bp; the union overlaps bins 15, 16, and 17. Again the bin with the highest frequency is 17.

An upper bound to the fixed-bin match probability is the total frequency of the three bins overlapped by the match window; that frequency is 0.167.

The floating-bin frequency is the proportion of bands in the database that lie in the match window, and is about 0.071. The fixed-bin estimate, 0.086, is therefore slightly conservative. (Note: the floating-bin frequency cannot be calculated from Table 4.4, but requires the FBI database.)

If the more accurate Equation 5.7a had been used, the match window would have been 2,613 to 2,888 bp. The widely used approximation, Equation 5.7b, is clearly quite accurate, although the exact formula would be theoretically preferable.

CONFIDENCE INTERVALS FOR MATCH PROBABILITIES

Match probabilities are calculated from a database. Those data are a sample from a larger population, and another sample might yield different match probabilities. To account for the fact that match probabilities are based on different databases and might change if another data set were used, it is helpful to give confidence intervals for those probabilities. A confidence interval is expected to include the true value a specified percentage of the time. In symbols, a $100(1 - \alpha)\%$ confidence interval is expected to include the true value $100(1 - \alpha)\%$ of the time. Typical values are 95% ($\alpha = 0.05$) or 99% ($\alpha = 0.01$). The confidence interval will depend on the genetic model, the actual probabilities, and the size of the database. We consider only the simplest case, a population in HW and LE proportions.

For such a population, the probability of a multilocus genotype is the product of the constituent allele frequencies, which are estimated from the database, with a factor of 2 included for each heterozygous locus involved (see Chapter 4). The product form of the relation suggests that it is most convenient to find a confidence interval for the natural logarithm of the probability and then transform it back to the probability, as is often done in data analysis (see Sokal and Rohlf 1981).

The contribution to the match probability of a single homozygous locus is p_i^2 (or $2p_i$ if a conservative estimate is desired) and, for a heterozygous locus, it is $2p_ip_j$. In practice, the true probability is unknown and is replaced by the estimate, $\hat{p}_k$, which is taken to be the proportion of the k-th allele in the database of N persons (2N genes per locus). We approximate the expectation of each logarithm by the logarithm of the expectation. The approximate variances of the logarithms are

$$A_iA_i: V[\ln(2\hat{p}_i)] \approx (1 - p_i)/(2Np_i) \text{ (for single bands),} \qquad (5.8a)$$

$$A_iA_j: V[\ln(2\hat{p}_i\hat{p}_j)] \approx (p_i + p_j - 4p_ip_j)/(2Np_ip_j), \qquad (5.8b)$$

$$A_iA_i: V[\ln(\hat{p}_i^2)] \approx 2(1 - p_i)/(Np_i). \qquad (5.8c)$$

If $Np_i >> 1$ for each allele and every locus, the logarithm of the genotype frequency is approximately normally distributed (Cox and Snell 1989). Because of the independence of the loci, the variance of the logarithm of the multilocus estimate is the sum of the values for each locus. If z_α is the standard-normal deviate associated with a symmetric confidence interval of $100(1 - \alpha)\%$, then the confidence interval for the logarithm of the genotypic frequency is equal to the estimated value $\pm z_\alpha s$, where s is the square root of the multilocus variance. These limits are then transformed back by antilogs.

A similar procedure was given by Chakraborty, Srinivasan, and Daiger (1993).

If more loci are added, the estimated probability will be smaller, but additional variability in the estimate implies that on the log scale the interval will be wider.

A smaller database also will lead to wider intervals. The width of the confidence interval on the log scale is inversely proportional to the square root of the size of the database. Thus, for a database one fourth as large as the one in Box 5.2, the confidence limits would be $-17,263 \pm (1.96)(0.329)(2)$. On the original scale, the limits are 8.76×10^{-9} and 1.156×10^{-7}, a range of about 13-fold, which is more than three times as large as the confidence interval for the database in Box 5.2. We can also write confidence intervals for values calculated with Equations 4.10.[7]

Box 5.2.   Calculating Confidence Limits: A Numerical Example

As a numerical example, consider again the data for the white population illustrated in Box 4.3, using data from Table 4.8. The profile is $A_6 - B_8 B_{14} C_{10} C_{13} D_9 D_{16}$. The A-locus variance component is estimated to be

$$(1 - \hat{p}_i)/(2N\hat{p}_i) = (1 - 0.035)/[1584(0.035)] = 0.01741.$$

For the B-locus, the component is

$$(\hat{p}_i + \hat{p}_j - 4\hat{p}_i\hat{p}_j)/(2N\hat{p}_i\hat{p}_j) = [(0.029 + 0.068 - 4(0.029)(0.068)]/$$
$$[1,190(0.029)(0.068)] = 0.03797.$$

For the C-locus, the component is 0.01475, and for D it is 0.03807. Adding those four components yields a sum of 0.10820, the square root of which is 0.32893. The estimated genotype frequency (Box 4.3) is 3.182×10^{-8}; its natural logarithm, $(2.303 \log_{10})$, is -17.263.

For a 95% confidence interval, $z_\alpha = \pm 1.96$, so the confidence limits of the logarithm are $-17.263 \pm (1.96)(0.329)$. Taking antilogs (exponentiating), the confidence limits for the match probability are 6.06×10^{-8} and 1.67×10^{-8}. The width of the 95% confidence interval is about a factor of 3.6, or roughly a factor of 1.9 in either direction.

---

[7]If Equations 4.4 or 4.10 are used to evaluate match probabilities, a prescription for calculating confidence intervals can be similarly derived, although the detailed formulae will be somewhat different. Since knowledge of the range of reasonable values of $\bar{\theta}$ is obtained from an accumulating body of population-genetics studies, one might give a range of confidence intervals based on a range of values of $\bar{\theta}$. Alternatively, when applying Equations 4.10, one could obtain a conservative approximation to match probabilities by using a value of $\bar{\theta}$ that is slightly larger than that found in most studies. For example, for a confidence interval based on Equations 4.10, at each locus the contribution to the variance of the estimated value of the logarithm of Equation 4.10a equals approximately

$$\{1/[2\bar{\theta} + (1-\bar{\theta})p_i] + 1/[3\bar{\theta} + (1-\bar{\theta})p_i]\}^2(1-\bar{\theta})^2(1+\bar{\theta})p_i(1-p_i)/(2N);$$

for Equation 4.10b, the corresponding formula is

$$\{p_i(1-p_i)/[\bar{\theta} + (1-\bar{\theta})p_i]^2 + p_j(1-p_j)/[\bar{\theta} + (1-\bar{\theta})p_j]^2 -$$
$$2p_ip_j/[\bar{\theta} + (1-\bar{\theta})p_i][\bar{\theta} + (1-\bar{\theta})p_j]\}(1-\bar{\theta})^2(1+\bar{\theta})/(2N).$$

Although calculation of confidence intervals is desirable, they do not include the effects of all the sources of error. A more inclusive estimate of uncertainty, which is usually larger, is considered later in the chapter.

ALLELES WITH LOW FREQUENCY

VNTRs have a very large number of alleles. Consequently, some bins—especially those at the ends of the size distribution for a locus—have very low frequencies. An estimate of an allele frequency can be very inaccurate if the allele is so rare that it is represented only once or a few times in a database; and some rare alleles might not be represented at all. Several procedures have been suggested to alleviate the problems caused by such inaccuracies. One approach is to add 0.5 to the observed number of occurrences of each rare allele (Cox and Snell 1989); another is to replace all rare-allele proportions by an arbitrary upper bound, as has been done for paternity analysis (Walker 1983, p 449). That was also recommended by Chakraborty (1992) and for STRs, by Evett et al. (1996).

It is common in some statistical tests to pool very rare classes, and that is what the FBI has done by *rebinning*. If a bin in the database contains fewer than five entries, it is pooled with adjacent bins so that no bin has fewer than five. We recommend this procedure for VNTRs and for other systems in which an allele is represented fewer than five times in the database. For a floating-bin analysis, the bin frequency is determined only after the evidence sample is typed. A similar expedient for rare alleles is to use the maximum of 5 and k, where k is the actual number of alleles from the database that fall within the match window.

Rare alleles can produce substantial departures from HW proportions, even if the populations from which they are drawn are in random-mating proportions. This is illustrated in the data in Table 4.4. Estimates of θ_{ii} obtained by randomly combining the data from Table 4.4 are all positive, as expected, and are each less than 0.004. Estimates of θ_{ij} are more variable and can be either positive or negative; about 1/5 of the values are outside the range -0.1 to 0.1. Large negative values can mean that HW calculations can be serious underestimates and thus biased against the defendant. However, these values are the result of random fluctuations between databases. In actual populations, we expect θ_{ij} to be positive unless it is very close to zero.

INDIVIDUAL VARIABILITY AND EMPIRICAL COMPARISONS

Confidence intervals derived from the simplifying assumptions of sampling theory do not take account of all possible sources of uncertainty that can affect the accuracy of a match probability or likelihood ratio. To examine the degree to which other sources of variation may affect the accuracy of our calculations, we have looked to empirical studies.

The FBI has compiled many data from the United States and other parts of the world (FBI 1993b; Budowle, Monson, Giusti, and Brown 1994a, 1994b). We can use those data to examine frequencies of a given genotype in different data sets.

We are mainly concerned with the effects of population subdivision, leading to different allele frequencies in different areas or in people with different ethnic backgrounds. Such differences are obscured in the averages. We examine only allele frequencies, because multilocus genotypes are much too rare to study. But the close agreement of the data with HW and LE proportions (Chapter 4), together with conservative assumptions, lend credence to our analyses.

Geographical Subdivision

One question is whether local regions differ appreciably from the national average. The FBI has compiled data from different sources throughout the world. One representative example is a comparison between blacks in the United States as a whole and those in Georgia. Assume that the source of evidence DNA from a particular crime in Georgia is known to be black. To make the most appropriate estimate of the probability that a profile from a randomly selected black person from this area would match the evidence profile, we would use the Georgia database. But suppose that we do not have local data and use the national average instead. How much of an error would that entail?

The relevant data (from FBI 1993b) are graphed in Figure 5.3. Each point on the graph represents a specific genotype for one or more of four VNTR loci, D1S7, D2S44, D4S139, and D10S28. For each genotype on the graph, the estimated frequency from the general US black database is given by the ordinate; its estimated frequency in the local Georgia database is given by the abscissa. In calculating the genotypic frequencies, LE and HW proportions were assumed, and single bands were assigned a frequency of 2p.[8] The two lines on either side of the diagonal represent 10-fold deviations from the expected proportions. The US population is probably more heterogeneous than the Georgia subset. The graph shows that if one were investigating a crime in Georgia but used nationwide figures, the estimate would practically always lie between the two lines, that is, it is within a factor of 10 either way from the frequency of the same profile in the more relevant local database.

As stated earlier, the points on these graphs are calculated from the databases under the assumptions that HW and LE ratios prevail within the population

---

[8]Figures 5.2–5.4 appear to show more very large values than expected (near the lower left corner). That is caused by the conventions used in the preparation of the graphs. First, each single band was given a value of twice the bin frequency (that is, the 2p rule was applied). Second, some of the points are for small numbers of loci, sometimes as few as one. Third, greater errors are likely to occur in measuring very large and very small fragments; therefore, such fragments were each assigned a value of one. In general, the more loci represented by a data point, the farther to the upper right the point lies.

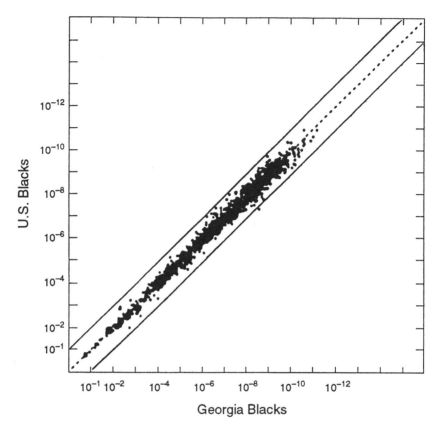

FIGURE 5.3   A scatter plot for US black populations. Each point represents a specific genotype from one to four VNTR loci, whose estimated frequency in the overall US black population is given by the ordinate and in the Georgia black population by the abscissa. The upper and lower lines represent values that deviate from equality by a factor of 10. Note: $10^{-6} = 1/10^6 = 0.000001$. From FBI (1993b, p 1233).

represented in each database. Departures from these assumptions could, of course, lead to greater uncertainty. In Chapter 4, however, we noted that typical values of $\bar{\theta}$ are less than 0.01 and departures from LE are similarly small. Therefore, we believe that the uncertainties caused by deviations from HW and LE expectations are much less than those caused by differences in allele frequencies in different subgroups.

The FBI compendia (FBI 1993b; Budowle, Monson, Giusti, and Brown 1994a, 1994b) contain a large number of graphs with many different comparisons. Figure 5.3 is typical of several other geographical comparisons. Geographical data for whites and Hispanics are in general agreement with those for blacks. We conclude that individual within-race profile frequencies from different geographic areas in the United States usually differ by less than a factor of 10 in either direction.

Differences Among Subgroups

The US white population consists of people of various European origins who have been partially mixed in the "melting pot." How much difference does this substructure make? It is difficult to identify relevant homogeneous groups within the United States. A better way to answer the question is to use data from Europe; those data better reflect the characteristics of the ancestral groups and should exaggerate between-group differences that have been diluted in the mixing of populations in the United States. Because of its large database, we compare the data set from Denmark with that from the United States (Figure 5.4). As the graph shows, if we substitute average frequencies for US whites for frequencies from the Danish data set, the error is almost always less than 10-fold in either direction. Graphs of Swiss, German, Norwegian, Spanish, and French data show similar patterns when compared with the United States. The percentage deviations tend to be larger in the upper right-hand part of the graphs—that is, where the probabilities become small. With probabilities of one in 100 million or less, an error of 10-fold either way is not likely to affect the conclusion.

The European populations have mixed less than the corresponding US groups that descended from European migrants. Therefore, the effects of subdivision should be less among white populations in the United States than in Europe. It seems safe to say that for those groups, an estimate using a nationwide rather than a subgroup database is likely to be less than 10-fold too low or too high. Data for Hispanics and East Asians are similar.

Different Races

When we compare data from different racial groups, a different picture emerges from that found within racial groups—the profile frequencies can differ considerably. Figure 5.5 compares US whites and blacks. Although the great majority of the points lie within a ± 10-fold range, an appreciable fraction are found outside this range. If, for example, we used the white database when we should have used the black, the error would sometimes be greater than 10-fold (that is, a substantial fraction of the data points are outside the two lines on either side of the diagonal in the figure), and a few points differ by 100-fold or more. That suggests a conservative procedure that can be used if it is not known whether the perpetrator is black or white: a match probability could be calculated from both databases and the higher of the two values used. If only one database is used, it might be the wrong one, and the result might be misleading.

It is not surprising that differences between races are considerably larger than those between subgroups within races (Devlin and Risch 1992; Devlin,

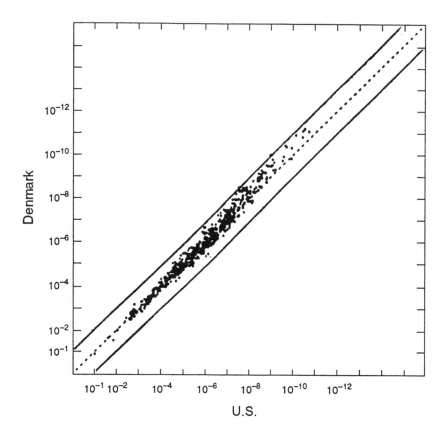

FIGURE 5.4 A scatter plot for the white population. The abscissa gives estimated frequencies in the US white population and the ordinate those in a Danish population. White frequencies are from Cellmark; Danish frequencies from Institute of Forensic Genetics in Copenhagen. From FBI (1993b, p 1267).

Risch, and Roeder 1993, 1994). That has been known by population geneticists for a long time and for various genes. The 1992 NRC report relied on a single study (Lewontin 1972) that appeared to support the opposite view, but that study has not been confirmed by other, more extensive ones (for example, Latter 1980). The 1992 report took the view of Lewontin and Hartl (1991) that examination of differences in databases from different racial groups might actually underestimate the degree of divergence within races, rather than overestimate it as we have seen to be the case from the VNTR studies discussed above. The recent compilations by the FBI, as well as numerous other studies (e.g., Hartmann et al. 1994), confirm the intuitively reasonable expectation that differences between ethnic groups within races are smaller than differences between races. But the

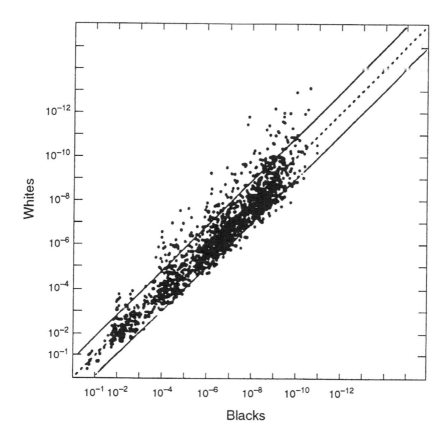

FIGURE 5.5   A scatter plot comparing the estimated white population frequencies (ordi-nate) with the black population (abscissa). Note the considerably greater spread than in Figures 5.2 and 5.3, which plot data from within the same racial group. From FBI (1993b, p 1230).

far more important conclusion, and the one that makes VNTR and other forensic loci so useful, is that most of the variation is not among groups but among persons, as population geneticists, including Lewontin (1972), have repeatedly emphasized.

We have referred to only some of the available data above. Several other studies have used deliberately wrong or artificially stratified databases and showed that such manipulations do not produce grossly wrong results (Evett and Pinchin 1991; Berry, Evett, and Pinchin 1992).

As mentioned earlier, in the data compiled by TWGDAM there was only one four-locus match in the white population and one in the Hispanic population among 58 million pairwise comparisons. There were no five- or six-locus matches.

That was not true for the American Indian population, where two four-locus matches were found among 1.7 million pairs. Those were not instances where the same person was entered twice into the database, because the profiles did not match at the other loci tested. As we have emphasized earlier, there is considerably more subdivision in American Indians, so four-locus matches within a tribe are not as unusual (R. Chakraborty, unpublished data).

The data and studies that we have reviewed support the argument that multilocus VNTR comparisons are very powerful tests of identity. Unless there is reason to believe that close relatives are involved or that the suspect and donor of the evidence DNA, if not the same person, are from the same subpopulation, the product rule (with the 2p rule) is appropriate (see Chapter 4).

The data for PCR-based systems are far more limited than those for VNTRs. However, the numbers are increasing. Chakraborty, Jin, et al. (1995) show graphs of different populations within racial groups for Polymarkers, plotted in the manner of Figures 5.3 to 5.6. The numbers for Polymarkers are much smaller than those for VNTRs, but as with VNTRs, the points all fall within 10-fold above or below the line corresponding to perfect agreement. Comparable data exist for STRs.

As mentioned before, the graphs in Figures 5.3 and 5.4 assume HW and LE. On the average, as we have repeatedly emphasized, departures from these assumptions are small. Yet, with several loci, despite some cancellation, small errors can accumulate. That is most important for rare alleles, where random fluctuations can generate appreciable departures from HW and LE.

In a recent study of the TWGDAM data, Chakraborty (personal communication) has calculated the values of θ_{ij} for VNTRs. Even though the mean value is close to zero and the distribution is approximately symmetrical, individual values show appreciable departures, especially for very rare alleles. The variability is mainly, if not entirely, due to uncertainties in the databases, but such variations may also occur in the population if there is localized subdivision.

MORE CONSERVATIVE FORMULAE

Some workers (Balding and Nichols 1994, 1995) have advocated the use of Equations 4.10 rather than the simpler Equations 4.1, which assume HW proportions (see Chapter 4). Figure 5.6 illustrates the effect of using Equations 4.10 for a rather extreme example (Roeder et al. 1995). On the ordinate are the frequencies of various genotypes for an artificial 50:50 pooled mixture of whites and blacks; on the abscissa are frequencies for whites. If we assume that the evidence DNA is from a white person, and if we falsely assume that the pooled mixture of whites and blacks is in HW and LE proportions, then the graph shows the range of error that would exist if the pooled database were used instead of the more appropriate database for whites. In the top graph in the figure, a point that is below and to the right of the diagonal line overestimates the true probability

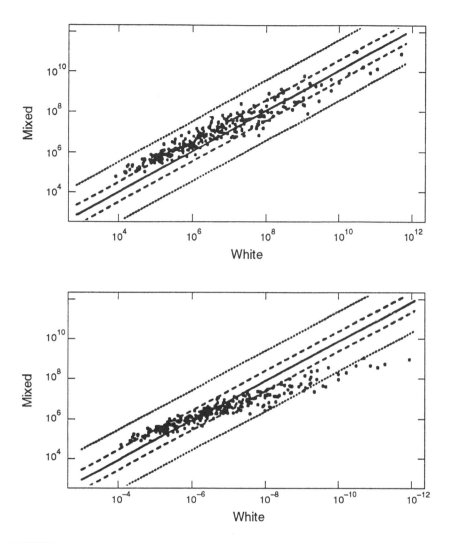

FIGURE 5.6 A scatter plot comparing the white population (abscissa) with an equal mixture of whites and blacks (ordinate). In the upper graph, the HW rule was used; in the lower, Equations 4.10 with $\bar{\theta} = 0.01$. The dashed lines represent deviations by a factor of 5 and the dotted lines by a factor of 15. Data from Lifecodes (Roeder et al. submitted).

of a match (that is, it errs in favor of the defendant). The majority of the points in the regions of higher probabilities are above the 45° line; that is, they are biased against the defendant. That is the effect that was of concern in the 1992 NRC report, but with respect to ethnic differences within racial groups rather than between racial groups. We have chosen an extreme example for illustration. Even so, all the points are within 15-fold of the 45° diagonal line in the graph.

The bottom graph in Figure 5.6 shows the effect of using Equations 4.10 for the mixed population rather than using the HW formula, Equation 4.1. The value of $\bar{\theta}$ was taken to be 0.01, which is the value estimated from this data set (Roeder et al. 1995). It is clear from the graph that using Equations 4.10 usually leads to a conservative estimate, except for the higher probabilities shown in the lower left part of the graph. That makes sense, for it is clear from Equations 4.10 that when p is large, $\bar{\theta}$ has little effect on profile-frequency estimates.

We conclude that, even if an artificial, intentionally inappropriate database of mixed profiles from whites and blacks is used, Equations 4.10 are conservative. We further note that when fixed bins are used in the manner recommended in the section in this chapter on statistical aspects of VNTR analysis, the procedure is usually conservative, and that applying the 2p rule increases the conservatism of the method. Finally, using Equations 4.10 with fixed bins adds to the conservatism.

To summarize: Within a racial group, geographic origin and ethnic composition have very little effect on the frequencies of forensic DNA profiles, although there are larger differences between major groups (races). It is probably safe to assume that within a race, the uncertainty of a value calculated from adequate databases (at least several hundred persons) by the product rule is within a factor of about 10 above and below the true value. If the calculated profile probability is very small, the uncertainty can be larger, but even a large relative error will not change the conclusion. If there is good reason to think that the suspect and the source of the evidence are from the same subpopulation, Equations 4.10 can be used.

THE CEILING PRINCIPLES

The 1992 NRC report assumed that population substructure might exist and recommended procedures for calculating profile frequencies that could be expected to be sufficiently conservative to accommodate the presence of substructure. Two such procedures are recommended in the 1992 report, the "ceiling principle" and the "interim ceiling principle."

The ceiling principle (NRC 1992, p 82-85) places a lower limit on the size of the profile frequency by giving thresholds for the allele-frequency values used in the calculation. To determine the thresholds, the report recommended that 100 persons be sampled from each of 15-20 genetically homogenous populations spanning the racial and ethnic diversity of groups represented in the United States. For each allele the highest value among the groups sampled, or 5%, whichever was larger, would be used. Then the product rule would be applied to those values to determine the profile frequency. The choice and sampling of the 15-20 populations was to be supervised by the NCFDT (see Chapter 3), which has not come into being. The necessary ground work for applying the ceiling principle has not been done, and there have been few attempts to apply it. We share the view of many experts who have criticized it on practical and statistical grounds and who see no scientific justification for its use.

The 1992 report recommended that until the ceiling principle could be put into effect, the interim ceiling principle be applied. In contrast to the ceiling principle, the interim ceiling principle has been widely used and sometimes misused. The rule (NRC 1992, p 14-15, 91-93) is: "In applying the multiplication rule, the 95% upper confidence limit of the frequency of each allele should be calculated for separate US 'racial' groups and the highest of these values or 10% (whichever is the larger) should be used. Data on at least three major 'races' (e.g., whites, blacks, Hispanics, east Asians, and American Indians) should be analyzed." The report also stated that the multiplication (that is, product) rule should be applied only when there is no significant departure from HW and LE, even though the ceiling principle was introduced specifically to accommodate deviations from HW and LE.

If the interim ceiling principle is applied to four loci, the minimum probability, assuming that there are no single bands, is $[2(0.1)(0.1)]^4 = (1/50)^4 = 1/6,250,000$. With five loci the minimum probability becomes about one in 300 million. But if the 2p rule is used for single bands and any locus found to depart from HW proportions is not used, the probability can be much larger. For example, if only three loci are used and one is homozygous, the minimum is $2(0.1)(1/50)^2 = 1/12,500$.

Is the interim ceiling principle logical? Is it unnecessarily conservative? In view of all the accumulated data we have discussed, is it needed? The interim ceiling principle has the advantage that in any particular case it gives the same answer irrespective of the racial group. That is also a disadvantage, because it does not permit the use of well-established differences in frequencies in different races; it is inflexible and cannot be adjusted to the circumstances of a particular case.

The ceiling principles have been widely discussed, usually critically (Chakraborty and Kidd 1991; Cohen 1992; Morton 1992, 1995; Evett, Scranage, and Pinchin 1993; Kaye 1993, 1995a; Lempert 1993; Weir 1993a; Balding and Nichols 1994; Devlin, Risch, and Roeder 1994; Lander and Budowle 1994; TWGDAM 1994c; Morton 1995). Here are some of those criticisms:

• The 10% value is completely arbitrary, and there is no scientific justification of its choice as a ceiling value.

• Although calculation of an upper 95% confidence limit for an individual allele is justified as a standard statistical procedure, multiplication of those values is not.

• The ceiling principles do not make use of the large amount of allele-frequency data now available from different groups and subgroups.

• They do not make use of standard procedures long used by population geneticists to study subdivided populations.

• It is excessively conservative. (Actually it is not always conservative, for one can contrive examples in which it is not [Slimowitz and Cohen 1993], but in realistic examples it is conservative.)

• The report's lack of specific instructions as to which population groups should be included has led some experts and attorneys to focus on extreme examples, perhaps involving small databases with large sampling errors or irrelevant populations; that practice was not foreseen by the writers of the 1992 report.

We agree with the criticisms listed above. Our view is that sufficient data have been gathered that neither ceiling principle is needed. We have suggested alternative procedures, all of which are conservative to some degree. We believe that estimates based on the formulae outlined in Chapter 4—and with proper attention to uncertainties—are now appropriate. In special cases in which there is no appropriate database, such as for some American Indian tribes, the estimates (based on the methods in this report) for several related groups should be used.

TWGDAM (1994c) has recently issued a report on the ceiling principle. TWGDAM "cannot recommend the application of the ceiling principle. The basis for the need for a ceiling principle is flawed. . . . The current methods employed by forensic scientists have been demonstrated to be robust scientifically" (p 899).

If the interim ceiling principle is used despite that recommendation, TWG-DAM recommends an approach intended to overcome some of the criticisms of the 1992 NRC report. The recommended approach differs from that in the 1992 report in several ways:

• When the measurement error spans a fixed-bin border, take the frequency of the most frequent of the bins instead of summing the overlapped bins, as recommended by the 1992 report.

• Native-American databases are not to be used to generate values for the ceiling; the groups to be used are whites, blacks, Hispanics, and east Asians.

• The multiple of the standard deviation for an upper 95% confidence limit should be 1.64, not 1.96, which was given in a footnote on page 92 of the 1992 report. NRC (1992) confused one-tailed and two-tailed confidence coefficients.

We agree with the TWGDAM recommendations and add the following interpretations, which we believe are consistent with the 1992 report.

• The ceiling principles are intended for criminal, not civil cases. They are therefore inappropriate for paternity testing, unless that is part of a criminal proceeding.

• The ceiling principles were intended for VNTRs with many alleles, no one of which has a very high frequency. They are not applicable to PCR-based systems, which ordinarily have few alleles. For example, applying the upper 95% confidence limit produces allele frequencies that add up to more than one, and, with two alleles, to heterozygote frequencies that can be greater than the HW maximum of 1/2.

• As originally presented (NRC 1992, p 91), the ceiling principle would use only those loci not differing significantly from HW and LE. But populations with the least reliable numbers (that is, the smallest databases) are the very ones most likely not to show a statistically significant departure from HW and LE. Thus, an analyst who uses the interim ceiling principle will often be forced to reject more reliable loci in favor of less reliable ones. Furthermore, the purpose of the ceiling principles is to allow for differences in allele frequencies in different subgroups, for which HW and LE are insensitive measures. Therefore, we believe that all loci in the selected databases should be used in the calculation.

In summary, the procedures we have recommended in Chapter 4 are based on population genetics and empirical data and can encompass suitable degrees of conservatism. With such procedures available, we believe that the interim ceiling principle is not needed and can be abandoned.

DIRECT COUNT FROM A DATABASE

The 1992 NRC report stated (p 91) that "the testing laboratory should check to see that the observed multilocus genotype matches any sample in the population database. Assuming that it does not, it should report that the DNA pattern was compared to a database of N individuals from the population and no match was observed, indicating its rarity in the population." The Committee noted that if there were no occurrences of a profile in 100 samples, the upper confidence limit is 3%. It went on to say (p 76) that "such estimates produced by straightforward counting have the virtue that they do not depend on theoretical assumptions, but simply on the sample's having been randomly drawn from the appropriate population. However, such estimates do not take advantage of the full potential of the genetic approach."

The ceiling method uses random-mating theory but does not make full use of population data. The counting method does not even combine allele frequencies and thereby loses even more information. In addition, very small probabilities cannot be estimated accurately from samples of realistic size; modeling is required. In fact, most profiles are not found in any database, so there must be a convention as to how to handle zeros. Since we believe that the abundant data make the ceiling principles unnecessary, this is true *a fortiori* for the direct counting method.

Some statisticians and others have questioned the accuracy of using population-genetics theory that incorporates estimated allele distributions in forensic calculations. Somewhat comparable calculations are available that do not use this information. For a Poisson distribution, an upper $100(1 - \alpha)\%$ confidence limit L for the expected number of events when zero events have been observed is $L = -\ln(\alpha)$. For a 95% confidence limit, $\alpha = 0.05$ and $L = 3$. For illustration, the TWGDAM data included about 7,000 persons in the white database. That yields $(7,000)(6,999)/2 = 24.5$ million pairs of profiles. Only one four-locus match was found and none for five or more. Let us assume that all persons were tested at five loci—the same five loci—and regard these pairs as a random sample. Then a Poisson approximation similar to that leading to Equation 5.5 (but without assuming HW and LE) leads to the conclusion that an upper 95% confidence limit for the probability of a match between suspect and evidence DNA at those five loci is 3/(24.5 million), or about 1 in 8 million. This calculation illustrates the possibility of procedures that do not employ estimated allele distributions and population-genetics theory but still give very small match probabilities, provided that sufficiently large databases of genotype profiles are available.

However, such a method is inappropriate, and we do not recommend it. It gives an approximate upper bound to the mean value, but not conditioned on the particular profile in question; it does not answer the question we are most interested in, the probability of a match of the particular evidence and suspect profile. It has not been demonstrated to be robust with respect to various database problems; for example, the same loci may not always have been tested. Also, it does not use available information about allele frequencies and thus does not permit sharper inferences conditional upon that information. Finally, the value is strongly dependent on the size of the database.

The population-genetic assumptions that we use are robust, are accurate within the limits discussed elsewhere in this report, and make sensible use of information about allele frequencies.

CONCLUSIONS AND RECOMMENDATIONS

Statistical Issues

Confidence limits for profile probabilities, based on allele frequencies and the size of the database, can be calculated by methods explained in this report. We recognize, however, that confidence limits address only part of the uncertainty. For a more realistic estimate, we examined empirical data from the comparison of different subpopulations and of subpopulations with the whole. The empirical studies show that the differences between the frequencies of the individual profiles estimated by the product rule from different adequate subpopulation databases (at least several hundred persons) are within a factor of about 10 of each other, and that provides a guide to the uncertainty of the determination for a single profile. For very small estimated profile frequencies, the uncertainty can be greater, both because of the greater relative uncertainty of individually small probabilities and because more loci are likely to be multiplied. But with very small probabilities, a large relative error is not likely to change the conclusion.

Database Searches

If the suspect is identified through a DNA database search, the interpretation of the match probability and likelihood ratio given in Chapter 4 should be modified.

Recommendation 5.1: When the suspect is found by a search of DNA databases, the random-match probability should be multiplied by N, the number of persons in the database.

If one wishes to describe the impact of the DNA evidence under the hypothesis that the source of the evidence sample is someone in the database, then the likelihood ratio should be divided by N. As database searches become more extensive, another problem may arise. If the database searched includes a large proportion of the population, the analysis must take this into account. In the extreme case a search of the whole population should, of course, provide a definitive answer.

Uniqueness

With an increasing number of loci available for forensic analysis, we are approaching the time when each person's profile will be unique (except for identical twins and possibly other close relatives). Suppose that, in a population of N unrelated persons, a given DNA profile has probability P. The probability (before a suspect has been profiled) that the *particular* profile observed in the evidence sample is not unique is at most NP.

A lower bound on the probability that *every* person is unique depends on the population size, the number of loci, and the heterozygosity of the individual loci. Neglecting population structure and close relatives, 10 loci with a geometric mean heterozygosity of 95% give a probability greater than about 0.999 that no two unrelated persons in the world have the same profile. Once it is decided what level of probability constitutes uniqueness, appropriate calculations can readily be made.

In any particular case, the chance that the DNA profile for the evidence sample is unique is of more concern than the chance that all DNA profiles are unique. Hence, the calculation in the first paragraph will be the one more often employed.

Matching and Binning

VNTR data are essentially continuous, and, in principle, a continuous model should be used to analyze them. The methods generally used, however, involve taking measurement uncertainty into account by determining a match window. Two procedures for determining match probabilities are the floating-bin and fixed-bin methods. The floating-bin method is statistically preferable but requires access to a computerized database. The fixed-bin method is more widely used and understood, and the necessary data tables are widely and readily available. When our fixed-bin recommendation is followed, the two methods lead to very similar results. Both methods are acceptable.

Recommendation 5.2. If floating bins are used to calculate the random-match probabilities, each bin should coincide with the corresponding match window. If fixed bins are employed, then the fixed bin that has the largest frequency among those overlapped by the match window should be used.

Ceiling Principles

The abundance of data in different ethnic groups within the major races and the genetically and statistically sound methods recommended in this report imply that both the ceiling principle and the interim ceiling principle are unnecessary.

Further Research

The rapid rate of discovery of new markers in connection with human gene-mapping should lead to many new markers that are highly polymorphic, mutable, and selectively neutral, but which, unlike VNTRs, can be amplified by PCR and for which individual alleles can usually be distinguished unambiguously with none of the statistical problems associated with matching and binning. Furthermore, radioactive probes need not be used with many other markers, so identification can be prompt and problems associated with using radioactive materials can be avoided. It should soon be possible to have systems so powerful that no statistical and population analyses will be needed, and (except possibly for close relatives) each person in a population can be uniquely identified.

Recommendation 5.3. Research into the identification and validation of more and better marker systems for forensic analysis should continue with a view to making each profile unique.

APPENDIX 5A

Mixed stains introduce a number of complexities. We limit our consideration to cases in which the stain comes from two persons, but only one suspect is identified. The case where four bands are observed, two of which match the suspect, was given in the text. Here we consider circumstances in which fewer than four bands are found in the evidentiary DNA. This may mean that either the suspect or the other contributor to the stain produced a single band. Thus, the 2p rule may be needed. It is also possible that there are only two bands, but other loci indicate that the stain is mixed. These cases are summarized in Table 5.1.

TABLE 5.1   Likelihood Ratios for Mixed Stains[a]

Crime scene	Suspect	Rule	Likelihood Ratio
$A_1A_2A_3A_4$	A_1A_2	—	$\dfrac{1}{12p_1p_2}$
$A_1A_2A_3$	A_2A_3	$2p$	$\dfrac{1 + p_2 + p_3}{4p_2p_3(3 + p_1 + p_2 + p_3)}$
		p^2	$\dfrac{p_1 + 2p_2 + 2p_3}{12p_2p_3(p_1 + p_2 + p_3)}$
$A_1A_2A_3$	A_1	$2p$	$\dfrac{1}{4p_1(3 + p_1 + p_2 + p_3)}$
		p^2	$\dfrac{1}{6p_1(p_1 + p_2 + p_3)}$
A_1A_2	A_1A_2	$2p$	$\dfrac{p_1 + p_2 + p_1p_2}{2p_1p_2(2 + 2p_1 + 2p_2 + p_1p_2)}$
		p^2	$\dfrac{(p_1 + p_2)^2}{2p_1p_2(3p_1p_2 + 2p_1^2 + 2p_2^2)}$
A_1A_2	A_1	$2p$	$\dfrac{1 + p_1}{2p_1(2 + 2p_1 + 2p_2 + p_1p_2)}$
		p^2	$\dfrac{2p_1 + p_2}{2p_1(3p_1p_2 + 2p_1^2 + 2p_2^2)}$

[a]For each combination of crime-scene and suspect genotypes, the likelihood ratio is given for each of two rules for dealing with single bands (or homozygotes).

APPENDIX 5B

If the database is not homogeneous, that is, if $P(M_i)$ is different for different values of i, then the inequality in Equation 5.3 is still valid, so

$$P(M) \leq \Sigma_i P(M_i), \tag{5.9}$$

where $P(M_i)$ can be evaluated by the methods of Chapter 4. Many of the terms in the sum will be the same. In the simplest case, in which the database contains N persons, all with the same ethnic background, the effect is just to multiply an individual match probability by N, leading to Equation 5.3.

If we assume that the database consists of n_1 whites and n_2 blacks, then Equation 5.9 simplifies to

$$P(M) \leq n_1 P(W) + n_2 P(B), \tag{5.10}$$

where W denotes the event that a randomly selected white profile matches the evidence-sample profile and B denotes the same match event for a randomly selected black profile.

Remark. An approximation that will often be somewhat closer to P(M) than Equation 5.9 is

$$P(M) \approx 1 - \exp[-\Sigma_i P(M_i)]. \tag{5.11}$$

That approximation will give approximately the same answer as Equation 5.9 when $\Sigma_i P(M_i)$ is small, and that is the case of practical importance.

The event M involves all markers tested, both those employed for identification purposes and any additional markers used for confirmation. If we let $M_{i,1}$ denote the event of a match of the i-th profile on the initial batch of markers tested for the purpose of the database search, and $M_{i,2}$ the event of a match of the i-th profile on the subsequent markers tested, then under the assumption of linkage equilibrium, $P(M_i) = P(M_{i,1})P(M_{i,2})$. That same factorization would hold under the assumption of linkage equilibrium for an arbitrary division of the markers into two subsets.

From a Bayesian viewpoint, there are other methods to deal with database searches, although the final result is much the same as that given above (see also Balding and Donnelly 1995). Although the assignment of prior probabilities is problematic and appears to have been used rarely if at all in criminal forensic investigations in the United States, some related ideas can be useful in clarifying certain issues. Let Q be the probability of the event E that some person whose profile is in the database left the evidence sample, with $1 - Q$ being the probability of event E^c that the evidence sample was left by someone whose profile is not in the database. Suppose that there is a match between the evidence-sample profile and at least one profile in the database. Assuming that $P(M|E) = 1$ and $P(M|E^c) = P(M)$, where P(M) is evaluated as above, we find the posterior odds that the evidence sample was left by someone whose profile is in the database to be $P(E|M)/P(E^c|M) = Q/[(1-Q)P(M)]$. Since the posterior odds equals the prior odds times the likelihood ratio, the likelihood ratio is $1/P(M)$, as above.

If there is a unique match in the database, the preceding argument, which implicates the database as a whole, would, of course, implicate the person with the unique matching profile. The following alternative argument focuses directly on such a person. Let E_i denote the event that the i-th person whose profile is in the database left the evidence sample, and let M_i be the event that the profile of the i-th person matches that of the evidence sample. Let U_i be the event that the i-th person has a unique matching profile. Let q_i denote the prior probability of E_i, so that $Q = \Sigma_i q_i$, and let $p = P(M_i|E^c)$ be the conditional probability of a random match under the condition E^c that no one profiled in the database left the evidence sample. The posterior odds implicating the i-th person as the source of the evidence sample are $P(E_i|U_i)/P(E_i^c|U_i) = q_i P(U_i|E_i)/[(1-q_i)P(U_i|E_i^c)]$. Under the assumption that all possible sources of the evidence sample are unrelated, it can be shown that this ratio equals $q_i/(1-Q)p$, and even without that assumption, the same expression is a lower bound for the posterior odds. In the special case in which $q_i = Q/N$, where N is the size of the database, the formula becomes

$Q/[(1-Q)Np]$; when Np is small, this is essentially the same as the preceding case. A Bayesian analysis is particularly well-suited to deal with the case where the database can be expected to contain almost all reasonable suspects. In that case, the prior odds, $Q/(1-Q)$, would be large.

APPENDIX 5C

Equation 5.5 can be derived as follows. Let M denote the number of pairwise matches in the population when K loci are typed. To evaluate the probability that $P\{M \geq 1\}$ we let $E = \Sigma Q_v^2$, where Q_v is the probability of the v-th genotype in some fixed enumeration of the set of all possible genotypes. As an application of the "birthday problem" with unequal probabilities (Aldous 1989, p 109), we have

$$P\{M \geq 1\} \approx 1 - \exp(-N^2E/2) \qquad (5.12)$$

if N is large and $\max(Q_v)$ is small. The contribution to E of a single locus, expressed in terms of the allele frequencies p_i and homozygosity f at that locus, is

$$\Sigma_{i<j}(2p_ip_j)^2 + \Sigma_i p_i^4 = 2f^2 - \Sigma_i p_i^4 \leq 2f^2.$$

Taking the product over all loci, we find that an upper bound for E is $\Pi_L[2f_L^2]$. Hence, a simple approximate upper bound for the desired probability is

$$1 - \exp(-N^2 2^{K-1}f^{2K}) \leq N^2 2^{K-1}f^{2K}, \qquad (5.13)$$

where $f = (\Pi f_L)^{1/K}$, the geometric mean of the homozygosities.

If the homozygosity of some loci is moderate or high, as for some PCR loci, the following refinement of our approximate upper bound can be useful because it shows that a smaller number of loci may yield uniqueness at each given probability level. In the above derivation, instead of dropping $\Sigma_i p_i^4$, note from Jensen's inequality (see, for example, James and James 1959) that $\Sigma_i p_i^4 \geq (\Sigma_i p_i^2)^3 = f^3$. That leads to the approximate upper bound obtained by setting

$$E = \Pi_L f_L^2(2 - f_L) \qquad (5.14)$$

in Equation 5.12.

As an example, suppose $N = 5 \times 10^9$ and $f_L = 0.5$ for every L. If we insist that the probability of simultaneous uniqueness of all profiles exceed 0.99, then Equation 5.13 requires 71 loci, whereas Equations 5.12 and 5.14 show that 50 actually suffice.

6

DNA Evidence in the Legal System

In the preceding chapters, we have tried to clarify the scientific issues involved in forensic DNA testing. This chapter discusses the legal implications of the committee's conclusions and recommendations. It describes the most important procedural and evidentiary rules that affect the use of forensic DNA evidence, identifies the questions of scientific fact that have been disputed in court, and reviews legal developments.[1]

All forensic methods for individualization—fingerprints, dental impressions, striations on bullets, hair and fiber comparisons, voice spectrograms, neutron-activation analysis, blood-grouping and serum-protein and enzyme typing, as well as DNA profiling—demand an ability to match samples with reasonable accuracy with respect to characteristics that can help to differentiate one source from another. If such evidence is to be useful in court, scientifically acceptable procedures must permit the reliable measurement and comparison of physical features. Likewise, a scientific basis must exist for concluding that properly performed comparisons can distinguish possible sources.

As to the latter issue—the ability to differentiate between sources—the courts have demanded a more convincing showing of the exact degree of individualization yielded by DNA tests than by any other commonly used forensic technique. Some courts have deemed it necessary for experts not only to demonstrate that DNA profiles usually vary from one person to another, but also to produce

---

[1]Unless otherwise indicated, our observations apply to all the technologies for DNA analysis described in this report.

uncontroversial, quantitative estimates of how rare the identifying characteristics are within particular groups and subgroups. Whether many other forms of identification-evidence could survive comparable demands is doubtful.[2] Jurists and legal scholars have debated whether DNA evidence warrants this special treatment.[3] We take no sides in such legal debates, but we do emphasize that the two issues— the scientific acceptability of the laboratory method for comparing samples and the idea that the characteristics studied in the laboratory are probative of identity— are distinct. Consequently, this chapter describes the implications of our conclusions about the state of scientific knowledge both for testimony about the extent to which DNA samples match and for testimony about the probabilities of such matches.

LEGAL STANDARDS AND PROCEDURES

Whether scientific evidence is admissible in criminal cases depends on whether the evidence tends to prove or disprove a fact that, under the applicable law, might matter to the outcome of the case; whether the expert presenting the evidence is qualified; whether the information is derived from scientifically acceptable procedures; and whether the potential for unfair prejudice or time-consumption substantially outweighs the probative value of the information. We discuss those general principles and then consider their application to DNA evidence. We also describe pretrial and trial procedures that might help courts to reach decisions on admissibility and to improve the quality and use of the scientific evidence at trial. We begin with the intertwined procedural issues that arise in connection with a defendant's request for discovery, retesting, or expert assistance.

The Defendant's Right to Discovery

The 1992 National Research Council (NRC) report stated that "all data and laboratory records generated by analysis of DNA samples should be made freely available to all parties," and it explained that "all relevant information . . . can include original materials, data sheets, software protocols, and information about unpublished databanks" (NRC 1992, p 150, 148). Certainly, there are no strictly scientific justifications for withholding information in the discovery process, and in Chapter 3 we discussed the importance of full, written documentation of

---

[2] State v Bogan, 905 P.2d 515, 522-23 (Ariz. Ct. App. 1995), *rev. granted.*

[3] State v Bogan, 905 P.2d 515, 522-23 (Ariz. Ct. App. 1995), (dissenting opinion challenging the majority's conclusion that the "'tenuous distinction between molecular genetics and other scientific disciplines' should [not] cause DNA opinion evidence to be treated differently from other opinion testimony that is customarily allowed to support other kinds of scientific evidence") *rev. granted;* Neufeld and Colman (1990) (advocating more rigorous standards for forensic science generally); Saks and Koehler (1991) (calling for more rigorous validation of many forensic tests).

all aspects of DNA laboratory operations. Such documentation would facilitate technical review of laboratory work, both within the laboratory and by outside experts.

The rules of discovery determine the circumstances under which a defendant can compel the production of such records. Because many complex technical, scientific, and statistical issues affect the use of DNA evidence, there will be cases in which defendants will contend that without comprehensive and detailed information, they are unable to prepare for trial adequately.[4] Although some courts have ordered liberal discovery, providing access to the documentation and information would broaden the scope of discovery in some jurisdictions. Although some courts have ordered liberal discovery with regard to DNA testing,[5] other courts have taken a more restrictive approach.[6] In jurisdictions that interpret their discovery rules as applying only to written reports, the defense cannot obtain discovery of laboratory records if the DNA examiner fails to submit a written report or to incorporate a matter into a report, even if the examiner makes an oral report.[7] Our recommendation that all aspects of DNA testing be fully

---

[4]State v Schwartz, 447 N.W.2d 422, 427 (Minn. 1989) ("access to the data, methodology, and actual results is crucial so a defendant has at least an opportunity for independent expert review").

[5]See, e.g., United States v Yee, 129 F.R.D. 629 (N.D. Ohio 1990) (even before 1993 amendment to Federal Rule of Criminal Procedure 16(a)(1)(E), a federal magistrate judge granted discovery of matching criteria, environmental insult studies, population data, and proficiency tests as "predicate materials" essential to the defense in a DNA-testing case); State v Schwartz, 447 N.W.2d 422, 427-28 (Minn. 1989) (although a laboratory disclosed its protocol, laboratory notes, autoradiographs, and frequency tables, its refusal to supply "more specific information on its methodology and population data base" was a reason to exclude the findings); People v Davis, 196 A.D.2d 597, 601 N.Y.S.2d 174 (Sup. Ct. 1993) (Lifecodes was required on constitutional grounds to turn over statistical data underlying a DNA probability estimate); cf. State v Feldman, 604 A.2d 242, 244 (N.J. Super. 1992) (defense was entitled to discovery related to a databank search of the Automated Fingerprint Information Service). A few statutes governing the admissibility of DNA tests include provisions for pretrial discovery of the state's report. E.g., 10 Md. Code Ann. Cts. & Jud. Proc. § 10-915(3)(b).

[6]See, e.g., State v Dykes, 847 P.2d 1214, 1217-1218 (Kan. 1993) (request of a defendant claiming American Indian ancestry to obtain discovery of a data bank denied, but court permitted discovery of state laboratory's notes, autoradiographs and testing protocol); Spencer v Commonwealth, 384 S.E.2d 785, 791 (1989) (written laboratory reports discoverable, but rules expressly excluded discovery of expert's underlying "work notes [or] memorandum"), cert. denied, 110 U.S. 1171 (1990); cf. United States v Iglesias, 881 F.2d 1519, 1523 (9th Cir. 1989) (discovery of log notes, protocols, or other internal documents of chemists analyzing heroin was denied).

[7]See, e.g., United States v Shue, 766 F.2d 1122, 1135 (7th Cir. 1985) (oral report of FBI photographic expert not discoverable pursuant to Federal Rule 16), cert. denied, 484 U.S. 956 (1987). Rule 16 was amended in 1993 to require that the government disclose to a defendant a summary of the expert testimony that the prosecution intends to offer on direct examination and the bases therefore. It is still unclear whether this provision will cause experts to provide more detailed written documentation than they previously furnished. Many states do not have a counterpart to this subdivision. Other jurisdictions make all discovery related to scientific tests discretionary, and still others explicitly provide for the discovery of oral reports of examinations or tests. See Giannelli and Imwinkelried (1993), vol. 1, § 3.2.

documented is most valuable when this documentation is discoverable in advance of trial.

Expertise

Experts who present and interpret the results of DNA tests must be "qualified by knowledge, skill, experience, training or education" (Fed. R. Evid. 702). There is no well-defined threshold of knowledge or education that a witness must exceed to qualify as an expert. The question is whether the person has enough knowledge "to make it appear that his opinion or inference will aid the trier in the search for truth" (McCormick 1992, § 13, p 54).

Because DNA identification can involve testimony as to laboratory findings, statistical interpretation of these findings, and the underlying principles of molecular biology, expertise in several fields might be required. An expert who is qualified to testify about laboratory techniques might not be qualified to testify about molecular biology, to estimate population frequencies, or to establish that an estimation procedure is valid. Consequently, more than one expert witness might be needed.[8]

Nevertheless, if previous cases establish that the testing and estimation procedures are legally acceptable and if the computations are essentially mechanical,

---

[8]See generally McCormick 1992, § 203, p 875 n 40; Berger 1994, p 63; Kaye and Freedman 1994, p 337. In State v Carter, 246 Neb. 953, 524 N.W.2d 763 (1994), the Nebraska Supreme Court, in reversing a conviction involving a PCR DQA test on the grounds that the 1992 NRC report indicated lack of general acceptance of calculations that assumed Hardy-Weinberg proportions, noted the absence of testimony from a population geneticist. See also Swanson v State, 308 Ark. 28, 823 S.W. 812 (1992) (an argument that a serologist lacked a PhD and was not qualified as an expert in population genetics and therefore could not testify about probabilities was not preserved for appeal); Powell v State, 598 S.W.2d 829 (Tex. Ct. Crim. App. 1994) (argument that molecular biologist should not have been allowed to testify "concerning probabilities of matching DNA patterns because . . . the witness had not been qualified as an expert in the field of population genetics" not made at trial, and therefore not preserved for appeal). Trial judges ordinarily are accorded great discretion in evaluating the qualifications of a proposed expert witness, and the decisions depend on the background of each witness. E.g., United States v Davis, 40 F. 3d 1069 (10th Cir. 1994) (the court rejected the argument that a witness "was not qualified to testify regarding population genetics" because "acceptance of an expert's qualifications will be disturbed only for a clear abuse of discretion" and the witness "had thirteen years experience working for the FBI," "a Master's degree in cell biology," and "six months of specialized training in DNA profiling"); State v McFadden, 458 S.E. 2d 61 (S. Car. 1995) (there was no abuse of discretion in allowing a microbiologist employed by the state's forensic laboratory to testify as to the nature of databases and as to product-rule estimates of 1/(710 million) for blacks and 1/(1.7 billion) for whites); State v Lewis, 654 So. 2d 761 (La. Ct. App. 1995) (the court of appeals held that the trial court abused its discretion by denying expert status to a technician who presented herself as an expert in molecular biology and DNA analysis; the technician had been the assistant director of a laboratory for a year and had no doctoral degree, but belonged to invitational professional organizations, had received numerous academic awards, had testified as an expert in other cases, and had written 14 articles in collaboration with the laboratory director—in promotional rather than scientific publications).

then highly specialized statistical expertise is not essential. Reasonable estimates of allele frequencies in major population groups can be obtained from standard references, and many quantitatively literate experts could use the appropriate formulas in Chapters 4 and 5 to compute the relevant profile frequencies or probabilities. Limitations in the knowledge of a technician who applies a generally accepted statistical procedure can be explored on cross-examination,[9] and, if serious questions arise, more knowledgeable specialists can be called to address those questions.

In addition to hearing testimony from experts called by the parties, a court may appoint experts to report to it, rather than to the parties.[10] Suggestions that court-appointed experts should be used more in science-rich cases have frequently been made (e.g., Fienberg 1989, p 14), but surveys indicate that such appointments are rare (Cecil and Willging 1994, p 529 and n 2). Some issues that arise with regard to DNA testing seem particularly suitable for assistance from a neutral expert. Well-qualified experts could assist a court or jury in understanding basic principles of DNA testing, how such procedures such as RFLP- and PCR-based testing work, and the extent and effect of departures from Hardy-Weinberg (HW) proportions and linkage equilibrium (LE). Court-appointed experts could also provide information about the composition of databases and the scientific litera-ture dealing with specific issues. Some courts have appointed experts to address general questions related to DNA profiling. E.g., United States v Bonds, 12 F.3d 540 (6th Cir. 1993) and United States v Porter, 1994 WL 742297 (DC Super. Ct., Nov. 17, 1994). More controversial is whether a court should appoint its own expert instead of an expert for the defense when there are more specific disputes, such as the precise location of a band on an autoradiograph. A court might conclude that case-specific issues are better resolved with witnesses chosen by and reporting to the parties.[11]

A court can seek to narrow differences between opposing experts by a variety of techniques. A court could direct experts to address particular issues in their reports or pretrial summaries of testimony. After those have been exchanged,

---

[9]E.g., State v Colbert, 257 Kan. 896, 869 P.2d 1089 (1995) (in view of general acceptance of VNTR databases, estimate of match probability admissible despite expert's concessions that he was not a population geneticist and was not qualified to explain how the databases applied to the town of Coffeyville).

[10]In the federal courts, Federal Rule of Evidence 706 authorizes a court to appoint an expert. Many jurisdictions have similar rules. As with the appointment of defense experts, the federal courts have relied on the Criminal Justice Act § 06(A)(E).

[11]Cecil and Willging (1994, p 542). In some cases, defendants have sought court-appointed experts to review the work of the state's experts. E.g., Taylor v Commonwealth, 1995 WL 808189 (Va. Ct. App. 1995) (unpublished opinion refers to corroboration "by an independent DNA expert appointed by the trial court on defendant's motion"). Other opinions refer to independent experts without indicating the manner of their appointment. E.g., Williams v State, 265 Ga. 351, 455 S.E. 2d 836 (1995) (observing that "an independent geneticist concurred with the DNA findings").

the court could then instruct each side to identify all statements in an opposing expert's opinion that are disputed and to explain the basis for the disagreement. Controverted issues can be further narrowed at a pretrial conference (see Schwarzer 1994). Procedures such as these might, for instance, persuade statistical experts to furnish a best estimate in addition to a range of estimates so that the jury will have a better sense of the degree of disagreement between the two sides. Even if an expert responds that not enough is known as yet to make a statistically valid estimate, the court will have obtained additional information.

Having more information may aid a court in ruling on challenges to the admissibility of expert testimony and may enable it to make more effective plans for how the expert testimony should be handled at trial. In some cases, judges have departed from the traditional order of presenting testimony to enable opposing experts to testify consecutively rather than waiting for the prosecution to conclude its case. In appropriate circumstances, courts have allowed an expert's direct testimony to be presented in written or other recorded form rather than in person.

General Acceptance and Sound Methodology

The technology used to examine VNTRs, STRs, or other loci must satisfy the standard required of scientific evidence. In the United States, two major standards exist for deciding whether scientific findings will be admitted into evidence: the "general-acceptance" test and the "sound-methodology" standard. In addition, some jurisdictions have adopted special statutes that provide for the admissibility of genetic testing in general or of DNA analyses in particular in criminal or civil cases.[12] If a timely objection is raised, the judge must determine whether the applicable standard has been met.

The general-acceptance standard was first articulated in an influential 1923 federal case, *Frye v United States*, 293 F. 1013 (DC Cir. 1923). In jurisdictions

---

[12]Statutes applicable to criminal cases include 11 Del. Code § 3515; Ind. Code § 37-4-13; 15 La. Stat. Ann. § 441.1; 10 Md. Code Ann. § 915; Minn. Stat. § 634.25; Tenn. Code Ann. § 24-7-117 (1993 Supp.); Va. Stat. § 19.2-270.5; NRC 1992, p 141-142. The Tennessee statute, for example, provides that "in any civil or criminal trial, hearing or proceeding, the results of DNA analysis . . . are admissible in evidence without antecedent expert testimony that DNA analysis provides a trustworthy and reliable method of identifying characteristics in an individual's genetic material upon a showing that the offered testimony meets the standards of admissibility set forth in the Tennessee Rules of Evidence" (Tenn. Code Ann. § 24-7-117[b][1]). "DNA analysis" is defined broadly to mean "the process through which deoxyribonucleic acid (DNA) in a human biological specimen is analyzed and compared with DNA from another biological specimen for identification purposes" Id. at § 24-7-117(a). Some statutes explicitly identify a type of DNA analysis, e.g., 10 Md. Code Ann. § 915(b) ("an analysis that utilizes the restriction fragment length polymorphism analysis of DNA"). For discussions, see Moenssens, Starrs, Henderson and Inbau (1995, § 15.20) (surveying criminal and civil statutes); Kaye and Kanwischer (1988) (cataloging civil statutes); Liebeschuetz (1991); Jakubaitis (1991); O'Brien (1994).

that follow *Frye*, the proponent of the scientific evidence must establish that the underlying theory and methodology are generally accepted within the relevant portions of the scientific community. The biological and technological principles underlying the forensic methods for characterizing DNA variations have generated little controversy in court.[13] Indeed, the 1992 NRC report proposed that courts "take judicial notice of [the] scientific underpinnings of DNA typing,"[14] and many courts have done so.[15] Courtroom debate has revolved instead around the application of those principles to forensic samples and the procedures for declaring a match and interpreting its importance.

The sound-methodology standard is derived from phrases in the Federal Rules of Evidence. In *Daubert v Merrell Dow Pharmaceuticals*, 113 S.Ct. 2786 (1993), the Supreme Court held that these rules implicitly jettison general acceptance as an absolute prerequisite to the admissibility of scientific evidence. Instead of the *Frye* test, the court prescribed a broader framework for deciding whether proposed testimony has sufficient scientific validity and reliability to be admitted as relevant "scientific knowledge" that would "assist the trier of fact." In that

---

[13]For an unusual exception, see Kelly v State, 792 S.W. 2d 579 (Tex. App. 1990) (admitting a VNTR profile match where the state produced five experts who were seriously challenged by only one defense expert, who said that "radioactive technology was too new to be generally accepted in the scientific community"), *aff'd*, 824 S.W. 2d 568 (Tex. Crim. App. 1992). Although the vast bulk of the cases finding general acceptance have come in the context of VNTR profiling, similar principles and methods of molecular biology underlie the detection of coding DNA polymorphisms, STRs, minisatellite repeat mapping, and the like.

[14]When a court takes judicial notice, it accepts a matter as true without requiring that it be proved. Judicial notice is reserved for matters of common knowledge or those that are capable of "accurate and ready determination by resort to sources whose accuracy cannot be questioned" Fed. R. Evid. 201(b). The 1992 NRC report suggested that the following "underpinnings" would be subject to judicial notice (p 149): "The study of DNA polymorphisms can, in principle, provide a reliable method for comparing samples; each person's DNA is unique (with the exception of identical twins), although the actual discriminatory power of any particular DNA test will depend on the sites of DNA variation examined; [and] the current laboratory procedure for detecting DNA variation (specifically, single-locus probes analyzed on Southern blots without evidence of band shifting) is fundamentally sound, although the validity of any particular implementation of the basic procedure will depend on proper characterization of the reproducibility of the system (e.g., measurement variation) and the inclusion of all necessary scientific controls."

[15]E.g., United States v Perry, Crim. No. 92-474 (D.D.C. Jan. 11, 1994) (order taking "judicial notice of the reliability of the technique of DNA profiling"); State v Montalbo, 73 Haw. 130, 828 P.2d 1274 (1992) (taking judicial notice that "the DNA paradigm is not controversial and is widely accepted in the relevant scientific community"); People v Adams, 195 Mich. App. 267, 489 N.W.2d 192 (1992) ("trial courts may take judicial notice of the reliability of DNA identification testing," but "the prosecutor must establish in each particular case that the generally accepted laboratory procedures were followed"); State v Woodall, 182 W. Va. 15, 385 S.E.2d 253 (1989) (taking judicial notice of general scientific acceptance where there was no expert testimony, but holding that inconclusive results were properly excluded as irrelevant). But cf. State v Hammond, 221 Conn. 264, 604 A.2d 793 (1992) ("Unlike some courts . . . , we regard DNA typing as too novel for its reliability to be judicially noticed at this time.").

framework, the lack of general acceptance weighs against admissibility but is not invariably fatal. The court discussed other factors that might be considered. Its nonexhaustive list includes the extent to which the theory and technology have been tested, the existence of a body of peer-reviewed studies, and the known error rates of the procedure.

Before *Daubert*, many state and federal courts had construed their rules of evidence as not including a rigid requirement of general acceptance. The 1992 NRC report (p 137) described the "helpfulness standard" used in those jurisdictions as encompassing the following factors: "general acceptance of scientific principles," "qualifications of experts testifying about the new scientific principle, the use to which the new technique has been put, the technique's potential for error, the existence of specialized literature discussing the technique, and its novelty." Since *Daubert*, many state courts have suggested that their "helpfulness standard" was essentially identical with the approach articulated in *Daubert*; a few have characterized their rules as more permissive.[16]

Labels like "general acceptance," "sound methodology," and "helpfulness" are just that—labels. Cases decided in each jurisdiction help to define the scientific community in which the degree of scientific acceptance is to be ascertained, the extent of disagreement that can be tolerated, the information that may be used to gauge the extent of consensus, and the specific factors other than general acceptance that bear on relevance and helpfulness.[17] The degree of scientific consensus is important to the admissibility of scientific evidence in all jurisdictions, and pretrial hearings in hotly contested cases have lasted months and generated thousands of pages of testimony probing the opinions of experts on various aspects of DNA profiling. The courts have examined affidavits or testimony from scientists selected by the parties, specific papers in scientific periodicals, the writings of science journalists, the body of court opinions, and other scientific and legal literature, including the 1992 NRC report.

---

[16]E.g., State v Peters, 192 Wis. 2d 674, 534 N.W.2d 867 (Ct. App. 1995) ("Unlike judges in *Frye* and *Daubert* jurisdictions, this role is much more oblique and does not involve a direct determination as to the reliability of the scientific principle on which the evidence is based. . . . Although Wisconsin judges do not evaluate the reliability of scientific evidence, they may restrict the admissibility of such evidence through their limited gatekeeping functions."). For a survey of the reactions of state courts to *Daubert*, see Meaney (1995).

[17]McCormick (1992, § 203). With many, if not most, types of scientific evidence, admissibility does not seem to turn on the choice of the label. For example, by and large, polygraph evidence is inadmissible in both general-acceptance and sound-methodology jurisdictions. With DNA identification, however, a different pattern might be emerging. Over the last several years, appellate courts in *Frye* jurisdictions have seemed more prone than appellate courts in other jurisdictions to regard the admission of single-locus VNTR tests as error. See State v Anderson, 118 N.M. 284, 295-96, 881 P. 2d 29, 40-41 (1994) (collecting cases); State v Streich, 658 A. 2d 38 (Vt. 1995) ("We note that the courts that refuse to accept statistics based on the unmodified product method continue to rely on the more narrow *Frye* standard.").

Balancing and Weight

Even in jurisdictions where a DNA-identification technology meets the applicable standard of scientific acceptance or validity, the results of particular tests and the manner of their presentation can be subject to challenge. When the dangers of unfair prejudice, time-consumption, and confusion of the issues substantially outweigh the probative value of particular evidence, the trial court should exclude the evidence. E.g., Fed. R. Evid. 403; McCormick 1992, § 185. And even when the court admits expert testimony, the scientific basis and quality of the testimony can be attacked before the trier of fact. Not all expert testimony is equally convincing, and a trier of fact may choose to give admissible evidence little weight in reaching its verdict.

Trends in the Admissibility of DNA Evidence

Application of the standards for admitting scientific evidence to the admissibility of DNA profile evidence has produced divergent results. In the United States, the first wave of criminal cases involving DNA identification began in 1986.[18] The focus was on the problems raised in transferring the technology of modern molecular biology from the medical and genetics laboratories, which usually dealt in fresh samples and easily interpretable diallelic probes, to the forensic laboratory, which must handle aged and exposed stains and usually uses more complex, multiallelic genetic systems. Nevertheless, the underlying theory that DNA profiling is capable of helping to identify the source of a DNA sample was never in doubt, expert testimony for the prosecution was rarely countered, and courts readily admitted the findings of commercial laboratories.[19] In the wake of those early cases, many experts from several disciplines scrutinized the work of commercial and government laboratories (Kaye 1991, p 357 n 18). The resulting plethora of questions about laboratory procedures and analyses initiated a second wave of cases in which various courts—including the supreme courts of Georgia,[20]

---

[18]Blake et al. (1992, p 707) report that "[t]he first use of PCR in a criminal case" occurred in a 1986 Pennsylvania case entitled *Commonwealth v Pestinikis*. This application of an early form of the DQA test appears to be the first instance of forensic DNA testing of any kind in this country. The first appellate opinion on the admissibility of DNA testing is Andrews v State, 533 So. 2d 841 (Fla. Dist. Ct. App. 1988), and it involved VNTR profiling.

[19]See, e.g., Cobey v State, 559 A.2d 391 (Md. Ct. Spec. App. 1988) (prosecution produced five experts to testify to general acceptance of VNTR probes; defense called no experts); Kaye (1991, p 357 n 17); Thompson and Ford (1989).

[20]Caldwell v State, 393 S.E.2d 436 (Ga. 1990) (finding Lifecodes "straight binning method satisfactory," but because the laboratory's calculation that the frequency of the profile in the population was 1/24,000,000 rested on the assumption of HW proportions was inconsistent with its database, held that the more conservative figure of 1/250,000 derived from that database would have to be used).

Massachusetts,[21] and Minnesota[22]—excluded at least some aspects of DNA evidence.[23] Nevertheless, in most cases, the courts continued to hold DNA matches and probabilities admissible even in the face of conflicting expert testimony.[24]

After publication of the 1992 report, commentators pointed to "a third wave of cases . . . crashing down upon this battered legal shoreline" (Kaye 1993, p 103). Those cases focused less on the laboratory methods for characterizing and matching DNA and more on the statistical methods for interpreting the significance of similarities in DNA samples. Many opinions in that period lagged behind the scientific publications, which responded forcefully to early speculations and questionable analyses of the importance of departures from the assumptions of statistical independence of alleles within and among VNTR loci. Indeed, some courts reasoned that the movement of scientific opinion was essentially irrelevant under *Frye* as long as respected scientists continued to oppose the statistical methods. E.g., People v Wallace, 14 Cal. App. 4th 651, 17 Cal. Rptr. 2d 721(1993).

Even more recently, with the diffusion of PCR-based methods into the forensic realm, a fourth wave of cases has arrived. The newest cases involve attacks on the procedures for ensuring the accuracy of such analyses and questions about the quantitative interpretation of genetic typing. Again, the underlying theory is not seriously questioned, and laboratories' ability (at least in principle) to obtain informative results is not in dispute. As with the later VNTR profiling cases, defendants have questioned whether the protocols used for forensic work are sufficient to prevent false-positive results, and they have challenged the procedures for estimating the frequencies of the genotypes that are detected after PCR amplification. To clarify the legal relevance of our scientific conclusions

---

[21]   Commonwealth v Curnin, 565 N.E.2d 440 (Mass. 1991) (holding that Cellmark DNA evidence in a rape case had been erroneously admitted in the absence of a showing of the general acceptance of the validity of the product rule, which gave a frequency of 1/(59 million)).

[22]State v Schwartz, 447 N.W.2d 422, 428 (Minn. 1989) (responding to VNTR analysis, said to produce a "banding pattern [whose frequency] in the Caucasian population is approximately 1 in 33 billion," the court concluded that "DNA typing has gained general acceptance in the scientific community" but that "the laboratory in this case did not comport" with "appropriate standards," and further holding the statistical conclusion to be inadmissible because even if the computation is accurate, "we remain convinced that juries in criminal cases may give undue weight and deference to presented statistical evidence").

[23]Other courts have also refused to admit some forms of DNA evidence. See, e.g., United States v Two Bulls, 918 F.2d 56 (8th Cir. 1990), *vacated for rehearing en banc but appeal dismissed due to death of defendant*, 925 F.2d 1127 (8th Cir. 1991); People v Castro, 545 N.Y.S.2d 985 (Sup. Ct. 1989); cf. Perry v State, 586 So.2d 242 (Ala. 1991) (remanding for hearing on Lifecodes's adherence to proper procedures and acceptability of statistical methods).

[24]See, e.g., United States v Jakobetz, 747 F. Supp. 250 (D. Vt. 1990) (applying relevance standard), *aff'd*, 955 F.2d 786 (2d Cir. 1992), *cert. denied*, 113 S.Ct. 104 (1992); United States v Yee, 134 F.R.D. 161 (N.D. Ohio 1991) (applying general-acceptance standard), *aff'd sub nom.* United States v Bonds, 12 F.3d 540 (6th Cir. 1993); cf. State v Pierce, 597 N.E.2d 107 (Ohio 1992) (applying relevance standard, no defense experts); Satcher v Commonwealth, 421 S.E.2d 821 (Va. 1992) (applying general-acceptance standard and statute, no defense experts).

and recommendations related to typing methods and statistical issues, we turn now to a more detailed review of these issues as they have arisen in the cases and legal commentary.

TYPING METHODS

VNTR Profiling

Judicial recognition of the scientific acceptance of the foundations of DNA analysis is consistent with our conclusion that the methods of DNA analysis surveyed in this report are firmly grounded in molecular biology. When VNTR profiling is done with due care, the results are highly reproducible, and comparisons at four or more loci are almost certain to exclude the innocent. To the best of our knowledge, no state or federal court has held that VNTR profiling is inadmissible on the grounds that it is not scientifically accepted or sound.[25] Some courts have excluded VNTR matches because of misgivings over the statistical interpretation of the similarities in the profiles (we address this below), but there seems little doubt in the courtroom, as in the laboratory, that properly conducted VNTR profiling is a scientifically acceptable procedure to help to identify the origin of particular biological materials.[26]

The procedures for matching and binning VNTR fragments discussed in Chapter 5 have provoked more dissension. Defendants have argued that the "window" within which an examiner may declare that the electrophoretic bands of VNTRs from two samples of DNA match is too wide.[27] The few reported opinions to discuss the size of the match window, however, have simply held that the FBI's window is not so large as to render its analyses of VNTR test results inadmissible. As the explanation in Chapter 5 indicates, because wide windows increase the chance that a match will be declared—and at the same time increase the estimates of the frequency of a matching profile—a broad range of match windows is acceptable.[28]

---

[25]For reviews of the case law, see, e.g., Kaye (1993, 1994); Thompson (1993). It remains possible that some unreported cases have reached a contrary result.

[26]E.g., Fishback v People, 851 P.2d 884, 893 (Colo. 1993) (trial courts may take judicial notice of the acceptability of the techniques used in RFLP analysis); State v Moore, 885 P.2d 457 (Mont. 1994) ("the theory underlying DNA and RFLP technology is not open to serious attack"); State v Streich, 658 A.2d 38 (Vt. 1995) (this "part of the scientific debate has essentially ended in favor of DNA admissibility").

[27]United States v Jakobetz, 747 F. Supp. 250 (D. Vt. 1990), aff'd, 955 F.2d 786 (2d Cir. 1992), cert. denied, 113 S. Ct. 109 (1992); United States v Yee, 134 F.R.D. 161 (N.D. Ohio 1991), aff'd sub nom, United States v Bonds, 12 F.3d 540 (6th Cir. 1993). Those arguments have no application to PCR-based methods that use discrete markers.

[28]From a statistical standpoint, the window is best understood in terms of the "standard error" of measurement—a quantity that indicates the variability in repeated measurements of DNA fragments of the same size—and can differ from one laboratory to another. As explained in Chapter 5, match windows must be wider than the normal variability to permit a declaration that two fragments match in most of the cases when they are actually the same length. But the window should not be so wide

Calculations of the population or subpopulation frequency of VNTR profiles that satisfy the statistical criterion for a match require estimates of the allele frequencies in the reference group. We suggested in Chapter 5 that defining these alleles with floating bins is statistically preferable to the fixed-bin approach but requires access to a computerized database. That conclusion does not imply that the use of fixed bins is scientifically unacceptable.[29] Fixed bins are more widely used and understood, and when the recommendations in Chapter 5 are followed, they provide a satisfactory approximation to floating bins.

When fixed bins are used, a dispute sometimes arises as to the frequency of a fragment that lies near the border of two bins. In Chapter 5, we noted that summing the frequencies of both bins, as recommended in the 1992 NRC report, will always give an upper bound on the allele frequency. At least one court has concluded that, within the fixed approach, this summing is "the only methodology that can be characterized as being generally accepted" (United States v Porter, 1994 WL 742297 [DC Super. Ct. Nov. 17, 1994]). As we have noted, however, taking the allele frequency from the larger bin provides a better approximation to the more accurate figure obtained from floating bins.

PCR-Based Testing

Courts have had less experience with evidence derived from PCR-based testing. PCR-based test-evidence, however, is being introduced in a substantial number of cases,[30] and courts in each jurisdiction must decide whether this new mode of DNA typing satisfies the applicable test for admitting scientific evidence, regardless of whether RFLP-based evidence has been admitted.[31] In the reported

---

as typically to produce declarations of matches between fragments that are not about the same size (see Chapter 5). The result is a wide range of possible match windows. Cf. Roeder 1994, p 275 ("the 'objective' match criterion . . . is, in fact, simply an arbitrary rule"). In these circumstances, it has been suggested that expert testimony that narrower windows would have excluded a defendant is tautological and more prejudicial than probative (Kaye 1993, 1995). A brief argument to the contrary is made in Thompson (1993).

[29]Cf. People v Venegas, 36 Cal. Rptr. 2d 856 (Ct. App. 1995) (observing that because "the [1992] NRC report expressed approval of the fixed bin method as an alternative to the NRC's 'floating bin' method . . . there is no need for the FBI to abandon that method in order to find consensus in the NRC methodology"), *rev. granted*, 39 Cal. Rptr. 2d 408, 890 P. 2d 1117.

[30]See Blake et al. (1992, p 720) ("As of September 1991, the HLA-DQA test has been introduced as courtroom evidence into 44 cases and has been evaluated in 25 admissibility hearings in 20 different states"). As of November 10, 1995, 34 cases in which PCR-based DNA testing had been conducted could be retrieved from the Westlaw "allcases" database of court opinions. A survey with responses from 49 forensic laboratories, conducted in November 1994, revealed over 280 cases where PCR-based typing results were introduced in courts in 37 states (Perkin Elmer Corp. 1995, at 1).

[31]See, e.g., Harrison v State, 644 N.E.2d 1243, 1251 (Ind. 1995) ("The words 'DNA test results' are not magic words which once uttered cause the doors of admissibility to open."); State v Russell, 125 Wash.2d 570, 882 P.2d 747 (1995) ("The issue in this case is thus not whether the underlying

cases, judges, with the exception of a few dissenters, have held PCR-based techniques sufficiently reliable to establish matches between samples, under both the general-acceptance and the sound-methodology standards.[32] As we discuss later, however, the courts have been less hospitable to statistical calculations.

Some opinions differentiate VNTR testing from PCR-based testing. They characterize the former as capable of identifying a suspect but describe PCR-based testing as "answer[ing] the question of whether a suspect can be eliminated as a donor."[33] As described in Chapter 4, the individual loci used in current PCR-based tests are less polymorphic than VNTR loci; as a result, the multilocus genotype frequencies from PCR-based tests typically are not as small as those in VNTR typing.[34] But that is a quantitative difference rather than a sharp distinction. Furthermore, very small frequencies can be obtained by testing at additional loci.[35]

---

theory of DNA testing is generally accepted, but whether the PCR technique is generally accepted."); State v Grayson, No. K2-94-1298, 1994 WL 670312 (Minn. Dist. Ct. Nov 8, 1994) (although RFLP testing is accepted in Minnesota, court re-examined PCR-based testing according to the *Frye* standard). Consequently, judicial opinions on the admissibility of PCR-based evidence illuminate the procedures that judges use in determining the validity of a new DNA technology, in addition to elucidating particular legal issues generated by the PCR method of DNA typing. See, e.g., State v Gentry, 125 Wash.2d 570, 888 P.2d 1105 (1995) (1995) (6-week *Frye* hearing).

[32]Serritt v State, 647 So. 2d 1 (Ala. Crim. App. 1994); People v Amundson, 34 Cal. App. 4th 1151, 41 Cal. Rptr. 2d 127 (1995) ("Since [the 1992 NRC] report was written, the reliability of PCR testing for forensic use has consistently been proven by the testimony of experts, hundreds of authoritative scientific articles and other literature supporting this typing technique, and by the overwhelming acceptance of PCR testing in dozens of judicial decisions."); People v Groves, 854 P.2d 1310 (Colo. Ct. App. 1992) ; State v Hill, 859 P.2d 1238 (Kan. 1995) (generally accepted); State v Hoff, 904S.W.2d 56 (Mo. Ct. App. 1995) (generally accepted); State v Moore, 885 P.2d 457 (Mont. 1994) (DQA inclusion and exclusions satisfy Daubert standard); State v Williams, 599 A.2d 960 (N.J. Super. Ct. 1991) ("hundreds" of scientific articles); State v Lyons, 863 P.2d 1303 (Or. Ct. App. 1993) (PCR methodology used forensically in eight states and adopted by several state and private forensic laboratories and FBI; extensive peer-reviewed literature); Trimboli v State, 826 S.W.2d 953 (Tex. Crim. App. 1992); Clarke v State, 813 S.W.2d 654 (Tex. App. 1991); State v Gentry, 888 P.2d 1105 (Wash. 1995) (generally accepted); State v Russell, 125 Wash. 2d 24, 882 P. 2d 747 (1994) (court notes extensive validation studies on PCR testing in holding the *Frye* test satisfied).

[33]State v Carter, 524 N.W.2d 763, 769 (Neb. 1994); State v Grayson, No. K2-94-1298, 1994 WL 670312 (Minn. Dist. Ct. Nov 8, 1994) ("means to exclude possible defendants rather than identify"); State v Penton, No. 9-91-25, 1993 WL 102507 (Ohio Ct. App. Apr. 7, 1993) ("Unlike RFLP/DNA analysis, PCR/DNA can not get you down to one person but excludes a percentage of the population."), app. dismissed, 619 N.E.2d 698, 617 Ohio St. 3d 1464 (1993).

[34]In the reported cases, PCR typing usually was done with a DQ Alpha kit. But see People v Morales, N.Y.L.J., Oct. 26, 1994, at 34, col. 6 (Rockland County Ct.). (Amplitype PM or Polymarker test, as well as DQA test, admitted); cf. State v Russell, 125 Wash. 2d 24, 882 P. 2d 747, 768 (1994) (as other modes of testing are developed, "any concerns about implementation in a given case are matters to be addressed to the trial court pursuant to E[vidence] R[ule] 702").

[35]These loci can be analyzed with further PCR-based tests, with VNTR systems, or with traditional protein markers. See, e.g., People v Simpson, No. BA097211 (Super. Ct., Los Angeles Cty., 1995) (VNTR, DQA, Polymarker, ABO, and PGM markers); State v Gentry, 125 Wash.2d 570 (Wash.

In finding PCR evidence admissible, the courts have rejected a variety of objections, some of which rely on language in the 1992 report.[36] The principal concerns are the alleged lack of forensic experience with PCR testing[37] and the possibility of contamination.[38] Most courts have decided that those criticisms are pertinent to assessing the weight of the evidence but do not warrant the wholesale exclusion of PCR-based tests.[39]

LABORATORY ERROR

Defendants have challenged the admissibility of DNA results on the grounds that the protocols or procedures followed by the laboratory were inadequate to reduce the risk of error sufficiently, that the laboratory failed to adhere to the stated protocols, or that the laboratory failed to demonstrate its ability to type samples accurately on a series of external, blind proficiency tests. Courts have shown little inclination to exclude evidence on those grounds.[40] Although egregious departures from customary practices might well lead a court to exclude the evidence, the possibility of laboratory error ordinarily is said to affect the

---

1995) (using ABO, GM, haptoglobin, and PCR-based results, an expert testified that the combined frequency in the Caucasian population was 0.18%, whereas the frequency for the PCR type was 8%).

[36]E.g., People v Amundson, 41 Cal. Rprt. 2d 127 (Ct. App. 1995) ("'the report's observation that PCR analysis has not yet received 'full acceptance' for forensic use is not a valid criticism . . . a new scientific technique need only have gained 'general acceptance'''"), *rev. granted*; State v Russell, 882 P.2d 747, 762 (Wash. 1994). The 1992 NRC report expressed reservations about PCR-based testing for forensic use (p 70), the dangers of contamination (p 65-67), differential amplification (pp. 64-65), and misuse of testing kits by "nonexpert laboratories" (p 69).

[37]See State v Gentry, 125 P.2d 570 (Wash. 1995) (dissent cites 1992 report as establishing that PCR testing was "not yet generally accepted as a methodology capable of consistently producing reliable results on forensic samples").

[38]But see State v Russell, 882 P.2d 747, 767 (Wash. 1994) (also discussing dangers of differential amplification and misincorporation).

[39]E.g., State v Lyons, 863 P.2d 1303, 1309 (Or. Ct. App. 1993) ("The potential for contamination presents an 'open field' for cross-examination at trial, but does not indicate that the PCR method is inappropriate for forensic use."); State v Russell, 882 P.2d 747 (Wash. 1994) (discussing 1992 NRC report, but finding PCR-based evidence admissible after noting that over 30 forensic laboratories were performing DQA testing as of March 1991, that the FBI began using the Cetus kit in 1992, that the British Home Office had adopted DQA as its screening test, and that problems of laboratory error are "either detectable or preventable" when proper techniques and laboratory procedures are used). In theory, a court could find a particular PCR-based test performed in such a substandard way as to justify exclusion of the evidence. Cf. State v Moore, 885 P.2d 457, 474-75 (Mont. 1994) (DQA test results admissible despite concern about contamination expressed in 1992 NRC report because "the experts handling the piece of brain tissue were aware of the possibility of contamination, and took appropriate steps to avoid and detect contamination").

[40]State v Streich, 658 A.2d 38 (Vt. 1995) ("The [RFLP] process is not error-free, but adherence to accepted procedures and controls minimizes this error. . . . We cannot find any recent decision under any standard of admissibility which refuses to admit the DNA match result based on the invalidity or risk of error of the underlying technology.").

weight rather than the admissibility of the evidence, e.g., Hopkins v State, 579 N.E. 2d 1297 (Ind. 1991) (departures from protocol). At the same time, some courts, expressing concern over the impact of DNA evidence on jurors, have grafted a procedural safeguard onto the general-acceptance standard. Starting with *People v Castro*, 144 Misc. 2d 956, 545 N.Y.S. 2d 985 (Sup. Ct. 1989), a minority of courts have treated an inquiry into a laboratory's conforming in a particular case to a generally accepted protocol as an essential part of a pretrial hearing under *Frye*.[41]

We emphasized the importance of minimizing laboratory error in Chapter 3, where we called for scrupulous care in sample-handling and laboratory procedures, for regular participation in proficiency tests, and, whenever feasible, for procedures that would offer defendants the opportunity for a second test by an independent laboratory. Those recommendations rest not on a judgment that current error rates are so high that test results are scientifically unacceptable, but on a desire to reduce the incidence of errors to an extremely low value.

It is possible that courts will want to treat compliance with such recommendations as an aspect of admissibility to encourage laboratories to follow them.[42] That result is not compelled by *Daubert* or *Frye*, but in some jurisdictions a defendant does have the right to examine physical evidence held by the government, and this right has been construed to include the right to test or retest a sample in the government's control.[43]

---

[41]Compare United States v Two Bulls, 918 F.2d 56 (8th Cir. 1990), *vacated for rehearing en banc but appeal dismissed due to death of defendant*, 925 F.2d 1127 (1991); Perry v State, 586 So. 2d 242 (Ala. 1991); People v Barney, 8 Cal. App. 4th 798, 10 Cal. Rptr. 2d 731 (1992); Commonwealth v Curnin, 409 Mass. 218, 565 N.E.2d 440 (1991) (dictum); Commonwealth v Rodgers, 605 A.2d 1228 (Pa. Super. 1992); Barnes v State, 839 S.W.2d 118 (Tex. App. 1992) (requiring clear and convincing evidence of compliance) with State v Bible, 858 P.2d 1152 (Ariz. 1993), *cert. denied*, 114 S.Ct. 1578 (1994); People v Stremmel, 258 N.E.2d 93 (Ill. App. 1994); Davidson v State, 580 N.E. 2d 238 (Ind. 1991); State v Vandebogart, 616 A.2d 483 (N.H. 1992); State v Cauthron, 120 Wash. 2d 879, 846 P.2d 502 (1993).

[42]Cf. McCormick (1992, § 203, at 875 n.41) (proposing external proficiency testing as a prerequisite to admissibility); Jonakait (1991). Courts also could refer to regular participation in accreditation programs, proficiency-testing and independent audits when instructing the jury, allowing jurors to draw a negative inference from the absence of these quality-control mechanisms. In addition to providing the jury with valuable guidance, wide use of this instruction would encourage laboratories to participate in such activities. An instruction might read: ''In evaluating the quality of the DNA evidence, you might wish to consider the laboratory's participation or nonparticipation in the following quality-control activities: (1) accreditation; (2) proficiency-testing, particularly proficiency-testing with blind samples; and (3) independent audits.''

[43]In the federal courts, Rule 16(a)(1)(C) of the Federal Rules of Criminal Procedure—which authorizes, on defendant's request, inspection of tangible objects in the government's possession— has been interpreted to mandate a defendant's right to test or retest a sample in the government's control. See, e.g., United States v Butler, 988 F.2d 537 (5th Cir. 1993) (cocaine), *cert. denied*, 114 S.Ct. 413 (1993). Some states similarly construe their jurisdiction's criminal-discovery rules as mandating retesting (Annotation 1984). Other states have statutes or rules that specifically provide for the retesting of physical evidence. See, e.g., Iowa Code Ann. § 813.2, R. 13(2)(b)(1) (1979); La. Code Crim. Part 71 (West 1981); State v Schwartz, 447 N.W.2d 422, 427 (Minn. 1989) (relying on

A number of issues can arise even when the right to a second test is recognized. Does the prosecution have a right to be present?[44] When is the defendant's request timely? How specific a request must the defendant make?[45] Does retesting by another laboratory suffice, or must the testing be done under defense supervision?[46] Does it matter whether the laboratory is a government, rather than an independent nongovernment, laboratory?[47] Will the state pay if the defendant is indigent?

Of course, the right of indigent defendants to expert assistance at state expense extends beyond the right to retest. In some circumstances, the constitution requires that indigent defendants be provided with funds to retain suitable experts. The leading case is *Ake v Oklahoma*, 470 U.S. 68 (1985). In *Ake*, the Supreme Court reversed a conviction because the trial court had refused to appoint an expert to assist the indigent defendant, who was relying on an insanity defense. But *Ake* was a capital case in which the defense sought the assistance of a psychiatrist, and courts have differed in their interpretation of the holding (Harris 1992). Some courts have applied *Ake* broadly to authorize all types of expertise;

---

a Minnesota rule of criminal procedure giving defense counsel the right to "inspect and reproduce any results of any ... scientific tests, experiments or comparisons made in connection with the particular case" to conclude that, whenever practical, "a defendant should be provided with the actual DNA sample(s) in order to reproduce the tests"). In addition, some authority supports a constitutional right to retest, stemming from the requirement of due process. See, e.g., Moore v State, 748 P.2d 732, 735 (Ok. Crim. App. 1987) (Oklahoma constitution requires the state to afford the accused an opportunity to re-examine and retest unless the sample was consumed by government testing; illegal substance); State v Thomas, 421 S.E.2d 227, 234 (W.Va. 1992) (if the prosecution conducts a test, such as an electrophoretic blood test, that consumes the sample being tested, the state must "preserve as much documentation of the test as is reasonably possible to allow for a full and fair examination of the results by a defendant and his experts"). Other courts, however, have found that even when retesting was refused, sufficient protection for the accused was afforded by the right to cross-examine the prosecution's expert. See, e.g., Frias v State, 547 N.E.2d 809, 813 (Ind. 1989) (cocaine), *cert. denied*, 495 U.S. 921 (1990); People v Bell, 253 N.W.2d 726, 729 (1977); Montoya (1995).

[44]Compare State v Faraone, 425 A.2d 523, 526 (R.I. 1981) ("The court may [after the defendant moves for testing] in its discretion, provide for appropriate safeguards, including where necessary, the performance of such tests at the state laboratory under the supervision of the state's analyst.") with Prince v Superior Court, 8 Cal. App. 4th 1176, 1179, 10 Cal. Rptr. 2d 855, 857 (1992) (defendant entitled to independent testing).

[45]See, e.g., State v Faraone, 425 A.2d 523, 526 (R.I. 1981) (requiring defendant to file a motion "setting forth the circumstances of the proposed analysis, the identity of the expert who will conduct such analysis, his qualifications, and scientific background").

[46]See, e.g., Hicks v State, 352 S.E.2d 762, 769 (Ga.) (it is not an error to deny a request for independent analysis of blood samples if the trial court had offered the defendant an opportunity to have the state crime laboratory perform additional tests and had left open the possibility of a forensic expert for the defendant if necessity was shown; capital case), *cert. denied*, 482 U.S. 931 (1987).

[47]Cf. Harrison v State, 644 N.E.2d 1243, 1253 (Ind. 1995) (in finding no abuse of discretion in failing to appoint a defense expert, the court noted that "there was every reason to believe that" experts who had performed testing for the prosecution were neutral).

others have restricted *Ake* to its particular facts, focusing on the type of assistance requested and on whether the prosecution was seeking the death penalty (see Harrison v State, 644 N.E.2d 1243 [Ind. 1995]). Furthermore, courts differ in how much of a particularized showing of need and potential prejudice a defendant must make.[48] Those variations in the interpretation of *Ake* have produced conflicting results when indigent defendants have sought expert assistance with regard to DNA testing. Some courts have held that an expert must be provided,[49] and others have found no such need.[50]

Instead of providing a defendant with an expert, a court might appoint an expert to assist the court. As noted in the earlier discussion of expert witnesses, courts have been more inclined to use this procedure to investigate general scientific issues related to DNA profiling than to resolve controversies related to the particulars of the DNA testing in a given case. However, no rule of law clearly compels such a limitation on court-appointed experts.

Returning to the implications of recognizing a defendant's right to retesting whenever feasible, difficult issues can arise as to informing the jury of the defense's failure to retest or of the results of any retesting. May the prosecution comment on or introduce evidence about the defendant's failure to request retesting or to introduce DNA-testing results?[51] May it cross-examine defense experts

---

[48]Statutes also play a role; some set limits, which can be quite low, on the compensation for experts and other defense services. E.g., Tex. Crim. Proc. Code Ann. art. 26.05 § 1(d) (Vernon 1989 & Supp. 1994) (maximum, $1,000).

[49]See, e.g., Dubose v State, 662 So.2d 1189 (Ala. 1995) (it is a due-process violation not to provide an expert "to refute the testimony of the Lifecodes witnesses . . . to independently test the samples, to question whether the DNA results, in fact, showed a match, or to explain that scientific opinion may be divided"); Cade v State, 658 So. 2d 550 (Fla. Ct. App. 1995) (trial court abused its discretion under state statute by denying defense request for appointment of DNA expert even though there was no showing of specific need, but only the general observation that "I can't tell the Court what I'm looking for because it's so complicated"), *rev. denied*, 663 So. 2d 631 (Fla. 1995); Husske v Commonwealth, 448 S.E.2d 331, 335 (Va. Ct. App. 1994) (it depends on how important the scientific issue is in the case and how much help a defense expert could have given; it is an error not to provide an expert to challenge the numbers and assertions of a population geneticist).

[50]Harrison v State, 644 N.E.2d 1243 (Ind. 1995) (there is no error in failing to provide an expert in a capital case; the court stresses that *Ake* was concerned with expertise of a very subjective nature, whereas DNA testing involved precise physical measurements performed by an independent laboratory, and the defendant had not made any showing of what the laboratory might have done inaccurately); State v Harris, 866 S.W.2d 583 (Tenn. Crim. App. 1992) (insufficient showing of particularized need). The more detailed a showing the court requests as to precisely what issues in the case necessitate expert assistance, the less likely it is that a defense counsel unsophisticated about DNA testing will be able to satisfy the court.

[51]Many subsidiary questions can arise: Would such a comment chill the defendant's right to effective assistance of counsel because defendants would not avail themselves of the opportunity to retest if this provided ammunition for the prosecution? Would such a comment impermissibly shift to the defendant a burden to produce evidence? To what extent does it matter whether the defense has called witnesses in its behalf instead of merely cross-examining the prosecution's expert? Would such a comment be unfair if the defendant were indigent and the jurisdiction did not provide defendants with experts in DNA typing?

about a failure to retest?[52] May it obtain discovery or testimony from an expert who conducted retesting for the defense but whom the defense does not intend to call as a witness?[53] The law with regard to those questions is far from clear.[54] Implicated are state and federal constitutional concerns emanating from due-process[55] and effective-assistance-to-counsel provisions,[56] such evidentiary doctrines as the attorney-client[57] and work-product privileges,[58] and criminal-procedure issues related to discovery.[59]

---

[52]See State v Gentry, 888 P.2d 1105, 1121-1122 (Wash. 1995) (the trial court ruled that questions to experts about whether they had retested forensic samples were permissible but that questions about whether they could have done so were impermissible and gave curative instruction on the prosecution's burden of proof; appellate court stated: "While it is questionable whether asking scientific experts whether they did, or could have, conducted duplicate testing is error at all, in this case any possible error in confusing the jury as to the burden of proof was cured by the trial court's simultaneous curative instructions."). See also State v Jobe, 486 N.W.2d 407, 418 (Minn. 1992) (the court found that the prosecutor's question to the defense's DNA expert, who was critical of FBI's testing procedures, as to "whether he could do that type of procedure in his laboratory if samples were provided" did not impermissibly shift the burden of proof, because it did not suggest that the "appellant was obligated to pursue independent testing").

[53]When the defense calls its expert to testify, it waives some privileges: United States v Nobles, 422 U.S. 225, 239 (1975) (work product); United States v Alvarez, 519 F.2d 1036, 1046-47 (3d Cir. 1975) (attorney-client privilege).

[54]Compare Giannelli (1991, p 819) ("retesting comes with a price tag. The prosecution could introduce evidence that samples had been turned over to the defense with the opportunity for retesting and then comment to the jury on the defense's failure to introduce the test results.") with Scheck (1994, p 1969 n 33) ("there should be no requirement that the results [of defense tests] be disclosed").

[55]In Ake v Oklahoma, 470 U.S. 68 (1985), the Supreme Court rested its decision requiring the state to provide expert psychiatric assistance to the defendant on the due-process clause. It has been suggested that a rule that infringes on the right of a defendant to obtain expert assistance by making that right costly "subverts this due process right" (Maringer 1993, p 656 n 11). Due process also is implicated to the extent that a comment impermissibly shifts the prosecution's burden of proof to the defendant.

[56]See, e.g., Prince v Superior Court, 8 Cal. App. 4th 1176, 1179, 10 Cal. Rptr. 2d 855, 857 (1992) (an order that would require defendant to turn over the results of DNA testing even if it did not introduce this evidence at trial denied the defendant the effective assistance of counsel); State v Melvins, 382 A.2d 925 (N.J.Super.1978) (an order requiring production of copies of a defense expert's investigative reports violated the Sixth Amendment if the defense was not planning to call the expert as witness). But see State v McDaniel, 485 N.W.2d 630, 633 (Iowa 1992) (prosecution use of an expert provided an indigent defendant violates neither due process nor effective assistance of counsel).

[57]The majority rule appears to be that the attorney-client privilege covers communication between experts and attorneys and that consequently the privilege prevents the prosecution from calling a defense-retained expert as a government witness (see Giannelli and Imwinkelried 1993, § 5-10). There are, however, cases that find either that the expert is not an agent of the attorney or that the privilege applies only to experts, such as psychiatrists, who rely on the defendant's communication in reaching their opinions. *Id.* See also Mosteller (1986).

[58]See Imwinkelried (1990) (arguing that work product, rather than privilege, should apply so that prosecution can obtain a defense witness's opinion on a showing of need).

[59]Rule 16 of the Federal Rules of Criminal Procedure requires the defense to advise the prosecution of the results of scientific tests only if it intends to introduce the results in its case in chief. Especially when coupled with a requirement that defense applications for "investigative, expert or other services"

Beyond all that, the recommendation to give a defendant the opportunity to retest whenever possible leaves open the question of how to proceed when a sample is too small to permit splitting. Some opinions suggest that if the prosecution consumes the evidence in the course of testing, it will not be constitutionally barred from introducing the results as long as it acted in good faith.[60] The Supreme Court has held that even a negligent failure to preserve evidence does not offend due process.[61] However, as one commentator notes, a "situation in which lost evidence might be exculpatory differs from one in which inculpatory evidence will be offered. A higher duty of care should be required in the latter situation" (Giannelli 1991, p 820).

One possible response to the problem of testing that legitimately consumes the sample is to give the defendant the right to have an expert present if prosecution testing will consume the available sample. E.g., State v Gaddis, 530 S.W.2d 64, 69 (Tenn. 1975). However, additional steps might have to be taken to make this right meaningful.[62] When later independent testing is not possible and the defendant is not provided an opportunity to have an independent expert observe the testing, or the testing is performed before charges are filed, our recommendation that all stages of the testing process be fully documented becomes particularly important.[63] In such cases, experts who report to the defense or directly to

---

proceed ex parte (see 18 U.S.C. § 3006A (e)), in many instances this provision would preclude the prosecution from knowing a defendant's plans. With DNA evidence, however, the prosecution will know that the defense wishes to retest because the samples have to be turned over. Nevertheless, it has been suggested that the restriction on discovery should be interpreted as barring the prosecution from calling the defense expert (*Contra* State v McDaniel, 485 N.W.2d 630 [Iowa 1992]).

[60]See California v Trombetta, 467 U.S. 479 (1984) (failure to preserve a breath sample did not amount to a lack of due process). With the advent of PCR testing, the prosecution's choice of a method that will consume a sample, rather than replicate it, might become an issue. See, e.g., People v Griffin, 761 P.2d 103, 107, 46 Cal.3d 1011, 1021-1022, 251 Cal. Rptr. 643, 647-48 (1988) (en banc) (surveys cases in which courts have suggested that prosecution has burden of showing that its destruction of the sample was reasonable). When the defense tests a sample to which the prosecution has not had access, it may not keep the results secret if the testing consumes the sample. See, e.g., State v Cosey, 652 So.2d 993, 994 (1995); People v Cooper, 809 P.2d 865, 889, 53 Cal.3d 771, 815, 281 Cal. Rptr. 90, 114 (1991) (en banc).

[61]Arizona v Youngblood, 488 U.S. 51 (1988) (the prosecution's failure to preserve evidence and to perform genetic-marker tests did not amount to a denial of due process). But cf. Colo. Rev. Stat. § 16-3-309 (1986) (setting forth factors that a court should consider in deciding whether to admit results of a test that consumed a sample, making independent testing impossible).

[62]Obviously, the defense can make such an arrangement only if it is provided adequate notice of the prosecution's plans for testing and if it has retained an expert. See, e.g., Commonwealth v Gliniewicz, 500 N.E.2d 1324, 1327 (1986) (in holding that the prosecution's actions violated a pretrial agreement, the court noted that "defendants received no notice of the impending tests, and thus were not able to have their own expert present to observe and potentially to refute the subjective aspects of the [blood] testing"). The value of having defense experts present, however, has been questioned (see Wooley 1995).

[63]See, e.g., People v Garries, 645 P.2d 1306 (Colo. 1982) (test results were suppressed where blood samples were consumed, and the defendant had no opportunity to be present and no photographs

the court might be helpful in verifying that there are no ambiguities in the autoradiographs or that any ambiguities are properly accounted for.

Whereas our recommendations are directed at reducing the chance of error and detecting errors that do occur in rare cases, defendants and some legal commentators have contended that the risk of laboratory or handling errors that would falsely incriminate a suspect should be estimated from external, blind proficiency tests, and a few courts have held that a laboratory's record in proficiency tests must accompany its estimate of the probability of a matching profile. E.g., United States v Porter, 1994 WL 742297 (DC Super. Ct., Nov. 17, 1994). We believe that proficiency-testing is a valuable device for reducing errors of all kinds, should be implemented as a matter of social policy, and bears on the weight that should be accorded forensic test results. At the same time, for the reasons given in Chapter 3, we have concluded that it is exceedingly difficult to estimate relevant error rates from either industry-wide or laboratory-specific proficiency-test results.

A question arises as to the admissibility of proficiency-test statistics themselves. The 1992 NRC report stated that the probative value of such statistics, when balanced against their potential to mislead a jury, favored admissibility: "laboratory error rates must be continually estimated in blind proficiency testing and must be disclosed to juries" (p 89). Inasmuch as the purpose of our report is to determine what aspects of the procedures used in connection with forensic DNA testing are scientifically valid, we attempt no such policy judgment.

Population and Subpopulation Frequencies

As indicated earlier, the concern that has given courts the most pause in admitting DNA evidence involves the methods for characterizing the implications of an observed degree of similarity in DNA types. Impressed with the diversity of the views expressed in the scientific literature and in testimony, many courts concluded that a major scientific controversy is raging over the proper method for ascertaining the frequency of a given profile. Particularly in *Frye* jurisdictions, those courts have held some forms of testimony about DNA findings inadmissible.[64] This section outlines some of the objections to estimating profile frequencies and random-match probabilities that have been heard in court and the implications of our conclusions about them.

---

were taken); State v Schwartz, 447 N.W.2d 422, 427 (Minn. 1989) (because "forensic samples are often so small that the entire sample is used in testing, ... access to the data, methods, and actual results is crucial"). See also People v Griffin, 761 P.2d 103, 107, 46 Cal.3d 1011, 1021-1022, 251 Cal.Rptr. 643, 647-48 (1988) (en banc) (surveys cases in which courts have suggested that prosecution has burden of showing that its destruction of the sample was reasonable).

[64]State v Streich, 658 A.2d 38 (Vt. 1995) ("We note that the courts that refuse to accept statistics based on the unmodified product method continue to rely on the more narrow *Frye* standard," but the court reached the same result under the *Daubert* standard).

Convenience Samples

Estimates of the frequency of matching genotypes depend on estimated allele frequencies. As noted in Chapter 5, databases used to provide allele frequencies come from convenience samples gathered from sources as diverse as FBI agents, university students, blood bank donors, and parties in paternity cases. Some experts discussing DNA evidence in court have questioned the representativeness of convenience samples.[65] Most courts have held that the use of convenience samples does not make computations inadmissible, but a few courts have suggested that a database resulting from a convenience sample provides an unacceptable foundation for the probability or frequency estimates being offered.[66]

Nevertheless, the ideal alternative to convenience sampling—some form of random sampling—often is impractical, and convenience sampling can produce reasonable estimates in some circumstances. In Chapter 5, we explained why the allele-frequency estimates from existing databases are suitable for computing genotype frequencies. In other contexts, courts have accepted convenience sampling. For many years, courts in criminal cases and paternity suits have admitted calculations based on allele frequencies derived from convenience samples for genetic markers, such as blood groups, HLA types, and serum proteins and enzymes. Courts regularly admit surveys based on convenience samples in litigation over alleged trademark infringement and deceptive advertising (Jacoby and Handlin 1991). When such samples are drawn from the relevant population and there is no evidence that an important subgroup is underrepresented, sample estimates are widely accepted to prove the likelihood of consumer confusion between products (Diamond 1994, p 238-239).

However, the courts usually view the results of such convenience samples as rough indicators rather than as precise quantitative estimates, and an expert relying on a convenience sample would be well advised to provide evidence that respondents were selected in a manner that was unlikely to introduce bias (Diamond 1994, p 238-239). One widely accepted way to test the potential bias associated with a particular convenience sample is to compare the results obtained from multiple convenience samples selected with substantially different criteria. Thus, in Chapter 5, we suggested that the similarities among DNA samples from a variety of sources indicate that convenience samples used to construct DNA databases are likely to be representative of racial and geographic population groups.

---

[65]For example, one early criticism of the allele-frequency estimates focused on the FBI's reliance on a database consisting of FBI agents. E.g., United States v Jakobetz, 747 F. Supp. 250 (D. Vt. 1990), aff'd, 955 F.2d 786 (2d Cir. 1992), cert. denied, 113 S. Ct. 109 (1992); United States v Bonds, 12 F.3d 540 (6th Cir. 1993).

[66]State v Bible, 858 P.2d 1152, 1186 (Ariz. 1993); State v Buckner, 125 P.2d 915 (Wa. 1995) (although "the sample must be truly random," the ceiling calculation could account for a departure from randomness).

The Disagreement About Substructure

As explained in Chapter 4, the dispute about the "product rule" centers on the degree of population structure and the effect that it could have, in most situations, on the frequency of an incriminating profile in a racial group or, in a few cases, on the frequency within a particular subpopulation.[67] In the absence of any effects from population substructure, the product of the frequencies of the alleles (taking into account the factor of two for each heterozygous locus) closely approximates the frequency of the profile in the population.

At the time of the 1992 NRC report, however, little information was available on the extent to which the relative frequencies of VNTR alleles varied among subgroups within the racial groups, and the report described the conflicting views of population geneticists on the validity of simply multiplying allele frequencies. Many courts took the report's description of a "substantial controversy" as proof of a major scientific disagreement.[68]

Today, the debate is shifting in the direction of accepting the validity of using the assumptions of Hardy-Weinberg proportions and linkage equilibrium to estimate profile frequencies and match probabilities in major racial groups. Courts are beginning to cite this development to support the conclusion that "it is apparent that . . . RFLP DNA profiling has achieved 'a consensus drawn from a typical cross-section of the relevant, qualified scientific community.'"[69]

---

[67]Neither the courts nor the experts are always careful to specify the population that is of interest. Population structure is less of an issue when one seeks to estimate the frequency within a racial group than in a small, genetically isolated subpopulation. See, e.g., Kaye (1993) (suggesting that the published criticism of the usual multiplication procedure occurs only in the context of making subpopulation estimates).

[68]See, e.g., Lindsey v People, 892 P.2d 281 (Colo. 1995) (suggesting that general acceptance was more easily found before 1992 NRC report); State v Carter, 246 Neb. 953, 524 N.W.2d 763, 782 (1994) ("The report . . . is persuasive regarding the lack of general acceptance. . . . Before [its] issuance . . . statistical estimates calculated by forensic laboratories were routinely ruled admissible in most cases; however, since the issuance, an overwhelming majority of courts have excluded evidence of a match after finding that there is no general acceptance as to the statistical probability calculations due to the division in the scientific community on the issue of population substructure."). For a more complete review of the cases after the publication of the 1992 report, see Kaye (1995).

[69]People v Wilds, 37 Cal. Rptr. 2d 351 (Ct. App. 1995), *rev. granted*. See also People v Amundson, 41 Cal. Rptr. 2d 127 (Ct. App. 1995) ("the scientific landscape has once again changed"), *rev. granted*; People v Marlow, 41 Cal. Rptr. 2d 5 (Ct. App. 1995) ("Since Lewontin's and Hartl's article . . . numerous studies have been published in scientific journals compiling VNTR frequency data from around the world. These studies have empirically demonstrated the very conservative nature of the frequency calculation methods employed by forensic laboratories. . . . The weight of authority in the published peer-reviewed literature overwhelmingly supports the proposition that VNTR frequency differences due to ethnicity or substructuring have little impact on DNA population frequency estimates . . . ."), *rev. granted*; People v Soto, 35 Cal. Rptr. 2d 846 (Ct. App. 1994), ("We now have data showing that population substructuring is not 'forensically significant' in estimating the random likelihood of a particular DNA profile."), *rev. granted*; Taylor v State, 889 P.2d 319 (Okla. Ct. Crim. App. 1995) (reiterating the conclusion of People v Soto that "several scientific developments

Nevertheless, most courts have not had the opportunity to consider the implications of the data uncovered since 1992, and judges continue to express misgivings over the possible impact of population structure on estimated VNTR profile frequencies. In addition, some courts have questioned the scientific acceptance of computations for PCR-based systems.[70] Because our conclusions about the limited extent and effect of population structure are derived from studies of many genetic markers, they pertain to the systems that detect DQA, STRs, and other DNA polymorphisms. Although the data on variations among subpopulations are more limited for these systems than for VNTRs, the experience with VNTRs and other polymorphisms indicates that correcting for population structure should make little difference, and the procedures outlined in Chapter 5 can be expected to give fair estimates of the range of uncertainty in population and subpopulation frequency estimates for discrete allele systems.

Ceiling Frequencies in Court

Rather than giving a definitive answer to speculations about population structure, the 1992 NRC report assumed that population structure could be a serious threat to estimates of VNTR profile frequencies within the general population or within subpopulations. To counter the assumed threat, it proposed a procedure for placing an upper bound on the profile frequency—the "interim ceiling principle" discussed in Chapter 5 of the present report. The method, as described in the 1992 report, includes many refinements, and ambiguities or variations in the details have led to the presentation of markedly different values by prosecutors and defendants as the ceiling frequency.[71] We believe that combing

---

since the [1992] NRC . . . report have laid to rest any concern over the use of the product rule''); Lindsey v People, 892 P.2d 281 (Colo. 1995) (perceiving a "calming of the DNA waters" and suggesting that "the debate seems to have turned full circle").

[70]The supreme court of Nebraska, for example, while finding a PCR-based match sufficiently reliable to satisfy its *Frye* standard, reversed a conviction on the grounds that no general acceptance exists with regard to the calculation of the probability to which the state's experts testified: State v Carter, 524 N.W.2d 763 (Neb. 1994) (relies on 1992 NRC report as indicating lack of general acceptance and states that limiting statistical estimates to two racial groups when the racial or ethnic background of the perpetrator is unknown is prejudicial).

[71]People v Venegas, 36 Cal. Rptr. 2d 856 (Ct. App. 1995) (an FBI expert reported a three-locus match for "DNA characteristics as shared by one person out of 65,000 in the general population, and one out of 30,000 in the southwestern United States Hispanic population"; "the defense genetics expert . . . concluded that . . . depending on his choice of methodology, . . . one out of 35 or one out of 378 persons shared appellant's DNA profile."), *rev. granted*. Discrepancies sometimes occur in the figures quoted for ceiling frequencies by prosecution experts alone. E.g., People v Marlow, 41 Cal. Rptr. 2d 5 (Ct. App. 1995) (such estimates ranged from 1/105,000 to 1/27,000), *rev. granted*; cf. Taylor v State, 889 P.2d 319 (Okla. Ct. Crim. App. 1995) (the state's expert produced figures of 1/(97 billion), 1/(334 billion), and, "using Lifecodes's current, more conservative approach" of "straight binning," 1/(10 billion)). Discrepancies between unadjusted figures and ceiling frequencies are even more dramatic. E.g., *id.* (1/7,400,000-1/33,000,000 without adjustment); People v Wilds,

through VNTR data on many subgroups to find the largest allele frequencies, taking the upper end of a confidence interval for each such frequency, ignoring loci because large samples indicate that alleles for some other locus do not occur in Hardy-Weinberg proportions, and using fixed-bin frequencies with extremely wide bins (e.g., State v Guevara, No. K9-92-1873 [Minn. Dist. Ct., Dakota Cty., Jan 26, 1993] [Order]; and Weir 1993c) were neither contemplated by the 1992 committee nor reflect reasonable scientific judgments. Although we cannot recommend either the interim or final ceiling methods, in Chapter 5 we identified several guidelines for those who wish to use such methods. These guidelines make such misuses less likely.

In addition to disputes over the details of how a ceiling should be computed, questions as to implications of the recommendation to use a ceiling have surfaced. Are ceiling frequencies sufficiently valid or accepted in the scientific community to be admissible? If so, should they be the exclusive measure of the frequency of an incriminating profile in the reference population, or may they be presented along with other estimates for racial groups or subgroups?[72]

Shortly after the publication of the 1992 NRC report, appellate courts drew

---

37 Cal. Rptr. 2d 351 (Ct. App. 1995) ("Cellmark's original probability estimate of a random match included a calculation of 1 in 186 billion. Using a more conservative approach, the estimate was reduced to 1 in 66 million. At a pre-trial hearing, Dr. Kidd applied 'statistically unreasonably conservative' assumptions to Cellmark's data and calculated a probability of 1 in 1.86 million. Based on an expanded data base which was available at the time of trial, Dr. Kidd revised his probability estimate to 1 in 4.5 million."), *rev. granted*; Lindsey v People, 892 P.2d 281 Colo. 1995) (estimates of "the probability that Lindsey's DNA profile would match the profile of a randomly selected African American individual . . . ranged from one in 340 billion down to one in 21 million using more conservative frequency calculations"); Brim v State, 654 So. 2d 184 (Fla. Dist. Ct. App. 1995) ("the FBI procedure [used by the Florida state laboratory] generated a probability that only one out of 1.4 billion whites and one out of 2.5 million blacks would share the DNA code . . . The modified ceiling principle indicated that only one in just over 9,000 individuals would share the perpetrator's genetic DNA code.") ; Commonwealth v Lanigan, 419 Mass. 15, 641 N.E.2d 1342 (1994) (interim ceiling estimate changed VNTR probability "from only one in more than 2,000,000 . . . to a range of one in 311,000 to one in 108,000"). Still larger figures can be obtained with the "counting method." E.g., People v Marlow, 41 Cal. Rptr. 2d 5 (Ct. App. 1995) (the laboratory's expert witness reported figures ranging from high of 1 in 33 million to a low of 1 in 7.4 billion for the frequency of the defendant's four-locus VNTR profile in various populations; the defense expert reported that it "might be as common as one in 211"), *rev. granted*. Because the opinions are not always clear about which "conservative" method is being used, it is not always easy to discern how much of the variation in the estimates can be attributed to ambiguities in the interim ceiling method or to choices among other competing procedures.

[72]The 1992 report was not explicit on this point. The interim ceiling principle does not purport to measure the frequency of an incriminating profile in the reference population, but rather an upper limit of the random-match probability that is unrelated to the reference population. In late 1994, one of the authors of that report, and an early advocate of the ceiling procedure, expressed his belief that the committee intended to offer ceiling frequencies as a supplement rather than as a necessary substitute for estimates derived from data on the population or subpopulation of interest (Lander and Budowle 1994).

various inferences from the proposal to present ceiling frequencies in court. Some courts reasoned that willingness to advance the proposal undermined the use of population-specific estimates.[73] Others intimated that ceiling frequencies might well be admissible and remanded cases to lower courts to decide whether such calculations had achieved sufficient general acceptance to be admissible.[74] A few wrote or held that ceiling frequencies already had attained the requisite general acceptance.[75]

The earliest opinions discussing ceiling estimates did not mention the strident criticisms of the method made by some population geneticists and statisticians. In time, however, the courts began to assimilate this literature. Although a few courts interpreted the criticism as "precluding the admissibility of DNA evidence" under the general-acceptance standard,[76] most have recognized that much of the criticism amounted to claims that there was no need for subpopulation studies and ceiling frequencies in the first place or that the recommended procedure for estimating an upper bound was unnecessarily cautious in its details.[77] In

---

[73]State v Sivri, 646 A.2d 169 (Conn. 1994); State v Carter, 246 Neb. 953, 524 N.W.2d 763 (1994) (the NRC report indicates a lack of general acceptance of HW proportions, which renders testimony of a PCR-based DQA test result said to include about 7% of the population inadmissible under *Frye*).

[74]United States v Porter, 618 A.2d 629 (DC App. 1992); People v Watson, 629 N.E.2d 634 (Ill. App. 1994); Commonwealth v Lanigan, 596 N.E.2d 311 (Mass. 1992); State v Vandebogart, 616 A.2d 483 (Vt. 1992). In Franson v Mitchell, 206 Ill. Dec. 399, 645 N.E. 2d 404 (Ill. Ct. App. 1994), the court determined that questions about the effect of population structure made a "probability of paternity" of 99.99% and a "cumulative paternity index" (likelihood ratio) of 29,217,637 inadmissible under *Frye*. It remanded for a determination of whether the more conservative methods proposed in the 1992 report had achieved general acceptance for parentage determinations. As we observed in Chapter 5, however, the ceiling methods were not proposed or designed for computing a paternity index, and the 1992 report's call for "conservative" procedures was influenced by its interpretation of the "beyond a reasonable doubt" standard of proof used in criminal, but not civil, cases.

[75]People v Venegas, 36 Cal. Rptr. 2d 856 (Ct. App. 1995), *rev. granted*; State v Bloom, 516 N.W.2d 159 (Minn. 1994); State v Alt, 504 N.W.2d 38 (Minn. Ct. App. 1993); State v Streich, 658 A.2d 38 (Vt. 1995); State v Cauthron, 846 P.2d 502 (Wash. 1993).

[76]People v Wallace, 14 Cal. App. 4th 651, 17 Cal. Rptr. 2d 721 (1993). See also Hayes v State, 660 So. 2d 257 (Fla. 1995) (dictum); State v Hollis, No. 92-1-04603-9 (Wash. Super Ct. King County, June 1993), appeal pending, No. 3307-1-L.

[77]State v Johnson, 183 Ariz. 623 (Ct. App. 1995) ("'most of the remaining debate stems from criticisms that the ceiling method is too conservative, that evidence of population substructure is lacking, and that further study is needed to determine the best means of presenting probability statistics to juries, not [from any doubts about] the ceiling method's validity as a reliable and highly conservative forensic tool"), *rev. granted*; People v Venegas, 36 Cal. Rptr. 2d 856 (Ct. App. 1995) (noting general agreement that interim ceiling calculations have "forensic reliability"), *rev. granted*; United States v Porter, 618 A.2d 629 (DC Ct. App. 1992); Commonwealth v Lanigan, 419 Mass. 15, 641 N.E.2d 1342 (1994) ("the great weight of opinion appears to be" that "the answer given by the ceiling principle is . . . either irrationally conservative and thus absurd or a reasonable means of producing admissible probability evidence untainted by potential problems of population substructuring"); State v Alt, 504 N.W.2d 38 (Minn. Ct. App. 1993); State v Vandebogart, 616 A.2d 483 (N.H. 1994) (affirming trial court's findings on remand "that there is 'universal' consensus in the scientific community of geneticists and forensic DNA scientists that the interim ceiling principle properly accounts for the possibility of population substructure by providing a highly conservative

jurisdictions that admit scientific evidence on the basis of the sound-methodology standard, ceiling estimates (as well as population-specific estimates) usually have fared well.[78]

In Chapter 5, we concluded that the ceiling method is unnecessarily conservative. With estimates of the uncertainty in the computed frequencies, population-specific computations of frequencies are scientifically valid. The ceiling procedure is simply one possible method for producing VNTR-profile frequency estimates that are expected to be larger than their true values. If, for courtroom use, advocates desire or courts require probable upper bounds on the true value of the frequency, the ceiling approach should yield a very high upper bound. Although we note that there is no convincing scientific reason to insist on such conservative procedures (see Chapter 5), we discuss the legal policies relevant to presentation of frequency estimates or related statistics later in this chapter.

A few courts have required the application of a "ceiling principle" in

---

estimate" and that, although those estimates "may be so conservative as to be deemed not accurate, it is nonetheless generally accepted . . . that any possible errors in such estimates favor the defendant"); State v Streich, 658 A.2d 38 (Vt. 1995) ("There is general acceptance within the scientific community that the ceiling principle over-compensates for any population substructure or allele linkage.").

[78]For example, in United States v Chischilly, 30 F.3d 1144 (9th Cir. 1993), a jury convicted the defendant of raping and murdering a woman in a remote part of the Navajo Indian reservation in Arizona. Single-locus VNTR tests performed by the FBI indicated a match between sperm found on the victim and a sample of the defendant's blood. A population geneticist testified that a probability of 1/2,563 would be a "conservative estimate" of the probability of a match with a randomly selected American Indian. That probability was not obtained with the 1992 NRC report's ceiling method, but by looking to the largest profile frequency among particular tribes represented in FBI's American Indian database. The US Court of Appeals for the Ninth Circuit upheld the admission of the testimony. It reasoned that "evidence of opposing academic camps in virtual scholarly equipoise amidst the scientific journals" demonstrated more than "minimal support within a [scientific] community" and that this degree of acceptance, in combination with the other considerations listed in *Daubert*, militated in favor of admission. Other federal and state courts, applying the scientific-soundness standard, have held far smaller genotype-frequency estimates—both ceiling and population-specific—admissible: United States v Jakobetz, 955 F.2d 786, 800 (2d Cir.), *cert. denied*, 113 S.Ct. 104 (1992) (pre-*Daubert* opinion holding population-specific frequencies admissible); United States v Bonds, 12 F.3d 540 (6th Cir. 1993); United States v Martinez, 3 F.3d 1191 (8th Cir. 1993), *cert. denied*, 114 S.Ct. 734 (1994); Commonwealth v Lanigan, 419 Mass. 15, 641 N.E.2d 1342 (1994) (interim ceiling estimate properly admitted under *Daubert* on retrial following reversal under *Frye* of original conviction obtained with usual product-rule estimate); State v Duran, 881 P.2d 48 (N.M. 1994); State v Peters, 192 Wis. 2d 674, 534 N.W.2d 867 (Ct. App. 1995) (ceiling frequency properly admitted with other estimates against American Indians under relevancy standard when the trial court found that the interim ceiling method satisfied *Daubert*); State v Springfield, 860 P.2d 435 (Wyo. 1993) (population-specific frequencies admissible when accompanied by ceiling frequency). But see State v Streich, 457 A.2d 440 (Vt. 1995) ("even under *Daubert* it is inappropriate to allow evidence based on the unmodified product method. In the lexicon of *Daubert*, we are concerned that the accuracy of the results cannot be ensured by testing, there is an unknown potential for error, and these calculations are not generally accepted within the scientific community. The endorsement of the ceiling principle by the NRC and more recently by leading advocates in the dispute, including a representative of the FBI, leads us to this conclusion.").

calculating frequencies or probabilities for a PCR-based test match or have held "unmodified" computations inadmissible.[79] Other courts have held ordinary "product-rule" estimates associated with the DQA test as generally accepted (State v Gentry, 125 Wash.2d 570, 888 P.2d 1105 [1995]). As indicated in Chapter 5, using the ceiling approach for genetic systems that have a small number of alleles per locus and moderate or large allele frequencies is especially difficult to justify.

EXPLAINING THE MEANING OF A MATCH

Once two samples are found to have similar profiles, the question arises as to what, if anything, the trier of fact may be told about the significance of this finding. Before forensic experts can conclude that DNA testing has the power to help identify the source of an evidence sample, it must be shown that the DNA characteristics vary among people. Therefore, it would not be scientifically justifiable to speak of a match as proof of identify in the absence of underlying data that permit some reasonable estimate of how rare the matching characteristics actually are.

However, determining whether quantitative estimates should be presented to a jury is a different issue. Once science has established that a methodology has some individualizing power, the legal system must determine whether and how best to import that technology into the trial process (Kaye 1995, p 104-105). If the results are sufficiently probative to be admissible, the conceivable alternatives for presentation range from statements of the posterior probability that the defendant is the source of the evidence DNA (see Chapter 5), to qualitative characterizations of this probability, to computations of the likelihood ratio for the hypothesis that the defendant is the source, to qualitative statements of this measure of the strength of the evidence, to the currently dominant estimates of profile frequencies or random-match probabilities, to unadorned reports of a match.

Few courts, if any, have examined the full range of alternatives, and courts have reached conflicting conclusions as to the acceptability of those modes of presentation that they have examined. Here, we outline the alternatives, identify the considerations that affect their suitability, and discuss the social science research that supplies some information on the possible effects of the various types of presentations on the jury.

---

[79]State v Carter, 246 Neb. 953, 524 N.W.2d 763 (1994) (1992 NRC Report indicates lack of general acceptance of HW proportions, which renders testimony of a DQA test result said to include about 7% of the population inadmissible under *Frye*); People v Morales (Rockland County Ct.), N.Y.L.J., Oct. 26, 1994, at 34, col. 6.

The Necessity for Quantitative Estimates

Many courts have held that unless the finding of a match is accompanied by some generally accepted or scientifically sound profile frequency or probability estimate, no testimony about DNA testing is admissible.[80] A few courts, thinking that existing estimates lack acceptance or validity, have excluded quantitative expressions of the frequency of the matching profile while allowing testimony about the match itself.[81] The insistence on quantitative estimation has been fueled by the observation in the 1992 NRC report (p 74) that "[t]o say that two patterns match, without providing any scientifically valid estimate (or, at least, an upper bound) of the frequency with which such matches might occur by chance, is meaningless." See, e.g., State v Carter, 246 Neb. 953, 524 N.W.2d 763, 783 (1994) (quoting 1992 report); Kaye (1995a).

Certainly, a judge's or juror's untutored impression of how unusual a DNA profile is could be very wrong. This possibility militates in favor of going beyond a simple statement of a match, to give the trier of fact some expert guidance about its probative value. As noted above, however, there are a variety of procedures— qualitative as well as quantitative—that might accomplish this objective.

Qualitative Testimony on Uniqueness or Infrequency

In Chapter 5, we asked whether DNA typing has advanced to the point where statements that a particular person is the source of an evidence sample of

---

[80]E.g., People v Wallace, 14 Cal. App. 4th 651, 17 Cal. Rptr. 2d 721 (1993); State v Hollis, No. 2-1-04603-9 (Wash. Super. Ct., King County, June, 1993), appeal pending, No. 3307-1-L; People v Barney, 8 Cal. App. 4th 798, 10 Cal. Rptr. 2d 731 (1992); People v Atoigue, DCA No. CR 91-95A (Guam Dist. Ct. App. Div. 1992); State v Carter, 246 Neb. 953, 524 N.W.2d 763, 782, 783 (1994) ("The calculation of statistical probability is an essential part of the process used in determining the significance of a DNA match . . .We hold that evidence of a DNA match will not be admissible if it has not been accompanied by statistical probability evidence that has been calculated from a generally accepted method."). *Contra* Commonwealth v Crews, 640 A.2d 395, 402 (Pa. 1994) ("The factual evidence of the physical testing of the DNA samples and the matching alleles, even without statistical conclusions, tended to make appellant's presence more likely than it would have been without the evidence, and was therefore relevant.").

[81]State v Bogan, 183 Ariz. 506, 905 P.2d 515 (Ct. App. 1995), *rev. granted*; State v Hummert, No. CR 90-05559 (Super. Ct. Maricopa Co. Apr. 16, 1991), *rev'd* for not excluding testimony thought to assert that match was unique, 183 Ariz. 493, 905 P.2d 493 (Ct. App. 1994), *rev. granted*; State v DeSpain, No. 15589 (Super. Ct. Yuma Co., Feb. 12, 1991); State v Pennell, 584 A.2d 513 (Del. 1989); State v Schwarz, 447 N.W.2d 422, 428 (Minn. 1989); State v Alt, 504 N.W.2d 38 (Minn. Ct. App. 1993); Polk v State, 612 So. 2d 381 (Miss. 1993) (the trial court admitted testimony of a match but excluded an accompanying population frequency estimate); State v Moore, 885 P.2d 457, 467, 468 (Mont. 1994) (the defendant was barred from challenging the fact that the trial court "refused to allow testimony concerning the statistics, but allowed the experts to testify that the RFLP and PCR test results were 'consistent' with [the defendant's DNA]," but "whether, and if so, to what extent we will allow DNA evidence without the accompanying statistical evidence in other criminal cases will be decided in a future case."); Rivera v State, 840 P.2d 933 (Wyo. 1992)

DNA can be scientifically justified. The 1992 report cautioned that "an expert should—given . . . the relatively small number of loci used and the available population data—avoid assertions in court that a particular genotype is unique in the population" (p 92). Because more population data and loci already are available, and still more will be available soon, we are approaching the time when many scientists will wish to offer opinions about the source of incriminating DNA.

In the context of a profile derived from a handful of single-locus VNTR probes, several courts have held that assertions of uniqueness are inadmissible,[82] and others have found such testimony less troublesome.[83] We can say only that after one reaches some threshold, the point at which DNA testing is extensive enough to warrant an opinion as to the identity of the source becomes a matter of judgment. Does a profile frequency of the reciprocal of twice the Earth's population suffice? Ten times? One hundred times? There is no "bright-line" standard in law or science that can pick out exactly how small the probability of the existence of a given profile in more than one member of a population must be before assertions of uniqueness are justified (see Chapter 1 for a discussion of how this problem was addressed for fingerprints; see Chapter 5 for discussion of statistical approaches to the problem for DNA typing). There might already be cases in which it is defensible for an expert to assert that, assuming that there has been no sample mishandling or laboratory error, the profile's probable uniqueness means that the two DNA samples come from the same person.[84]

(suggesting that the better practice is not to refer to probability estimates when introducing DNA results). But cf. Springfield v State, 860 P.2d 435 (Wyo. 1993) (a probability estimate was admissible).

[82]See State v Hummert 183 Ariz. 493, 905 P.2d 493 (Ct. App. 1994), *rev. granted*; State v Cauthron, 846 P.2d 502, 516, 518 (Wash. 1993) (experts from a testing laboratory presented no "probability statistics" but one expert claimed that "the DNA could not have from anyone else on earth"); State v Buckner, 890 P.2d 460 (Wash. 1995) (testimony that the profile "would occur in only one Caucasian in 19.25 billion" and that because "this figure is almost four times the present population of the Earth, the match was unique" was improper).

[83]State v Zollo, 36 Conn. App. 718 (1995) ("testimony that the chance that the DNA sample came from someone other than the defendant was 'so small that . . . it would not be worth considering'" was not inadmissible as an opinion on an ultimate issue in the case "because his opinion could reasonably have aided the jury in understanding the [complex] DNA testimony"); People v Heaton, 266 Ill. App. 3d 469, 640 N.E.2d 630 (1994) (an expert who used the product rule to estimate the frequency at 1/52,600 testified over objection to his opinion that the "defendant was the donor of the semen"); State v Pierce, No. 89-CA-30 (Ohio Ct. App. 1990) (affirming admission of testimony that the probability would be one in 40 billion "that the match would be a random occurrence," and "the DNA is from the same individual"), *aff'd*, 64 Ohio St. 3d 490, 597 N.E.2d 107 (1992); cf. State v Bogan, 905 P.2d 515, 522-23 (Ariz. Ct. App. 1995) (it was proper to allow a molecular biologist to testify, on the basis of a PCR-based analysis known as RAPD, that he "was confident the seed pods found in the truck originated from" a palo verde tree near a corpse); Commonwealth v Crews, 640 A.2d 395 (Pa. 1994) (testimony of an FBI examiner that he did not know of a single instance "where different individuals that are unrelated have been shown to have matching DNA profiles for three or four probes" was admissible under *Frye* despite objection to lack of a frequency estimate, which had been given at a preliminary hearing as 1/400).

[84]See, e.g., State v Bloom, 516 N.W.2d 159, 160 n.2 (Minn. 1994) (a population geneticist was prepared to testify that "in his opinion the nine-locus match constituted 'overwhelming evidence

Opinion testimony about uniqueness would simplify the presentation of evidence by dispensing with specific estimates of population frequencies or probabilities. If the basis of an opinion were attacked on statistical grounds, however, or if frequency or probability estimates were admitted, this advantage would be lost. Nevertheless, because the difference between a vanishingly small probability and an opinion of uniqueness is so slight, courts that decide on a criterion for uniqueness and determine that the criterion has been met may choose to allow the latter along with, or instead of, the former, when the scientific findings support such testimony.

Uniqueness is the limit as the frequency of a profile becomes smaller and smaller. But some experts might testify in qualitative terms even absent a claim of uniqueness; they might prefer to characterize profiles as "rare," "extremely rare," and the like. E.g., People v Venegas, 31 Cal. App. 4th 234, 36 Cal. Rptr. 2d 856, 865 n.13 (1995). At least one state supreme court has endorsed that more modest approach as a substitute to the presentation of more debatable numerical estimates.[85] Although different jurors might interpret the same words differently, the formulas provided in Chapters 4 and 5 produce frequency estimates for profiles of three or more loci that almost always can be conservatively described as "rare."

Quantitative Assessments: Frequencies and Match Probabilities

Except for strong claims of uniqueness, purely qualitative presentations suffer from ambiguity. Professional forecasters, physicians, science writers, students, and soldiers show high variability in translating verbal probability expressions to numerical expressions (Mosteller and Youtz 1990; Wallsten and Budesco 1990). Judges and jurors are likely to show a similar variability in interpreting the meaning of such verbal expressions.[86] To help a court or jury to understand the importance of a match, most experts provide quantitative, rather than qualitative, estimates of the frequency of an incriminating profile in one or more races or an upper bound on the frequency. Typically, the figures are presented as an estimated profile frequency or as the "probability of a random match" or "random-match probability." In some cases, probabilities that the profiles of close

---

that, to a reasonable degree of scientific certainty, the DNA from the victim's vaginal swab came from the [defendant], to the exclusion of all others'").

[85]State v Bloom, 516 N.W.2d 159, 166-67 (Minn. 1994) ("Since it may be impossible to reach a consensus on how to estimate, with any degree of precision, the probability of a random match, and given the great difficulty in educating the jury as to precisely what that figure means and does not mean, it might make sense to simply try to arrive at a fair way of explaining the significance of the match in a verbal, qualitative, nonquantitative, nonstatistical way."). See also Kreiling (1993).

[86]Cf. United States v Fatico, 458 F.Supp. 388, *aff'd*, 603 F .2d 1053 (2d Cir. 1979), cert. denied, 444 U.S. 1073 (1980) (a survey of district judges revealed that their assessment of the probability of guilt associated with the "beyond a reasonable doubt" standard ranged from 76% to 90%).

relatives would match are given as well. Chapters 4 and 5 describe methods for calculating those quantities. It is accurate to characterize the estimate obtained with those methods as match probabilities if it is established or assumed that the laboratory correctly characterized the human DNA in the samples and that the samples came from reported sources. Thus, the "match probability" might be called the "true match probability,"[87] and some experts use the phrase in this sense. In Chapters 4 and 5, all match probabilities are calculated on the assumption that no error has been made.

If a court concludes that the computations satisfy the general-acceptance or scientific-soundness standards, the opponent of the evidence may further argue that the quantitative testimony should be excluded because its prejudicial effect outweighs its helpfulness to the jury. E.g., People v Simpson, No. BA097211 (Super. Ct., Los Angeles Cty., Mar. 20, 1995) (Notice of Objections to Testimony Concerning DNA Evidence); and Taylor v State, 889 P.2d 319 (Okla. Ct. Crim. App. 1995). Three major sources of prejudice have been articulated: that the jury will be awed by small numbers and ignore other aspects of the case, that the jury will misconstrue the probability of a random match as the probability that the defendant is not the source of the incriminating DNA, and that the statement of a probability ignores the possibility of a match being declared due to sample mishandling or other blunders.

When the numbers have been presented as estimating the frequency of a profile or the probability of a random match and have not been mischaracterized as the probability that the defendant is not the source of the incriminating DNA, the argument that numbers will overwhelm the jury rarely has prevailed.[88] Only one jurisdiction has routinely excluded quantitatively framed testimony of probabilities or population frequencies in criminal cases for fear of unduly influencing lay jurors,[89] and the supreme court of that state carved out an exception to the exclusionary rule for ceiling calculations of DNA profile frequencies (State v Bloom, 516 N.W.2d 159 [Minn. 1994]). Nevertheless, some courts and legal scholars (e.g., Tribe 1971) have theorized that jurors will overvalue the quantitative evidence and undervalue other evidence. For example, the Massachusetts Supreme Judicial Court hypothesized in Commonwealth v Curnin, 565 N.E.2d 440, 441 (Mass. 1991), that "evidence of this nature [a random-match probability

---

[87]Some commentators distinguish between the probability of a reported match (including the risk of sample mishandling or laboratory error that would produce a false positive result) and the probability of a true (but coincidental) match for a person selected at random. E.g., Koehler 1993b.

[88]For cases rejecting this argument, see, e.g., United States v Chischilly, 30 F.3d 1144 (9th Cir. 1994) (citing cases); State v Weeks, 891 P.2d 891 P.2d 477 (Mont. 1995); State v Schweitzer, 533 N.W.2d 156, 160 (S.D. 1995) (reviewing cases).

[89]State v Carlson, 267 N.W.2d 160 (Minn. 1978); McCormick (1992, § 210). The opinions of the Minnesota Supreme Court also posit "a real danger that the jury will use the evidence as a measure of the probability of the defendant's guilt or innocence" (State v Schwarz, 447 N.W.2d 422, 428 [Minn. 1989], *quoting* State v Boyd, 331 N.W.2d 480, 483 [Minn. 1983]).

of 1 in 59 million], having an aura of infallibility, must have a strong impact on a jury.''

Empirical research does not support the common assertion that statistical evidence is overvalued. To the contrary, several studies with mock jurors suggest that decision-makers generally make smaller adjustments in their judgments in response to probability evidence than the statistical evidence warrants.[90] Nonetheless, the extremely low random-match probabilities associated with much DNA evidence might cause jurors to perceive the evidence as different in quality, as well as quantity. Virtually no studies of juror reactions have assessed the impact of probabilities as extreme as those in *Commonwealth v Curnin.*[91]

Courts that are especially concerned that small estimates of the match probability might produce an unwanted sense of certainty and lead a jury to disregard other evidence might wish to adopt procedures to reduce this risk. The party offering evidence has the primary responsibility of informing the jury about the evidence, but the legal system depends also on cross-examination, opposing witnesses, and judicial instructions to guide the jury. The efficacy of the first two approaches rests on the opposing party's capacity to enlist the assistance of informed counsel and well-qualified, expert witnesses. Issues related to the retention and appointment of experts were discussed earlier in this chapter. The third approach—instructing the jury—enables the court directly to address subjects likely to cause confusion or overweighting. Jurors commonly receive judicial instructions on factors to be considered in evaluating the credibility of witnesses. E.g., CALJIC No. 2.20 (3d ed. 1970), *cited with approval* in People v Hall, 28 Cal.3d 143, 167 Cal. Rptr. 844, 616 P.2d 826 (1980). Similarly, courts might wish to instruct a jury on, for example, factors that affect the adequacy of DNA analysis and the need to consider all the evidence in the case.

---

[90]For example, Goodman (1992) varied the frequency of the suspect's blood type in a hypothetical homicide case in which the sample of blood from the scene of the crime matched that taken from the defendant and not the victim. Although the mock jurors with frequency information were more likely to convict than those who received no frequency information, and although guilty verdicts decreased as the frequency of a random match went from 0.001 to 0.1, frequencies of 0.001, 0.01, and 0.05. did not produce differing rates of conviction. Other research on blood-type evidence has produced similar results (Faigman and Baglioni 1988; Thompson and Schumann 1987).

[91]See Kaye and Koehler 1991 (reviewing studies). Koehler and colleagues (1995) provided a brief written summary of a homicide case in which the case evidence was circumstantial and weak apart from the DNA evidence. In two studies, one with college students and a replication with jurors, respondents were assigned to one of three laboratory error-rate conditions (absent, 0.02, 0.001) and were either provided with a 1/(1 billion) probability of a random match or given no information on the probability of a random match. Conviction rates were influenced by the information on probability of a random match but unaffected by the presence or level of the laboratory error-rate information. Yet conviction rates with information on probability of a random match averaged 44% for the students (44% with and 44% without laboratory error information) and 49% for the jurors (54% with and 44% without laboratory error information), reinforcing the impression that jurors are not overwhelmed by statistical DNA evidence.

The second possible source of prejudice is the jury's potential misinterpretation of the probability of a random match as the probability that the defendant is not the source. Many court opinions and transcripts of expert testimony present the random-match probability as though it were the conditional probability that the defendant is not the source, given the evidence of a match.[92] The random-match probability is the conditional probability of the match, given that the defendant is not the source. Transposing the conditionals, as noted in Chapter 5, is sometimes called the "prosecutor's fallacy" and is often condemned in judicial dicta. E.g., State v Bible, 858 P.2d 1152 (Ariz. 1993); and State v Bloom, 516 N.W.2d 159 (Minn. 1994).

Nevertheless, few courts or commentators have recommended the exclusion of evidence merely because of the risk that jurors will transpose a conditional probability (McCormick 1992, § 212). The available research indicates that jurors may be more likely to be swayed by the "defendant's fallacy" than by the "prosecutor's fallacy." When advocates present both fallacies to mock jurors, the defendant's fallacy dominates. That fallacy, as noted in Chapter 5, consists of dismissing or undervaluing the matches with extremely high likelihood ratios because other matches are to be expected in unrealistically large populations of potential suspects. Furthermore, if the initial presentation of the probability figure, cross-examination, and opposing testimony all fail to clarify the point, the judge can counter both fallacies by appropriate instructions to the jurors that minimize the possibility of cognitive errors.[93]

Finally, defendants and some legal commentators have contended that the

---

[92]Examples are collected in Kaye (1993) and Koehler (1993a). See also, e.g., United States v Martinez, 3 F.2d 1191, 1194 (8th Cir. 1993) ("The second step of the DNA identification process then involves a determination of the probability that someone other than the contributor of the known sample could have contributed the unknown sample."); Greenwood v United States, 659 A.2d 825, 826 (DC Ct. App. 1995) ("The parties stipulated that DNA evidence established that the probability that Greenwood was the source of the semen found on the victim's underpants was not less than 2000 to 1."); People v Heaton, 266 Ill. App. 3d 469, 640 N.E.2d 630 (1994) (an expert was said to have testified that "the probability of another Caucasian . . . was 1 in 52,600"); Commonwealth v Crews, 640 A.2d 395, 400 (Pa. 1994) ("DNA analysis generally can provide only statistical probability; e.g., there is one chance in four hundred or one chance in four million that the DNA samples come from someone else."); Taylor v State, 889 P.2d 319 (Okla. Ct. Crim. App. 1995) (Lifecodes's expert was said to have "testified that the likelihood that an African American other than Taylor contributed the DNA . . . was one in 97 billion"); Taylor v Commonwealth, No. 1767-93-1, 1995 WL 80189 (Va. Ct. App. Feb. 28, 1995) (an unpublished opinion reporting that "DNA analysis of semen obtained from the victim and defendant's blood established a probability of 1 in 128 million that a black male other than defendant was the perpetrator").

[93]As regards the transposition fallacy, such an instruction might be framed along these lines: "In evaluating the expert testimony on the DNA evidence, you were presented with a number indicating the probability that another individual drawn at random from the [specify] population would coincidentally have the same DNA profile as the [blood stain, semen stain, etc.]. That number, which assumes that no sample mishandling or laboratory error occurred, indicates how distinctive the DNA profile is. It does not by itself tell you the probability that the defendant is innocent."

risk of a reported match due to laboratory or handling errors dwarfs the probability that a randomly selected profile will match the evidence DNA and renders any profile frequency or random-match probability estimate unfairly prejudicial (People v Barney, 8 Cal. App. 4th 798, 10 Cal. Rptr. 2d 731 [1992]; People v Simpson, No. BA097211 [Los Angeles Cty. Super. Ct., Oct. 4, 1994] [Defendant's Motion to Exclude DNA Evidence]; and Koehler, Chia, and Lindsey 1995). The argument that jurors will make better use of a single figure for the probability that an innocent suspect would be reported to match never has been tested adequately.[94] The argument for a single figure is weak in light of this lack of research into how jurors react to different ways of presenting statistical information, and its weakness is compounded by the grave difficulty of estimating a false-positive error rate in any given case. But efforts should be made to fill the glaring gap in empirical studies of such matters. Because of the potential power and probative value of DNA evidence, it is important to learn more about juror and judicial response to this evidence in the face of strong and weak nonstatistical evidence.[95]

Quantitative Assessments: Likelihood Ratios and Posterior Odds

Small values of the probability of a random match undermine the hypothesis (which we may abbreviate as S^C) that the defendant is not the source of incriminating DNA but just happens to have the same profile. Some statisticians prefer to use a likelihood ratio to explain the probative value of a match. As explained in Chapter 5, the likelihood ratio (LR) is related to competing hypotheses about the process that generated the data. With DNA measurements, the hypotheses of most interest are that the DNA samples have a common source (S) and that they do not (S^C). LR indicates how many times more probable it would be to

---

[94]The only study comparing reactions to separate and combined estimates found that subjects were insensitive to information on error rates when the random-match probability and the laboratory-error rate were presented separately (Koehler, Chia, and Lindsey 1995). The "evidence" in the mock case, however, was presented in the form of a single sentence unaccompanied by explanation or argument.

[95]In the short run, it is appropriate to alert jurors both to the value of the statistical evidence and to its limitations. In the longer run, research should be conducted to evaluate the impact of DNA testimony on juror decision-making and the effects of alternative approaches, such as likelihood ratios or instructions in applying Bayes's theorem, on jury comprehension. Studies are needed that test reactions to the kind of DNA evidence that is presented in the courtroom, along with witness explanations, attorney arguments, and judicial instructions. Such hypotheses as the suggestion that jurors faced with the estimated laboratory-error rate and the random-match probability might average the two (Lempert 1993) or that jurors will fail to use information on laboratory-error rates cannot be evaluated in a useful way if jurors are not provided with the kind of assistance that they would receive in the relevant legal setting. Additional research on juror reactions should test the ability of jury instructions, videotaped expert explanations, and other educational efforts to facilitate appropriate interpretation of DNA evidence.

observe the data if S, as opposed to S^C, were true. As long as LR is greater than 1, the DNA data support hypothesis S. The more LR exceeds 1, the greater the probative value of the data in supporting hypothesis S (see Lempert 1977).

Chapter 5 noted several LRs that might be used to describe the probative value of DNA data. With discrete allele systems and the match-binning analysis of VNTRs, we saw that the LR is 1/P, where P is the probability of a coincidental match.[96] For a profile such that P is, say, 1/1,000,000, the LR would be 1,000,000, and an expert might testify that the match is 1,000,000 times as probable under S than under S^C. More complicated VNTR-profile LRs do not use match windows and bins, but rather consider the extent of the matching at each allele and rely on a continuous representation of the frequency distribution of fragment lengths. With those models, a match that involves almost no separation in all the bands produces an LR that is greater than a match that involves separations at the edges of the match windows for all the bands. Indeed, because these LRs dispense with the somewhat arbitrary dichotomy between matches and nonmatches, they have been termed "similarity likelihood ratios" (Kaye 1995b) and advocated on the ground that they make better use of the DNA data—e.g., Berry 1991a; Evett, Scranage, and Pinchin 1993; Kaye 1995b; Roeder 1994. As with match probabilities, qualitative as well as overtly quantitative presentations can be devised (see Evett 1991, p 201, proposing "a verbal convention, which maps from ranges of the likelihood ratio to selected phrases," such as "strong evidence" or "weak evidence").

Although LRs are rarely introduced in criminal cases,[97] we believe that they are appropriate for explaining the significance of data and that existing statistical knowledge is sufficient to permit their computation. None of the LRs that have been devised for VNTRs can be dismissed as clearly unreasonable or based on principles not generally accepted in the statistical community. Therefore, legal doctrine suggests that LRs should be admissible unless they are so unintelligible that they provide no assistance to a jury or so misleading that they are unduly prejudicial. As with frequencies and match probabilities, prejudice might exist

---

[96]As discussed in Chapter 5, with match-binning, the numerator is slightly less than 1 because there is a very small chance that two measurements of the same band will not satisfy the match criteria (see Kaye 1995b).

[97]Likelihood ratios were used in State v Klindt, 389 N.W.2d 670 (Iowa 1986) (discussed later), and are admitted routinely in parentage litigation, where they are known as the "paternity index" (see Chapter 5). E.g., Kaye 1989; Aickin and Kaye 1983; McCormick 1992, § 212. Some state statutes use them to create a presumption of paternity (Kaye 1990a,b,c). The practice of providing a paternity index has been carried over into criminal cases in which genetic parentage is used to indicate the identity of the perpetrator of an offense. E.g., State v Skipper, 228 Conn. 610, 637 A.2d 1101 (1994); Davis v State, 476 N.E.2d 127 (Ind. Ct. App. 1985); State v Weeks, 891 P.2d 477 (Mont. 1995); State v Spann, 130 N.J. 484, 617 A.2d 247 (1993); State v Jackson, 320 N.C. 452, 358 S.E.2d 679 (1987). Some of the appellate courts in some of these cases disapproved of the biostatistical presentations, but none specifically condemned the use of the likelihood ratio.

because the proposed LRs do not account for laboratory error, and a jury might misconstrue even a modified version that did account for it as a statement of the odds in favor of S. As for the possible misinterpretation of LRs as the odds in favor of identity, that too is a question of jury ability and performance to which existing research supplies no clear answer.

The likelihood ratio is still one step removed from what a judge or jury truly seeks—an estimate of the probability that a suspect was the source of a crime sample, given the observed profile of the DNA extracted from samples. Recognizing that, a number of statisticians have argued that the LR should not be presented to the jury in its own right[98] but should be used to estimate the probability that a suspect is the source of a crime sample. E.g., Berry 1991a (but see Berry 1991b, p 203-204). Thus, a few experts have testified on this posterior probability in court.[99]

As noted in Chapter 5, the posterior odds (considering the DNA data) that the defendant is the source are the LR times the prior odds (those formed on the basis of other information). That procedure for updating probabilities has a rich history in statistics and law. Known as Bayes's rule, it has been the subject of protracted discussion among legal scholars and statisticians (see generally Allen et al. 1995; Symposium 1991; and Kaye 1988a). One of the more substantial issues raised in the legal scholarship revolves around specifying the prior odds to be updated. For courtroom practice, three methods of presentation have been proposed or used: "expert-prior-odds," "jury-prior-odds," and "variable-prior-odds" (Kaye 1993).

In the expert-prior-odds implementation, a scientist implicitly or explicitly selects a prior probability, applies Bayes's rule, and informs the jury that the scientific evidence establishes a single probability for the event in question. The prosecution relied on a Bayesian analysis of this type in *State v Klindt*, 389 N.W.2d 670 (Iowa 1986), a gruesome chainsaw-murder case decided before the emergence of DNA testing. The supreme court of Iowa affirmed the admission of a statistician's testimony as to a posterior probability in excess of 99% that a torso found in the Mississippi River was what remained of the defendant's missing wife. (It is doubtful, however, that the Iowa courts appreciated the basis of the calculation.) For years, courts in civil paternity cases that involved testing of antigens have routinely admitted testimony of posterior probabilities. E.g.,

---

[98]E.g., Evett 1991, p 201 ("Just leaving a court with a likelihood ratio does not seem enough."); cf. Fienberg 1992 (criticizing presentation of a relative likelihood function).

[99]See Smith v Deppish, 807 P.2d 144 (Kan. 1991) (the state's "DNA experts informed the jury that . . . there was more than a 99 percent probability that Smith was a contributor of the semen"); State v Thomas, 830 S.W.2d 546 (Mo. Ct. App. 1992) (a geneticist testified that "the likelihood that the DNA found in Marion's panties came from the defendant was higher than 99.99%"); Commonwealth v Crews, 640 A.2d 395, 402 (Pa. 1994) (an FBI examiner who at a preliminary hearing had estimated a coincidental-match probability for a VNTR match "at three of four loci" reported at trial that the match made identity "more probable than not").

Kaye 1989; Aickin and Kaye 1983; and McCormick 1992, § 212. However, the practice has met with much less favor in criminal cases where the experts failed to disclose that they had used an ad hoc prior probability of one-half.[100] The expert-prior-odds approach has been criticized as requiring a jury to defer to an expert's choice of the prior odds, even though the scientist's special knowledge and skill extend merely to the production of the likelihood ratio for the scientific evidence (Kaye 1993).

Jury-prior-odds implementation requires a jury to formulate prior odds, to adjust them as prescribed by Bayes's rule, and to return a verdict of guilty if the posterior odds exceed some threshold that expresses the point at which the reasonable-doubt standard is satisfied. But that procedure raises serious questions about a jury's ability to translate beliefs into numbers (see Tribe 1971; and Kaye, 1991) and about the desirability of quantifying the vague concept of reasonable doubt (See Nesson 1979, 1985; Shaviro 1989; and Tribe 1971).

Finally, with the variable-prior-odds method, an expert neither uses his or her own prior odds nor demands that jurors formulate their prior odds for substitution into Bayes's rule. Rather, the expert presents the jury with a table or graph showing how the posterior probability changes as a function of the prior probability.[101] Although the variable-prior-odds implementation of Bayes's rule has garnered the most support among legal scholars and is used in some civil cases, very few courts have considered its merits in criminal cases.[102] How much it would contribute to jury comprehension remains an open question, especially considering the fact that for most DNA evidence, computed values of the likelihood ratio (conditioned on the assumption that the reported match is a true match) would swamp any plausible prior probability and result in a graph or table that would show a posterior probability approaching 1 except for very tiny prior probabilities.

---

[100]State v Skipper, 228 Conn. 610, 637 A.2d 1101 (1994) (reasoning that this application of Bayes's theorem violated the presumption of innocence and suggesting in dictum that any use of Bayes's theorem would be impermissible); State v Hartman, 426 N.W. 2d 320 (Wis. 1988). The undisclosed use of a prior probability of one-half was standard in civil cases and first was criticized in Ellman and Kaye (1979). The courts that routinely admitted such testimony probably did not recognize the Bayesian nature of the "probability of paternity" laid before them, but courts unmistakably apprised of the foundations of these probabilities have continued to approve of them. A few courts have imposed restrictions on the practice. E.g., Commonwealth v Beausoleil, 490 N.E.2d 788 (Mass. 1986); Plemel v Walter, 735 P.2d 1209 (Or. 1987). For discussion and criticism, see Kaye (1988b, 1989).

[101]Finkelstein and Fairley (1970). For LR = 1,000,000, the posterior probability approaches 1 for all but invisible values of the prior probability. For example, the prior probability would have to be about 1/1,000,000 or less to keep the posterior probability to less than one-half.

[102]See State v Skipper, 228 Conn. 610 (1994) (stating in dictum that it would be an error to use the variable-prior-odds approach); State v Spann, 130 N.J. 484, 617 A.2d 247 (1993) (remanding for possible consideration of the use of a Bayesian graph of the probability of paternity). The *Skipper* opinion is criticized by many of the discussants in Allen et al. (1995).

Importance of Behavioral Research

To make appropriate use of DNA technology in the courtroom, the trier of fact must give the DNA evidence appropriate weight. However, unless the results and meaning of the DNA evidence are clearly communicated, the trier of fact may fail to grasp much of the technical merit of DNA profiling. No research has as yet tested the reactions of triers of fact to the detailed presentations of evidence on DNA profiling that are encountered in the courtroom. We do know that people can make frequent and systematic errors in tasks that require them to assess probabilities or to draw inferences using probabilistic information (see, for example, Bar-Hillel 1980; Edwards and von Winterfeldt 1986; Kahneman et al. 1982; Hogarth and Reder 1987; Nisbett and Ross 1980; Nisbett et al. 1983; Palmerini 1993; Poulton 1989). Yet, despite this plethora of research into information processing in other contexts, we know very little about how laypersons respond to DNA evidence and how to minimize the risk that they will give the DNA evidence inappropriate weight. For example, research generally shows that subjects tend to revise their probability estimates in light of new information less than Bayes's theorem would predict (reviewed by Beyth-Marom and Fischhoff 1983), and some research with mock jurors given written descriptions of blood-group evidence and various types of accompanying expert testimony also suggests that jurors will undervalue match probabilities (see Faigman and Baglioni 1988). However, the studies involve far higher match probabilities than the extreme probabilities associated with DNA evidence, which may evoke a different reaction (see Kaye and Koehler 1991).

Contextual features, such as the method of presenting a question, that are unrelated to a problem's formal structure may substantially influence probability judgments (Reeves and Lockhart 1993). The small amount of research on reactions to probabilistic evidence suggests that methods of presentation may strongly affect reactions to DNA evidence. Unexamined are the effects of testimony about extreme probabilities or laboratory error when DNA evidence is presented by expert witnesses who are subjected to cross-examination. To evaluate the reactions of laypersons to DNA evidence, research is needed in which the respondents are exposed to the methods of presenting DNA evidence typically used in trial settings.

Although scholars have suggested promising ways to present probabilistic assessments in the courtroom (Finkelstein and Fairley 1970; suggesting that jurors be presented with a range of plausible prior probabilities and information about what the likelihood ratio for the trace evidence implies in light of these prior probabilities), almost no empirical evidence yet exists on the effects of such modes of presentation on decisionmakers. Similarly, although some basic probability concepts can be taught to undergraduates in a half-hour with reasonable success (Fong et al. 1986), research is needed on the appropriate way to instruct jurors adequately on the more sophisticated probabilistic concepts at issue when DNA evidence is presented at trial. If courts are to make informed decisions about the expert presentations that will be allowed or preferred, further research is needed into alternative methods of trial presentation.

CONCLUSIONS

This chapter has described some of the legal principles and procedures governing the admission and use of DNA evidence in the courtroom and how this evidence has been received over the last decade. In assimilating scientific developments, the legal system necessarily lags behind the scientific world. Before making use of evidence derived from scientific advances, courts must scrutinize the proposed testimony to determine its suitability for use at trial, and controversy within the scientific community often is regarded as grounds for the exclusion of the scientific evidence. Although some controversies that have come to closure in the scientific literature continue to limit the presentation of DNA evidence in some jurisdictions, courts are making more use of the ongoing research into the population genetics of DNA profiles. We hope that our review of the research will contribute to this process.

In this chapter, we have also discussed how our conclusions and recommendations for reducing the risk of laboratory error, for applying human population genetics to DNA profiles, and for handling uncertainties in estimates of profile frequencies and match probabilities might affect the application of the rules for the discovery and admission of evidence in court. Many suggestions can be offered to make our recommendations most effective: for example, that every jurisdiction should make it possible for all defendants to have broad discovery and independent experts; that accreditation, proficiency-testing, and the opportunity for independent testing (whenever feasible) should be prerequisites to the admission of laboratory findings; that in resolving disputes over the adequacy or interpretation of DNA tests, the power of the court to appoint its own experts should be exercised more frequently; and that experts should not be barred from presenting any scientifically acceptable estimate of a random-match probability. We have chosen, however, to make no formal recommendations on such matters of legal policy; the single recommendation in the chapter concerns scientific evidence—namely, the need for behavioral research that will assist legal decision makers in developing standards for communicating about DNA in the courtroom:

Recommendation 6.1: Behavioral research should be carried out to identify any conditions that might cause a trier of fact to misinterpret evidence on DNA profiling and to assess how well various ways of presenting expert testimony on DNA can reduce such misunderstandings.

We trust that our efforts to explain the state of the forensic science and some of the social science findings that are pertinent to resolving these issues will contribute to better-informed judgments by courts and legislatures.

APPENDIX 6A

The following tables summarize the law in the United States on the admissibility of estimates of profile frequencies or random-match probabilities of DNA types. Table 6.1 lists the leading cases or statutes in each jurisdiction with a parenthetical explanation of the result in each case. Table 6.2 presents this information in a more abbreviated format. In many of the more recent cases, both an interim-ceiling and product-rule estimates were presented. The tables do not show whether an opinion holds or suggests that the product-rule estimate would have been inadmissible had the ceiling estimate not been included. Many other subtleties and issues that arise in these cases are not captured in this brief summary.

TABLE 6.1 Leading Cases and Statutes on Admissibility of Inclusionary DNA Evidence by Jurisdiction, as of June 1995

DC Cir.	United States v Perry, Crim. No. 92-474 (D.D.C. Jan. 11, 1994) (VNTR product estimate admissible)
2d Cir.	United States v Jakobetz, 955 F.2d 786 (2d Cir. 1992). *aff'd*, 955 F.2d 786 (2d Cir.), *cert. denied*, 113 S. Ct. 109 (1992) (VNTR product-rule estimate admissible under relevance standard)
6th Cir.	United States v Bonds, 12 F. 3d 540 (6th Cir. 1993) (VNTR product-rule estimate admissible under *Daubert*)
8th Cir.	United States v Martinez, 3 F. 3d 1191 (8th Cir. 1993) (testimony of VNTR match without frequency estimate admissible where defendant opposed admission of statistic), *cert. denied*, 114 S. Ct. 734 (1994)
9th Cir.	United States v Chischilly, 30 F. 3d 1144 (9th Cir. 1994) (VNTR product-rule estimate admissible under *Daubert*), *cert. denied*, 115 S. Ct. 946 (1995)
10th Cir.	United States v Davis, 40 F. 3d 1069 (10th Cir. 1994) (VNTR estimate admissible under *Daubert*, but estimation procedure not specified), *cert. denied*, 115 S. Ct. 1387, 1806 (1995)
Alabama	Dubose v State, 662 So.2d 1189 (Ala. 1995) (error not to appoint defense expert to counter what, presumably, was admissible VNTR product-rule estimate and opinion of uniqueness); Perry v State, 586 So. 2d 242 (Ala. 1991) (VNTR product-rule estimate remanded for *Frye* hearing), *on appeal from remand*, 606 So. 2d 224 (Ala. Crim. App. 1992) (admissible)
Alaska	Hilbish v State, 891 P.2d 841, 847 (Alas. Ct. App. 1995) (unstated DNA testing introduced, apparently without objection, to show that blood stain was the victim's to "a certainty of over 99.5 percent")
Arizona	State v Bible, 175 Ariz. 549, 858 P.2d 1152 (1993), *cert. denied*, 114 S.Ct. 1578 (1994) (VNTR product-rule estimate inadmissible under *Frye* because of controversy over sampling method, linkage equilibrium, and Hardy-Weinberg proportions); State v Johnson, 905 P.2d 1002 (Ariz. Ct. App. 1995) (VNTR ceiling estimate admissible under *Bible* and *Frye*); State v Bogan, 905 P.2d 515, 522-23 (Ariz. Ct. App. 1995) (RAPD match of DNA from tree and opinion as to source admissible), *rev. granted*; State v Hummert, 170 Ariz. Adv. Rep. 17 (Az. Ct. App. July 26, 1994) (testimony all but stating that matching VNTR profile is unique inadmissible)

TABLE 6.1   *Continued*

Arkansas	Swanson v State, 308 Ark. 28, 823 S.W. 812 (1992) (VNTR product-rule estimate admissible under relevance standard); Prater v State, 820 S.W.2d 429 (Ark. 1991) (same)
California	People v Admundson, 41 Cal. Rptr. 2d 127 (Ct. App. 1995) (unspecified PCR-based test as well as VNTR profiling) *rev. granted* (under California Rule of Court 976, opinions of the court of appeals that are under review by the state supreme court are considered unpublished unless the California Supreme Court orders their publication), People v Marlow, 41 Cal. Rptr. 2d 5 (Ct. App. 1995); People v Taylor, 33 Cal. App. 4th 262 (1995); People v Wilds, 37 Cal. Rptr. 2d 351 (Ct. App. 1995), *rev. granted*; People v Venegas, 36 Cal. Rptr. 2d 856 (Ct. App. 1995), *rev. granted*; People v Soto, 35 Cal. Rptr.2d 846 (Ct. App. 1994), *rev. granted*; People v Wallace, 14 Cal. App. 4th 651, 17 Cal. Rptr. 2d 721 (1993); People v Pizarro, 10 Cal. App. 4th 57, 12 Cal. Rptr. 436 (1992); People v Barney, 8 Cal. App. 4th 798, 10 Cal. Rptr. 2d 731 (1992); People v Axell, 235 Cal. App. 3d 836, 1 Cal. Rptr. 2d 411 (1991) (conflicting opinions on admissibility of VNTR product-rule and interim-ceiling estimates)
Colorado	Lindsey v People, 892 P.2d 281 (Colo. 1995) (VNTR product-rule and ceiling estimates admissible under *Frye* and relevance standards)
Connecticut	State v Sivri, 231 Conn. 115, 646 A.2d 169 (1994) (VNTR product-rule estimate admitted at trial, but case remanded for *Frye* hearing on necessity for interim-ceiling estimate in light of 1992 National Research Council report)
Delaware	Nelson v State, 628 A.2d 69 (Del. 1993) (trial court's exclusion of VNTR product-rule frequency "inherently inconsistent" with its admission of testimony of a match, because "without the necessary statistical calculations, the evidence of the match was 'meaningless' to the jury"); Del. Code Ann. § 3515 (1994)
DC	United States v Porter, 618 A.2d 629 (DC App. 1992) (remanding for *Frye* hearing on admissibility of VNTR ceiling estimates), *on remand,* 1994 WL 368405 (DC Super. Ct. 1994) (admissible)
Florida	Hayes v State, 660 So. 2d 257 (Fla. 1995) (VNTR ceiling estimate admissible under *Frye*; dictum); Andrews v State, 533 So. 2d 851 (1988) (VNTR product-rule estimate admissible under *Frye* and relevance standards)
Georgia	Caldwell v State, 260 Ga. 278, 393 S.E.2d 436 (1990) (VNTR product-rule estimate inadmissible because database shows departure from Hardy-Weinberg proportions, but a more-conservative estimate said to be derived without using any "population theory" admissible under *Frye*); Blige v State, 211 Ga. App. 771, 440 S.E.2d 525 (1994) (estimate produced by "downsizing" the numbers as in *Caldwell* admissible)
Hawaii	State v Montalbo, 73 Haw. 130 828 P.2d 1274 (1992) (VNTR product-rule estimate admissible under *Frye*)
Illinois	Franson v Micelli, 269 Ill. App. 3d 20 (1994) (summarizing the positions of each appellate district and holding inadmissible under *Frye* standard a VNTR paternity probability), *appeal allowed,* 161 Ill. 2d 525, 649 N.E. 2d 415 (1995); People v Heaton, 266 Ill. App. 3d 469, 640 N.E.2d 630 (1994) (VNTR product-rule estimate and opinion as to source admissible before 1992 National Research Council report); People v Stremmel, 258 N.E.2d 93 (1994) (VNTR product-rule estimate admissible under *Frye*); People v Watson, 257 Ill. App. 915, 629 N.E.2d 634 (1994) (VNTR product-rule estimate inadmissible under *Frye*; remanded for *Frye* hearing on admissibility of ceiling estimates); People v Lipscomb, 215 Ill. App. 3d 413, 574 N.E. 2d 1345 (1991) (VNTR product-rule estimate admissible under *Frye*)

TABLE 6.1 *Continued*

Indiana	Harrison v State, 644 N.E.2d 1243 (Ind. 1995) (remanding for *Frye* hearing on PCR-based tests); Davidson v State, 580 N.E. 2d 238 (Ind. 1991) (VNTR product-rule estimate admissible under *Frye*); Hopkins v State, 579 N.E. 2d 1297 (Ind. 1991) (same)
Iowa	State v Brown, 470 N.W.2d 30 (Iowa 1991) (VNTR product-rule estimate admissible under relevance standard)
Kansas	State v Haddock, 257 Kan. 964, 897 P.2d 152 (1995) (DQA test and frequency admissible under Frye); State v Hill, 257 Kan. 774, 859 P.2d 1238 (1995) (unspecified PCR-based test and frequency estimate admissible under *Frye*); State v Dykes, 252 Kan.556, 847 P.2d 1214 (1993) (VNTR product-rule estimate admissible under *Frye*)
Louisiana	State v Quatrevingt, 617 So.2d 484 (La. Ct. App. 1992) (VNTR product-rule estimate admissible under statute); aff'd, No. 93-KO-1644, 1996 WL 83873 (La. Feb. 28, 1996) (statute satisfies relevance requirement of *Daubert*, but Lifecodes's use of monomorphic probes was not shown to be scientifically sound under *Daubert*); La. Stat. Ann. § 441.1 (1992)
Maryland	Cobey v State, 80 Md. App. 31, 559 A.2d 391 (1989) (VNTR product-rule estimate admissible under statute); Md. Code Ann. Cts. & Jud. Proc. § 10-915(3)(b) (Michie Supp. 1992) ("evidence of a [RFLP] DNA profile is admissible")
Mass.	Commonwealth v Lanigan, 419 Mass. 15, 596 N.E. 2d 311 (1994) (VNTR ceiling estimate admissible under *Frye*), *appeal of remand from* 413 Mass. 154, 596 N.E.2d 311 (1992) (VNTR product-rule estimate inadmissible under *Frye*)
Michigan	People v Adams, 195 Mich. App. 267, 489 N.W.2d 192 (1992) (VNTR product-rule estimate admissible under *Frye*), *modified on other grounds*, 441 Mich. 916, 497 N.W.2d 182 (1993); People v Adell, 205 Mich. App. 326, 517 N.W.2d 785 (1994) (VNTR product-rule estimates admissible under *Adams*)
Minnesota	State v Bloom, 516 N.W.2d 159 (1994) (VNTR ceiling estimates admissible under *Frye*); Minn. Stat. Ann. § 634.25 (1989)
Mississippi	Polk v State, 612 So.2d 381 (1993) (VNTR match admissible under *Frye* without frequency estimates)
Missouri	State v Davis, 814 S.W.2d 593 (Mo. 1991) (VNTR product-rule estimate admissible under *Frye*), *cert. denied*, 502 U.S. 1047 (1992)
Montana	State v Weeks, 270 Mont. 63, 891 P.2d 477 (1995) (serological and VNTR tests along with paternity index of 1,900,000 calculated by unspecified method admissible to prove rape); State v Moore, 268 Mont. 20, 885 P.2d 457 (1994) (VNTR and DQA results admissible under *Daubert* without any statistical estimates where defendant had moved to exclude estimates as prejudicial)
Nebraska	State v Carter, 246 Neb. 953, 524 N.W.2d 763 (1994) (PCR DQA product estimate inadmissible under *Frye* in light of 1992 National Research Council report's discussion of Hardy-Weinberg proportions)
New Hamp.	State v Vandebogart, 136 N.H. 345, 616 A.2d 483 (1992) (VNTR product-rule estimate inadmissible under *Frye*; remanded for a *Frye* hearing on ceiling estimates), *appeal after remand*, 139 N.H. 145, 652 A.2d 671 (1994) (ceiling estimate admissible under *Frye*)
New Jersey	State v Williams, 252 N.J. Super. 369, 599 A.2d 960 (1991) (DQA product-rule estimate admissible under *Frye*)

TABLE 6.1 *Continued*

New Mexico	State v Duran, 118 N.M. 303, 881 P.2d 48 (1994) (VNTR ceiling estimate admissible under *Daubert*); State v Anderson, 118 N.M. 284, 881 P.2d 29 (1994) (VNTR product-rule estimates admissible under *Daubert*)
New York	People v Vann, 627 N.Y.S.2d 473 (App. Div. 3d Dep't 1995) (VNTR product-rule estimate admissible under *Frye* where the defendant objected that the test was not scientifically accepted but did not object to the frequency estimate); People v Palumbo, 162 Misc. 2d 650, 618 N.Y.S.23d 197 (Sup. Ct. 1994) (DQA test ordered following finding that DQA testing and population frequencies are generally accepted); People v Wesley, 83 N.Y.2d 417, 633 N.E.2d 451, 611 N.Y.S.2d 97 (1994) (VNTR product-rule estimate admissible under *Frye*); People v White, 621 N.Y.S.2d 728 (App. Div. 3d Dep't 1995) (VNTR test that identified defendant as father of aborted fetus admissible to prove rape)
North Car.	State v Pennington, 327 N.C. 89, 393 S.E.2d 847 (1990) (VNTR product-rule estimate admissible under relevance standard)
Ohio	State v Pierce, 64 Ohio St. 3d 490, 597 N.E.2d 107, 113 (1992) (VNTR product-rule estimate admissible under relevance standard); State v Penton, No. 9-91-25 (Ohio Ct. App. Apr. 7, 1993) (DQA estimate admissible under relevance standard)
Oklahoma	Taylor v State, 889 P.2d 319 (Okla. Ct. Crim. App. 1995) (VNTR product-rule estimate admissible under *Daubert*)
Oregon	State v Lyons, 124 Or. App. 598, 863 P.2d 1303 (1993) (DQA product-rule estimate admissible under relevance standard), *review allowed*, 319 Or. 406, 879 P.2d 1284 (1994); State v Futch, 123 Or. App. 176, 860 P.2d 264 (1993) (VNTR product-rule and [apparently] ceiling estimates admissible under relevance standard), *review allowed*, 319 Or. 406, 879 P.2d 1284 (1994)
Pennsylvania	Commonwealth v Crews, 536 Pa. 508, 640 A.2d 395 (1994) (testimony that VNTR match "at three of four loci" made identity "probable" admissible under *Frye* despite objection to lack of frequency estimate)
South Car.	State v Ford, 301 S.C. 485, 392 S.E.2d 781 (1990) (VNTR product-rule estimate admissible under *Frye* and relevance standards)
South Dakota	State v Schweitzer, 533 N.W.2d 156, 160 (S.D. 1995) (VNTR estimate admissible under *Daubert*; method of estimation not specified); State v Wimberly, 467 N.W.2d 499 (S.D. 1991) (VNTR product-rule estimate admissible under *Frye*)
Tennessee	State v Steele, No. 03C01-9207-CR-233, 1993 WL 415836 (Tenn. Ct. Crim. App. Oct. 13, 1993) (VNTR product-rule estimate admissible under *Daubert*); State v Harris, 866 S.W.2d 583 (Tenn. Ct. Crim. App. 1992) (VNTR product-rule estimate admissible under *Frye*, relevance standard, and special statute)
Texas	Campbell v State, 910 S.W.2d 475 (Tex. Crim. App. 1995) (DQA estimate admissible under "reliability" standard); Flores v State, 871 S.W. 2d 714 (Tex. Crim. App. 1993) (VNTR product-rule estimate admissible under relevance standard); Kelly v State, 824 S.W. 2d 568 (Tex. Crim. App. 1992) (same); Fuller v State, 827 S.W. 2d 919 (Tex. Crim. App. 1992) (same); Clarke v State, 839 S.W.2d 92 (Tex. Crim. App. 1991) (DQA product-rule estimate admissible under relevance standard)
Vermont	State v Streich, 658 A.2d 38 (Vt. 1995) (VNTR product-rule estimate, as opposed to a ceiling estimate, inadmissible under *Daubert*)

TABLE 6.1 *Continued*

Virginia	Mickens v Commonwealth, 247 Va. 395, 442 S.E.2d 678 (1994) (VNTR and DQA results admitted at trial but not discussed on appeal); Satcher v Commonwealth, 244 Va. 220, 421 S.E.2d 821 (1992) (VNTR product-rule estimate admissible under special statute); Spencer v Commonwealth, 238 Va. 295, 384 S.E. 2d 785 (1989) (same), *cert. denied*, 493 U.S. 1093 (1990); Spencer v Commonwealth, 240 Va. 78, 393 S.E.2d 609 (1989) (DQA test result admissible under statute), *cert. denied*, 498 U.S. 908 (1990); Va. Code Ann. § 19.2-207.5
Washington	State v Buckner, 125 Wash.2d 915, 890 P.2d 460 (1995) (testimony that VNTR profile with product-rule estimate of 1/19.5 billion inadmissible); State v Gentry, 125 Wash.2d 570, 888 P.2d 1105 (1995) (DQA product-rule estimate admissible under *Frye*); State v Cauthron, 120 Wash. 2d 879, 846 P.2d 502 (1993) (VNTR testimony of a VNTR match said to prove that defendant was the source of the incriminating DNA inadmissible under *Frye* because it was "unsupported by valid probability statistics," but ceiling estimate would be admissible)
West Virginia	State v Satterfield, 193 W.Va.503, 457 S.E.2d 440 (1995) (unspecified DNA test results admitted at trial but not discussed on appeal)
Wisconsin	State v Peters, 192 Wis. 2d 674, 534 N.W. 2d 867 (Ct. App. 1995) (VNTR product-rule and interim-ceiling estimates admissible under relevance standard)
Wyoming	Springfield v State, 860 P.2d 435 (Wyo. 1993) (VNTR ceiling estimate admissible under relevance standard)

TABLE 6.2   Admissibility of Inclusionary DNA Evidence by Jurisdiction, as of June 1995

I[103]	II	III	IV	V	VI	VII	VIII
				Opinion As	Only Fact Of		
	Standard Of		Method Of	To Source	Match	Product	Ceiling
Jurisdiction	Admissibility	DNA Test	Computation	Admissible?	Admissible?	Admissible?	Admissible?
DC Cir		RFLP	Product			Yes	
2d Cir	R	RFLP	Product			Yes	
6th Cir	F	RFLP	Product			Yes	
8th Cir	D	RFLP	Product			Yes	
9th Cir	D	RFLP	Product			Yes	
10th Cir	D	RFLP	?			?	?
Ala	F	RFLP	Product	Yes		Yes	
Ariz	F	RFLP	Product	No	Yes	No	Yes
		RAPD	Ceiling	Yes			
			None				
Ark	R	RFLP	Product			Yes	
Cal	F	RFLP,PCR	Product			Yes-No	Yes-No
			Ceiling			Yes-No	Yes-No
Colo	F,R	RFLP	Product			Yes	Yes
			Ceiling				
Conn	F	RFLP	Product			?	
Del	F,S	RFLP	Product			Yes	
DC	F	RFLP	Product			No	Yes
			Ceiling				
Fla	F	RFLP	Product			Yes	Yes (Dictum)
			Ceiling				
Ga	F	RFLP	?			?	
Haw	R	RFLP	Product			Yes	
Ill	F	RFLP	Product			Yes-No	
Ind	F,S	RFLP PCR	Product			Yes	
Iowa	R	RFLP	Product			Yes	
Kan	F	RFLP	Product				Yes
		DQA	Product				Yes
La	R,S	RFLP	Product			Yes	
Md	S	RFLP	Product			Yes	
Ma	D	RFLP	Product			No	Yes
			Ceiling				
Mich	F	RFLP	Product			Yes	
Minn	F,S	RFLP	Ceiling				Yes
Miss	F	RFLP	None		Yes		
Mo	F	RFLP	Product			Yes	
Mont	D	RFLP PCR	Product			Yes	
Neb	F	RFLP PCR	Product			Yes	
NH	F	RFLP	Product			No	Yes
			Ceiling				
NJ	F	PCR	Product			Yes	
NM	D	RFLP	Product			Yes	Yes
			Ceiling			Yes	Yes
NY	F	RFLP	Product			Yes	

TABLE 6.2 *Continued*

I[103] Jurisdiction	II Standard Of Admissibility	III DNA Test	IV Method Of Computation	V Opinion As To Source Admissible?	VI Only Fact Of Match Admissible?	VII Product Admissible?	VIII Ceiling Admissible?
NC	R	RFLP	Product			Yes	
Ohio	R	RFLP	Product			Yes	
		PCR				Yes	
Okla	D	RFLP	Product			Yes	
Ore	R	RFLP	Product			Yes	
		PCR					Yes
Pa	F	RFLP	None		Yes		
SC	F,R	RFLP	Product			Yes	
SD	F	RFLP	Product			Yes	
Tenn	F,D,R,S	RFLP	Product			Yes	
Tex	R	RFLP	Product			Yes	
		DQA, PCR					
Vt	D	RFLP	Product Ceiling			No	Yes
Va	R,S	RFLP	Product			Yes	
		DQA	Product			Yes	
Wash	F	RFLP	Product	No		No	Yes
		PCR					
Wisc	R	RFLP	Product Ceiling			Yes	Yes
Wyo	R	RFLP	Product Ceiling				Yes

[103] I. Federal or state jurisdiction in which at least one court opinion on the admissibility of DNA test results that incriminated the defendant was reported.

II. *Frye* (F), *Daubert* (D), relevance-helpfulness (R), or special statutory (S) standard applied. R refers to cases applying a non-*Frye* standard adopted before *Daubert*; all federal courts are now required to apply the *Daubert* standard.

III. Type of DNA test performed.

IV. Procedure used to compute probability or frequency offered in the case.

V. Is expert-opinion testimony that defendant is the source or that the type is unique admissible?

VI. Is only the fact of a match admissible?

VII. Is the product-rule estimate admissible?

VIII. Is the interim-ceiling-principle estimate admissible?

Abbreviations

α	Designating a significance-level probability or confidence coefficient; a measure of the uncertainly of a band measure with VNTRs.
θ	A measure of the degree of population subdivision; equivalent to F_{ST}.
χ^2	A measure used to assess statistical significance. From the value of χ^2 and the number of degrees of freedom, the probability of a deviation from the expected value as large as or larger than that observed can be determined.
2p rule	A conservative adjustment for a single VNTR band possibly being from a heterozygote; $2p_i$ replaces p_i^2.
A	Adenine; also used to designate an arbitrary genetic locus.
ABC	American Board of Criminalistics.
AMP-FLP	Amplified fragment length polymorphism.
ANSI/ASQC	American National Standards Institute/American Society for Quality Control.
ASCLD	American Society of Crime Laboratory Directors.
ASCLD-LAB	American Society of Crime Laboratory Directors, Laboratory Accreditation Board.
C	Cytosine, covariance (also Cov).
CAP	College of American Pathologists.
CODIS	The FBI national DNA identification index.
DISJ	A designation of a VNTR. I designates the chromosome; J is a

	numerical indentifier. D1S79 is number 79 on chromosome 1.
DNA	Deoxyribonucleic acid, the genetic material.
DQA	A gene locus associated with HLA and used in forensic analysis; the gene product is called DQα.
FBI	The US Federal Bureau of Investigation.
F_{ST}	Wright's measure of population subdivision; same as θ when mating within subpopulations is random.
G	Guanine.
GYPA	Glycophorin A gene locus.
HBGG	Hemoglobin b gamma globin gene locus.
HLA	Human leukocyte antigen gene locus.
HW	Hardy-Weinberg (proportions).
K562	A human cell line whose DNA sample is used as a standard.
LDLR	Low-density lipoprotein receptor gene locus.
LE	Linkage equilibrium.
LR	Likelihood ratio.
MVR	Minisatellite variant repeat.
NIST	National Institute of Standards and Technology.
PCR	Polymerase chain reaction.
p_i	A symbol used to designate the frequency of the i-th allele; the subscript may be dropped.
PM	Polymarker.
QA	Quality assurance.
QC	Quality control.
RFLP	Restriction fragment length polymorphism.
s or σ	Standard deviation.
STR	Short tandem repeats.
T	Thymine.
TWGDAM	Technical Working Group on DNA Analysis and Methods.
V	Variance (also Var).
VNTR	Variable number of tandem repeats. (These are RFLPs.)

Glossary[1]

Adenine—a purine base; one of the constituents of DNA; abbreviated A.

Allele—one of two or more alternative forms of a gene. In DNA analysis the definition is extended to any DNA region used for analysis.

Amplification—increasing the number of copies of a DNA region, usually by PCR.

Autoradiograph (autoradiogram; autorad)—a photographic recording of the position on an X-ray film where radioactive decay of isotopes has occurred.

Autosome—any chromosome other than the X or Y.

Band—the visual image representing a particular DNA fragment on an autoradiograph.

Band shift—the phenomenon in which DNA fragments in one lane of a gel migrate at a different rate from that of identical fragments in other lanes of the same gel.

Base pair—two complementary nucleotides in double-stranded DNA; these are AT or GC.

Biased—systematically deviating from the true value, as a conservative estimate.

Binning—grouping VNTR alleles into sets of similar sizes, necessary because the individual alleles are too similar to differentiate; two binning processes are fixed and floating bins (see Chapter 5).

Blind proficiency test—a proficiency test in which the laboratory personnel do not know that a test is being conducted.

Blot—see Southern blot.

---

[1]Adapted from NRC (1992).

Chromosome—a physical structure in the cell nucleus, made of DNA, RNA, and proteins. The genes are arranged in linear order along the chromosome.

Ceiling principle—a procedure for setting a minimum profile frequency. One hundred persons from each of 15-20 genetically homogeneous populations spanning the range of racial groups in the United States are sampled. For each allele, the highest frequency among the groups sampled, or 5%, whichever is larger, is used for calculations. (cf. *interim ceiling principle*)

Confidence interval, confidence limits—An interval, based on a sample, that is expected to include the population mean value a specified proportion of the time. $100(1-\alpha)\%$ confidence limits are expected to include the population value $100(1-\alpha)\%$ of the time. Conventional values are 90% ($\alpha = 0.10$), 95%, and 99%.

Conservative—favoring the defendant. A conservative estimate is deliberately chosen to be more favorable to the defendant than the best (unbiased) estimate would be.

Convenience sample—a sample chosen because of availability or similar reason; not a random sample.

Covariance (Cov, C)—for paired numbers, the average of the product of the deviation from its mean of each member of a pair.

Crossing over—the exchange of parts between homologous chromosomes during meiosis; recombination.

Cytosine—a pyrimidine base; one of the constituents of DNA; abbreviated C.

Degradation—the breaking down of DNA by chemical or physical means.

Denaturation—separation of a double stranded DNA into single strands.

Deoxyribonucleic acid (DNA)—the genetic material; a double helix composed of two complementary chains of paired nucleotides.

Diploid—having two sets of chromosomes (cf. *haploid*).

DNA polymerase—the enzyme that catalyzes the synthesis of double-stranded DNA.

DNA probe—see *probe*.

EDTA—a preservative added to blood samples.

Electrophoresis—a technique in which different molecules are separated by their rate of movement in an electric field.

Enzyme—a protein that is capable of speeding up, and therefore facilitating, a specific chemical reaction; a biological catalyst.

Ethidium bromide—a molecule that binds to DNA and fluoresces under ultraviolet light; used to identify DNA.

F statistics—Wright's measures of inbreeding and population structure; in this report population subdivision is measured by F_{ST} or θ.

Gamete—a haploid reproductive cell; sperm or egg.

Gametic equilibrium—see *linkage equilibrium*.

Gel—a semisolid medium used to separate molecules by electrophoresis.

Gene—the basic unit of heredity; a functional sequence of DNA in a chromosome.

Gene frequency—the relative frequency (proportion) of an allele in a population.

Genetic drift—random fluctuation in allele frequencies.

Genome—the total (haploid) genetic makeup of an organism. In the human this comprises 3 billion base pairs.

Genotype—the genetic makeup of an organism, as distinguished from its physical appearance (phenotype); usually designated by allele symbols, e.g., A_1A_2 designates the genotype of an individual with alleles A_1 and A_2. The word may be used to designate any number of loci, from one to the total number.

Guanine—a purine base; one of the consituents of DNA; abbreviated G.

Haploid—having one set of chromosomes, as a gamete (cf. *diploid*).

Hardy-Weinberg proportions—the state, for a genetic locus in a population, in which the alleles making up the genotypes are in random proportions; abbreviated HW.

Heterozygosity—the proportion of a population that is heterozygous for a particular locus.

Heterozygote—a fertilized egg (zygote) with two different alleles at a designated locus; by extension, the individual that develops from such a zygote.

Heterozygous—having different alleles at a particular locus (cf. *homozygous*).

Homologous—corresponding; used to describe the relationship between two members of a chromosome or gene pair.

Homozygote—a fertilized egg (zygote) with two identical alleles at a designated locus; by extension, the individual that develops from such a zygote.

Homozygous—having the same allele at a particular locus (cf. *heterozygous*).

Hybridization—the pairing of complementary single strands of DNA.

Inbreeding coefficient—the probability that two homologous genes in an individual are descended from the same gene in an ancestor; a measure of the proportion by which the heterozygosity is reduced by inbreeding; designated by F.

Interim ceiling principle—For each allele, the highest frequency (adjusted upward for statistical uncertainty) found in any racial group, or 10%, whichever is higher, is used in product-rule calculations. (cf. *ceiling principle*)

Isotope—an alternative form of a chemical element; used particularly in reference to radioactive forms, or radioisotopes.

Kilobase (kb)—1,000 bases.

Kinship coefficient—the probability that two randomly chosen genes, one from each of two individuals in a population, are identical (i.e. both descended from the same ancestral gene, or one from the other); equivalent to the inbreeding coefficient of a (perhaps hypothetical) offspring; designated by F.

Linkage—inheritance together of two or more genes on the same chromosome.

Linkage equilibrium—the state in which two or more loci in a gamete are in random proportions (i.e., the gamete frequency is the product of the allele frequencies; abbreviated LE).

Locus (pl. loci)—the physical location of a gene on a chromosome.

Marker—an easily detected gene or chromosome region used for identification.

Match—Two DNA profiles are declared to match when they are indistinguishable in genetic type. For loci with discrete alleles, two samples match when they display the same set of alleles. For VNTRs, two samples match when the pattern of the bands are similar and the positions of the corresponding bands at each locus fall within a preset distance.

Meiosis—the two cell divisions that occur in the development of a sperm or egg, during which the chromosome number is halved.

Membrane—the matrix (usually nylon) to which DNA is transferred from a gel during Southern blotting.

Nucleic acid—DNA or RNA.

Nucleotide—a unit of nucleic acid composed of phosphate, a sugar, and a purine or pyrimidine base.

Phenotype—the manifestation of the genotype; it may be externally visible, as eye color, or observed by a special technique, as blood groups or enzymes.

Polymerase chain reaction—an in vitro process for making many copies of a fragment of DNA; abbreviated PCR.

Polymorphism—the presence of more than one allele at a locus in a population; in forensic loci, the most common allele usually has a frequency less than 0.6.

Probe—a short segment of single-stranded DNA, labeled with a radioactive or chemical tag, that is used to detect the presence of a particular DNA sequence through hybridization to its complementary sequence.

Proficiency test—a test to evaluate the quality of performance of a laboratory.

Purine—the larger of the two kinds of bases found in DNA and RNA; A and G are purines.

Pyrimidine—the smaller of the two kinds of bases found in DNA and RNA; C and T are pyrimidines.

Quality assurance—a program conducted by a laboratory to ensure accuracy and reliability of tests performed; abbreviated QA.

Quality audit—a systematic and independent examination and evaluation of a laboratory's operations.

Quality control—activities used to monitor the quality of DNA typing to satisfy specified criteria; abbreviated QC.

Random match—A match in the DNA profiles of two samples of DNA, where one is drawn at random from the population.

Random-match probability—The chance of a random match. As used in this report, it is the probability that the DNA in a random sample from the population has the same profile as the DNA in the evidence sample.

Random sample—a sample chosen so that each sample of the population has a known chance of being represented. In a simple random sample each member has an equal chance of being represented.

Rebinning—grouping adjacent bins whose absolute number in the data base is fewer than five.

Replication—the synthesis of new DNA from existing DNA.

Restriction enzyme, restriction endonuclease—an enzyme that cuts a DNA molecule at a specified short base sequence.

Restriction fragment length polymorphism—variation in the length of a stretch of DNA; abbreviated RFLP.

Ribonucleic acid—a class of nucleic acid; it is synthesized from DNA and is part of the process of translating a DNA sequence into a phenotype; abbreviated RNA.

Sex chromosomes—the X and Y chromosomes.

Short tandem repeat—a tandem repeat in which the repeat units are three, four, or five base pairs; abbreviated STR.

Significant, statistically significant—two values are significantly different if the probability of obtaining a difference as large as or larger than that found is less than α when the true difference is zero. Conventionally, α is taken as 0.05, although other values, such as 0.01, are also used.

Somatic cells—cells other than those in the cellular ancestry of egg and sperm.

Southern blotting—the technique for transferring DNA fragments that have been separated by electrophoresis from the gel to a nylon membrane.

Standard deviation—the square root of the variance; abbreviated s or σ.

Tandem repeat—multiple copies of an identical DNA sequence arranged in direct succession in a particular region of the chromosome.

Thymine—a pyrimidine base; one of the constituents of DNA; abbreviated T.

Variable number of tandem repeats—repeating units of a DNA sequence; a class of RFLPs; abbreviated VNTR.

Variance (Var,V)—for a series of numbers, the average of the squared deviation of each number from the mean.

Zygote—the diploid cell resulting from the fusion of egg and sperm.

Biographical Information

COMMITTEE CHAIR

James F. Crow is Professor Emeritus of Genetics at the University of Wisconsin. He holds a PhD degree from the University of Texas. His research has been in *Drosophila* genetics and population genetics. He has been President of the Genetics Society of American and of the American Society of Human Genetics. Dr Crow has served as Chairman of the Genetics Study Section and the Mammalian Genetics Study Section of the National Institute of Health. He is a member of the National Academy of Sciences, the American Philosophical Society, and the American Academy of Arts and Sciences, and is a foreign member of the Japan Academy.

COMMITTEE MEMBERS

Margaret A. Berger is a Professor of Law at Brooklyn Law School, who teaches Evidence, Civil Procedure and a number of related courses. In addition to numerous articles, she is the co-author of *Weinstein's Evidence* (Matthew Bender) and of *Cases and Materials on Evidence* (Foundation Press). On behalf of the Carnegie Commission on Science, Technology and Government, she submitted an amicus curiae brief in Daubert v Merrill Dow Pharmaceuticals Inc, the recent Supreme Court case on the admissibility of scientific evidence. She also wrote the Evidentiary Framework chapter for *the Federal Judicial Center's Reference Manual on Scientific Evidence*. She currently serves as the Reporter to the Advisory Committee on the Federal Rules of Evidence. She received her

AB magna cum laude from Radcliffe College and her JD from the Columbia University School of Law.

Shari S. Diamond is Professor of Psychology and Criminal Justice at the University of Illinois at Chicago and Senior Research Fellow at the American Bar Foundation. She holds a PhD degree in social psychology from Northwestern University and a JD from the University of Chicago. Her research involves judicial and jury decision making and interactions between science and law. She has been President of the American Psychology-Law Society and has served as Editor of the Law & Society Review. She has been a member of the Law and Social Sciences Panel of the National Science Foundation and the National Academy of Sciences Committee on Law and Justice. She is a fellow of the American Psychological Association and the American Psychological Society.

David H. Kaye is Regents' Professor of Law at Arizona State University and was Director of the university's Center for the Study of Law, Science and Technology. He holds a JD from the Yale Law School and received degrees in astronomy and physics from Harvard University and MIT. He practiced law with a private law firm and served on the Watergate Special Prosecution Force. Professor Kaye writes extensively on scientific and statistical evidence. His work has appeared in treatises, books, and journals of law, statistics, psychology, medicine, and genetics. He has served as editor or an editorial board member of six journals. He is a member of the American Association for the Advancement of Science and the American Statistical Association.

Haig H. Kazazian, Jr is the Chairman of the Department of Genetics and Seymour Gray Professor of Molecular Medicine in Genetics at the University of Pennsylvania School of Medicine. He received his MD from The Johns Hopkins University School of Medicine. His research has concentrated on mutation analysis in genetic disease, notably hemoglobin disorders and hemophilia, and on the biology of human transposable elements. He has also had a long interest in DNA diagnosis of genetic disease. Dr Kazazian has served on numerous NIH committees and editorial boards and is the founding coeditor of the journal *Human Mutation*. He is a member of the Institute of Medicine of the National Academy of Sciences, Association of American Physicians, American Society of Clinical Investigation, American Pediatric Society, and the American Society of Human Genetics.

Arno G. Motulsky is Professor Emeritus (active) of Medicine and Genetics at the University of Washington, Seattle, Washington. He obtained his MD degree at the University of Illinois in 1947, and trained in internal medicine and medical genetics. He was President of the American Society of Human Genetics, and editor of the *American Journal of Human Genetics*. He serves on multiple editorial boards, including the *Proceedings of the National Academy of Sciences*. Dr Motulsky is a member of the National Academy of Sciences, the Institute of Medicine, and the American Academy of Arts and Sciences. In the 1970s he participated in the NRC committee on genetic screening and in the 1980s he served on the President's Commission for the Study of Ethical Problems in Medicine and Biomedical and Behavioral Research. He has received a variety of awards for his work. Dr. Motulsky has authored over 300 scientific publications, is coauthor of an influential textbook in his field, and has trained many medical geneticists.

Thomas Nagylaki is Professor of Ecology and Evolution and of Genetics at the University of Chicago. He holds a PhD in theoretical physics from the California Institute of Technology. His research is in theoretical population genetics, especially geographical variation, natural selection, random genetic drift, and gene conversion in multigene families. He has been a member of the editorial board of the *SIAM Journal on Applied Mathematics* and an associate editor of *Theoretical Population Biology* and is an editor of the *Journal of Mathematical Biology*.

Masatoshi Nei is Evan Pugh Professor of Biology and the Director of the Institute of Molecular Evolutionary Genetics at The Pennsylvania State University. He received his PhD from Kyoto University, Japan, in Quantitative Genetics. He is a theoretical population geneticist, and his career has been almost entirely devoted to understanding the cause and mechanism of evolution and developing statistical methods for analyzing and interpreting data on molecular evolution and population genetics. Dr Nei has served on numerous national and international committees and editorial boards and is the founding coeditor of the journal *Molecular Evolution and Biology*. He has been a Council Member and the President of the Society of Molecular Biology and Evolution. He is a Fellow of the American Academy of Arts and Sciences and an Honorary Member of the Genetics Society of Japan.

George F. Sensabaugh, Jr is Professor of Forensic Science and Biomedical Sciences in the School of Public Health, University of California, Berkeley. He received his doctorate in Criminology from the University of California, Berkeley, and did post-doctoral research at the University of California, San Diego, and the National Institute for Medical Research, London, England. His research interests include applications of DNA technology in forensic science and epidemiology. He serves on the editorial boards of the *Journal of Forensic Sciences*, *Science and Justice*, and *Forensic Science Reviews*. His professional memberships include the American Association for the Advancement of Science, the American Society of Human Genetics, the American Academy of Forensic Sciences, the International Society for Forensic Hemogenetics, and the American Chemical Society. He was a member of the National Research Council Committee on DNA Technology in Forensic Science.

David Siegmund earned his PhD in Mathematical Statistics from Columbia University in 1966. Since then he has taught at Columbia and at Stanford University, where he is currently Professor of Statistics and Associate Dean for the Natural Sciences. He has also been a visiting faculty member at the Hebrew University, the University of Zurich, the University of Heidelberg and Oxford

University. His research interests include sequential statistical analysis and statistical genetics. He is a Fellow and past President of the Institute of Mathematical Statistics and is a Member of the American Academy of Arts and Sciences.

Stephen M. Stigler is the Ernest DeWitt Burton Distinguished Service Professor of Statistics and member of the Committee on the Conceptual Foundations of Science at the University of Chicago. He received his PhD in statistics from the University of California at Berkeley. His research has included work in mathematical statistics, the application of statistics in the social and behavioral sciences, and the history of statistics and its applications, including in biological science. He is a member of the American Academy of Arts and Sciences and several professional societies; he has edited the *Journal of the American Statistical Association* and is Chairman of the Board of Trustees of the Center for Advanced Study in the Behavioral Sciences.

COMMITTEE ADVISOR

Victor A. McKusick is University Professor of Medical Genetics at Johns Hopkins. He received his MD from the Johns Hopkins University School of Medicine. Dr McKusick is the founding coeditor of the international journal *GENOMICS* and served as founding president of the Human Genome Organisation (HUGO). Dr. McKusick is a member of the National Academy of Sciences and served as a member of the Academy's Committee on Mapping and Sequencing the Human Genome and chair of its Committee on DNA Technology in Forensic Science. He also belongs to the American Society for Clinical Investigation, Association of American Physicians, American Philosophical Society, American Academy of Arts and Sciences, Royal College of Physicians (London), and Académie Nationale de Médecine (France).

STAFF

Eric A. Fischer is Director of the Board on Biology and the Institute of Laboratory Animal Resources at the National Research Council. He received his PhD in zoology from the University of California at Berkeley. Before coming to the National Research Council, he served on the faculty in psychology at the University of Washington in Seattle, worked on science policy for the US Senate Budget Committee as a AAAS Congressional Science Fellow, was Deputy Director of the Smithsonian Tropical Research Institute in Panama, and was Senior Vice President for Science and Sanctuaries at the National Audubon Society. His major scientific research interest is the evolutionary ecology of life history patterns.

Lee R. Paulson is Program Director for Information Systems and Statistics for the Board on Environmental Studies and Toxicology at the National Research Council and Associate with the Report Review Committee of the National Academy of Sciences. Before that, she was a research associate with the Committee on National Statistics. Her primary interest is in information technology and environmental applications.

Miron L. Straf is the Director of the Research Council's Committee on National Statistics. He holds a PhD degree in Statistics from the University of Chicago. He has served on the faculties of the University of California, Berkeley, and the London School of Economics and Political Science. His research interests include the use of statistics in law and for public policy.

John R. Tucker has been Director of the Board on Mathematical Sciences at the National Research Council since June 1994. He earned a BA in Mathematics from Washington College, an MPhil in mathematics and a PhD in mathematics from the George Washington University. He has been a researcher at Chi Associates Inc, an assistant professor at Virginia Commonwealth University and Mary Washington College, and, from 1989 to 1994, program officer and senior program officer at the NRC. His interests include nonlinear dynamics, order and disorder, and mathematics and statistics applications, particularly to biology and medicine.

Paulette A. Adams is Administrative Assistant to the Board on Biology. She is a graduate of Thames Valley University, London, England. Before joining the National Research Council she worked for several years in the British Civil Service, and for two years at the University of Houston College of Optometry. She is a member of the Institute of Qualified Private Secretaries, London, England.

Acknowledgments

During the course of its deliberations, the committee requested and received input from experts worldwide. The panel expresses its appreciation for the more than 50 written comments it received. The panel also acknowledges with appreciation presentations and input from the following persons:

Ivan Balazs, Lifecodes Corporation, Stamford, Connecticut.
Ranajit Chakraborty, University of Texas Graduate School of Medical Science, Houston.
Howard C. Coleman, GeneLex Corporation, Seattle, Washington.
Robin Cotton, Cellmark Diagnostics, Germantown, Maryland.
Harold A. Deadman, US Department of Justice, Washington, DC.
Peter Donnelly, University of Chicago, Illinois.
George T. Duncan, Broward Sheriff's Office, Ft Lauderdale, Florida.
Debra Endean, American Association of Blood Banks, Milwaukee, Wisconsin.
Peter Gill, The Forensic Science Service, Birmingham, United Kingdom.
John W. Hicks, Alabama Department of Forensic Sciences, Birmingham, Alabama.
Keith Inman, California Association of Criminalists, Oakland, California.
Jonathan J. Koehler, The University of Texas at Austin.
Kenneth C. Konzak, Bureau of Forensic Science, Berkeley, California.
CC Li, University of Pittsburgh, Pennsylvania.
Frederick R. Millar Jr, Office of California Attorney General, San Diego.
Laurence D. Mueller, University of California, Irvine.
David Reiser, Public Defender Service for the District of Columbia.

Patricia A. Riley, US Department of Justice, Washington, DC.
Kathryn Roeder, Carnegie Mellon University, Pittsburgh, Pennsylvania.
Richard L. Tanton, Palm Beach Sheriff's Crime Laboratory, West Palm Beach, Florida.
Elizabeth Thompson, University of Washington, Seattle.
Victor W. Weedn, Armed Forces Institute of Pathology, Rockville, Maryland.
David J. Werrett, The Forensic Science Service, Birmingham, United Kingdom.

Special thanks are due to Paul Ferrara of the Division of Forensic Sciences of the State of Virginia, and to Neal Risch of the Stanford University School of Medicine, who served as consultants to the committee and reviewed an earlier version of the report. The committee also wishes to thank the following people for their help and advice:

David Balding, University of London, United Kingdom.
Vivian Chang, Arizona State University College of Law, Tempe.
Angela Chen, Pomona College, Claremont, California.
Carter Denniston, University of Wisconsin, Madison.
Martin Kreitman, University of Chicago, Illinois.
Harvey Motulsky, New York City, New York.
Joseph Peterson, Department of Criminal Justice, Chicago, Illinois.
William Thompson, University of California, Irvine.
Bruce Weir, North Carolina State University, Raleigh.
Sandy Zabell, Northwestern University, Evanston, Illinois.

References[2]

AABB. 1994. Standards for parentage testing laboratories. Bethesda, MD: Am Assoc Blood Banks.

Aickin M, Kaye D. 1983. Some mathematical and legal considerations in using serological tests to prove paternity. In: Walker RH, editor. Inclusion probabilities in parentage testing. Arlington, VA: Am Assoc Blood Banks. p 155-168.

Aitken CGG. 1995. Statistics and the Evaluation of Evidence for Forensic Scientists. Chichester, England: J Wiley.

Aitken CGG, Stoney DA, editors. 1991. The use of statistics in forensic science. New York: Ellis Harwood.

Aldous DJ. 1989. Probability approximations via the Poisson clumping heuristic. New York: Springer-Verlag.

Allen R, Balding D, Donnelly P, Friedman R, Kaye D, LaRue L, Park R, Robertson B, Stein A. 1995. Probability and proof in State v Skipper: an internet exchange. Jurimetrics J 35: 277-310.

Anonymous. 1892. Review of "Finger Prints" by Francis Galton. The Athenaeum, December 24, p 893.

Annotation. 1984. Right of accused in state courts to have expert inspect, examine or test physical evidence in possession of prosecution. Modern cases. ALR 4th 27: 1188-1255.

ANSI/ASQC A3-1978. Quality systems terminology. Milwaukee: Am Soc Qual Control.

---

[2]For an extensive list of relevant literature, see Weir (1995).

Armour JAL, Jeffreys AJ. 1992. Biology and applications of human minisatellite loci. Curr Opinion Genet Dev 2: 850-856.

ASCLD. 1987. Guidelines for forensic laboratory management practices. Crime Lab Dig. 14: 39-46.

Balazs, I. 1993. Population genetics of 14 ethnic groups using phenotypic data from VNTR loci. In: Pena SDJ, Chakraborty R, Epplen JT, Jeffreys AJ, editors. DNA fingerprinting: state of the science. Basel, Switzerland: Birkhäuser Verlag. p 193-210.

Balazs I, Baird M, Clyne M, Meade E. 1989. Human population genetic studies of five hypervariable DNA loci. Am J Hum Genet 44: 182-190

Balding DJ, Donnelly P. 1994a. How convincing is DNA evidence? Nature 368: 285-286.

Balding DJ, Donnelly P. 1994b. The prosecutor's fallacy and DNA evidence. Crim Law Rev 1994: 711-721.

Balding DJ, Donnelly P. 1995. Inference in forensic identification. J Roy Stat Soc Ser A 158: 21-53.

Balding DJ, Donnelly P, Nichols RA. 1994. Comment: some causes for concern about DNA profiles. Stat Sci 9: 248-251.

Balding DJ, Nichols RA. 1994. DNA profile match probability calculations: how to allow for population stratification, relatedness, database selection and single bands. Forensic Sci Int 64: 125-140.

Balding DJ, Nichols RA. 1995. A method for quantifying differentiation between populations at multi-allelic loci and its implications for investigating identity and paternity. In: Weir B, editor. Human identification: the use of DNA markers. Dordrecht, Netherlands: Kluwer Acad. p 3-12.

Ballantyne J, Sensabaugh G, Witkowski J. 1989. Banbury Report 32: DNA technology and forensic science. New York: Cold Spring Harbor Lab Pr.

Bar-Hillel M. 1980. The base-rate fallacy in probability judgements. Acta Psychologica 44: 211-233.

Barnes WM. 1994. PCR amplification of up to 35-kb DNA with high fidelity and high yield from λ bacteriophage templates. Proc Natl Acad Sci USA 91: 2216-2220.

Berger M. 1994. Evidentiary framework. In: Reference manual on scientific evidence. Washington DC: Federal Judicial Center. p 37-117.

Berry D. 1991a. Inferences using DNA profiling in forensic identification and paternity cases. Stat Sci 6: 175-205.

Berry D. 1991b. Rejoinder. Stat Sci 6: 202-205.

Berry DA, Evett IW, Pinchin R. 1992. Statistical inference in crime investigations using desoxyribonucleic acid profiling (with discussion). J Roy Stat Soc Ser C 41: 499-531.

Beyth-Marom R, Fischhoff B. 1983. Diagnosticity and pseudodiagnosticity. J Pers Soc Psychol 45: 1185-1195.

Bever RA, Creacy S. 1995. Validation and utilization of commercially available

STR multiplexes for parentage analysis. In: Fifth international symposium on human identification 1994: proceedings. Madison, WI: Promega. p 61-68.

Blake E, Mihalovich J, Higuchi R, Walsh PS, Erlich H. 1992. Polymerase chain reaction (PCR) amplification and human leukocyte antigen (HLA)-DQα oligonucleotide typing on biological evidence samples: casework experience. J Forensic Sci 37: 700-726.

Brace CL. 1995. Region does not mean "race"—reality versus convention in forensic anthropology. J Forensic Sci 40: 171-175.

Brenner C, Morris JW. 1990. Paternity index calculations in single locus hypervariable DNA probes: validation and other studies. In: International symposium on human identification 1989: proceedings. Madison, WI: Promega. p 21-53.

Buckleton J, Walsh KJ, Triggs CM. 1991. A continuous model for interpreting the positions of bands in DNA locus-specific work. J Forensic Sci Soc 31: 353-363.

Budowle B, Baechtel FS, Adams DE. 1991. Validation with regard to environmental insults of the RFLP procedure for forensic purposes. In: Farley MA, Harrington JJ, editors. Forensic DNA technology. Chelsea, MI: Lewis. p 83-91.

Budowle B, Baechtel FS, Giusti AM, Monson KL. 1990. Data for forensic matching criteria for VNTR profiles. In: International symposium on human identification 1989: proceedings. Madison, WI: Promega. p 103-115.

Budowle B, Baechtel FS, Smerick JB, Presley KW, Giusti AM, Parsons G, Alevy MC, Chakraborty R. 1995. D1S80 population data in African Americans, Caucasians, southeastern Hispanics, southwestern Hispanics, and Orientals. J Forensic Sci 40: 38-44.

Budowle B, Giusti AM, Waye JS, Baechtel FS, Fourney RM, Adams DE, Presley LA, Deadman HA, Monson KL. 1991. Fixed-bin analysis for statistical evaluation of continuous distributions of allelic data from VNTR loci for use in forensic comparisons. Am J Hum Genet 48: 841-855.

Budowle B, Lindsey JA, DeCou JA, Koons BW, Giusti SM, Comey CT. 1995. Validation and population studies of the loci LDLR, GYPA, HBGG, D7S8, and Gc (PM loci), and HLA-DQα using a multiplex amplification and typing procedure. J Forensic Sci 40: 45-54.

Budowle B, Monson KL, Anoe K, Baechtel K, Bergman D. 1991. A preliminary report on binned general population data on six VNTR loci in Caucasians, Blacks and Hispanics from the United States. Crime Lab Dig 18: 9-26.

Budowle B, Monson KL, Giusti AM. 1994. A reassessment of frequency estimates of PvUII-generated VNTR profiles in a Finnish, an Italian and a general US Caucasian database: no evidence for ethnic subgroups affecting forensic estimates. Am J Hum Genet 55:533-539.

Budowle B, Monson KL, Giusti AM, Brown BL. 1994a. The assessment of frequency estimates of Hae III-generated VNTR profiles in various reference databases. J Forensic Sci 39: 319-52.

Budowle B, Monson KL, Giusti AM, Brown BL. 1994b. Evaluation of Hinf I-generated VNTR profile frequencies determined using various ethnic databases. J Forensic Sci 39: 988-1008.

Cavalli-Sforza LL, Menozzi P, Piazza A. 1994. The history and geography of human genes. Princeton, NJ. Princeton Univ Pr.

Cecil JS, Willging TE. 1994. Court appointed experts. In: Reference manual on scientific evidence. Washington, DC: Federal Judicial Center. p 525-573.

Chakraborty R 1991. Statistical interpretation of DNA typing data. Am J Hum Genet 49: 895-897.

Chakraborty R. 1992. Sample size requirements for addressing the population genetic issues of forensic use of DNA typing. Hum Biol 64: 141-159.

Chakraborty R 1993. Analysis of genetic structure of populations: meaning, methods, and implications. In: Majumder PP, editor. Human population genetics: a centennial tribute for JBS Haldane. New York: Plenum. p 189-206.

Chakraborty R, Danker-Hopfe H. 1991. Analysis of population structure: a comparative study of different estimators of Wright's fixation indices. In: Rao CR, Chakraborty R, editors. Handbook of statistics 8: statistical methods in biological and medical sciences. Amsterdam, Netherlands: North-Holland. p 203-254.

Chakraborty R, de Andrade M, Daiger SP, Budowle B. 1992. Apparent heterozygote deficiencies observed in DNA typing data and their implications in forensic applications. Ann Hum Genet 56: 45-57.

Chakraborty R, Jin L, Zhong Y, Deka R. 1995. Intra- and Inter-population variation at VNTR, short tandem repeat and polymarker loci and their implications in forensic and paternity analysis. In: Fifth international symposium on human identification 1994: proceedings. Madison, WI: Promega. p 29-41.

Chakraborty R, Jin L, Zhong Y, Srinivasan M, Budowle B. 1993. On allele frequency computation from DNA typing data. Int J Legal Med 106: 103-106.

Chakraborty R, Kidd KK. 1991. The utility of DNA typing in forensic work. Science 254: 1735-1739.

Chakraborty R, Srinivasan MR, Daiger SF. 1993. Evaluation of standard error and confidence interval of estimated multilocus genotype probabilities and their implications in DNA forensics. Am J Hum Genet 52: 60-70.

Cockerham CC. 1969. Variance of gene frequencies. Evolution 23: 72-84.

Cockerham CC. 1973. Analysis of gene frequencies. Genetics 74: 679-700.

Cohen J. 1990. DNA fingerprinting for forensic identification: potential effects on data interpretation of subpopulation heterogeneity and band number variability. Am J Hum Genet 46: 358-368.

Cohen J. 1992. The ceiling principle is not always conservative in assigning genotype frequencies for forensic DNA testing. Am J Hum Genet 51: 1165-1168.

Collins A, Morton NE. 1994. Likelihood ratios for DNA identification. Proc Natl Acad Sci USA 91: 6007-6011.

Comey CT, Budowle B, Adams DE, Baumstark AL, Lindsey JA, Presley LA. 1993. PCR amplification and typing of the HLA DQα gene in forensic samples. J Forensic Sci 38: 239-249.

Cosso S, Reynolds R. 1995. Validation of the AmpliFLP™ D1S80 PCR amplification kit for forensic casework analysis according to TWGDAM guidelines. J Forensic Sci 40: 424-434.

Cox DR, Snell EJ. 1989. Analysis of binary data. New York: Chapman and Hall.

Crow JF, Denniston C. 1993. Population genetics as it relates to human identification. In: Fourth international symposium on human identification 1993: proceedings. Madison, WI: Promega. p 31-6.

Developments. 1995. Confronting the new challenges of scientific evidence. Harvard Law Rev 108: 1481-1605.

Devlin B, Krontiris T, Risch N. 1993. Population genetics of the HRAS1 minisatellite locus. Am J Hum Genet 53: 1298-1305.

Devlin B, Risch N. 1992. Ethnic differentiation at VNTR loci, with special reference to forensic applications. Am J Hum Genet 51: 534-548.

Devlin B, Risch N, Roeder K. 1990. No excess of homozygosity at loci used for DNA fingerprinting. Science 249: 1416-1420.

Devlin B, Risch N, Roeder K. 1992. Forensic inference from DNA fingerprints. J Am Stat Assoc 87: 337-350.

Devlin B, Risch N, Roeder K. 1993. Statistical evaluation of DNA fingerprinting: a critique of the NRC's report. Science 259: 748-749, 837.

Devlin B, Risch N, Roeder K. 1994. Comments on the statistical aspects of the NRC's report on DNA typing. J Forensic Sci 39: 28-40.

Diamond SS. 1994. Reference guide on survey research. In: Reference manual on scientific evidence. Washington DC: Federal Judicial Center. p 221-271.

Edwards A, Hammond HA, Jin L, Caskey CT, and Chakraborty R. 1992. Genetic variation at five trimeric and tetrameric tandem repeat loci in four human population groups. Genomics 12: 241-253.

Edwards W, von Winterfeldt D. 1986. Cognitive illusions and their implications for the law. S Cal Law Rev 59: 225-276.

Ellman I, Kaye D. 1979. Probabilities and proof: Can hla and blood group testing prove paternity? NYU Law Rev 54: 1131-1162.

Evett IW. 1991. Comment. Stat Sci 6: 200-201.

Evett IW. 1992. Evaluating DNA profiles in the case where the defense is it was my brother. J Forensic Sci Soc 32: 5-14.

Evett IW, Buffery C, Willott G, Stoney D. 1991. A guide to interpreting single locus profiles of DNA mixtures in forensic cases. J Forensic Sci Soc 31: 41-47.

Evett IW, Gill PD, Scranage JK, Weir BS. 1996. Establishing the robustness of short-tandem-repeat statistics for forensic applications. Am J Hum Genet 58: 398-407.

Evett IW, Pinchin R. 1991. DNA single locus profiles: tests for the robustness of statistical procedures within the context of forensic science. Int J Legal Med 104: 267-272.

Evett IW, Scranage J, Pinchin R. 1992. An efficient statistical procedure for interpreting DNA single locus profiling data in crime cases. J Forensic Sci Soc 32: 307-326.

Evett IW, Scranage J, Pinchin R. 1993. An illustration of the advantages of efficient statistical methods for RFLP analysis in forensic science. Am J Hum Genet 52: 498-505.

Faigman DL, Baglioni AJ. 1988. Bayes' theorem in the trial process: instructing jurors on the value of statistical evidence. Law Hum Behav 12: 1-17.

FBI. 1990. Procedures for the detection of restriction fragment length polymorphisms in human DNA. mimeographed. 31 p.

FBI. 1993a. The application of forensic DNA testing to solve violent crimes. Washington, DC: US Dept Justice.

FBI. 1993b. VNTR population data: a worldwide survey. 5 vol. Quantico, VA: FBI Academy.

Federal Judicial Center. 1994. Reference manual on scientific evidence. Washington, DC: Federal Judicial Center.

Fienberg SE, editor. 1989. The evolving role of statistical assessments as evidence in the courts. New York: Springer-Verlag.

Fienberg SE. 1992. Comment: the increasing sophistication of statistical assessments as evidence in discrimination litigation. J Am Stat Assoc 77: 784-787.

Finkelstein MO, Fairley WB. 1970. A Bayesian approach to identification evidence. Harvard Law Rev 83: 489-517.

Finkelstein MO, Levin B. 1990. Statistics for lawyers. New York: Springer-Verlag.

Fisher, RA. 1951. Standard calculations for evaluating a blood group system. Heredity 5:95-102.

Fong G, Krantz D, Nisbett R. 1986. The effects of statistical training on thinking about everyday problems. Cog Psychol 18:253-292.

Galton F. 1892. Finger prints. London: Macmillan.

Geisser S, Johnson W. 1992. Testing Hardy-Weinberg equilibrium on allelic data from VNTR loci. Am J Hum Genet 51: 1084-1088.

Geisser S, Johnson W. 1993. Testing independence of fragment lengths within VNTR Loci. Am J Hum Genet 53: 1103-1106.

Giannelli PC. 1991. Criminal discovery, scientific evidence, and DNA. Vanderbilt Law Rev 44: 791-825

Giannelli P, Imwinkelried EJ. 1993. Scientific evidence. 2nd ed. Charlottesville, VA: Michie.

Gill P, Evett I. 1995. Population genetics of short tandem repeat (STR) loci. In: Weir B, editor. Human identification: the use of DNA markers. Dordrecht, Netherlands: Kluwer Acad. p 69-87.

Goodman J. 1992. Jurors' comprehension and assessment of probabilistic evidence. Am J Trial Advoc 16: 361-389.

Haldane JBS. 1949. The association of characters as a result of inbreeding and linkage. Ann Eugen 15: 15-23.

Hammond HA, Jin L, Zhong Y, Caskey CT, Chakraborty R. 1994. Evaluation of 13 short tandem repeat loci for use in personal identification applications. Am J Hum Genet 55: 175-89.

Harris DA. 1992. The constitution and truth seeking: a new theory on expert services for indigent defendants. J Crim Law Criminol 83: 469-525.

Hartl DL, Clark AG. 1989. Principles of population genetics. 2nd ed. Sunderland, MA: Sinauer.

Hartmann J, Keister R, Houlihan B, Thompson L, Baldwin R, Buse E, Driver B, Kuo M. 1994. Diversity of ethnic and racial VNTR RFLP fixed-bin frequency distributions. Am J Hum Genet 55: 1268-1278.

Helmuth R, Fildes N, Blake E, Luce MC, Chimera J, Gorodezky C, Stoneking M, Schmill N, Klitz W, Higuchi RM, Erlich HA. 1990. HLA-DQα allele and genotype frequencies in various human populations, determined by using enzymatic amplification and oligonucleotide probes. Am J Hum Genet 47:515-523.

Herrin G Jr. 1993. Probability of matching RFLP patterns from unrelated individuals. Am J Hum Genet 52: 491-497.

Herrin G, Fildes N, Reynolds R. 1994. Evaluation of the Amplitype® PM DNA test system on forensic case samples. J Forensic Sci 39: 1247-1253.

Hogarth RM, Reder MW, editors. 1987. Behavioral foundations of economic theory. Chicago, IL: Univ Chicago Pr.

Huang NE, Budowle B. 1995. Fixed bin population data for the VNTR loci D1S7, D2S44, D4S139, D5S110, and D17S79 in Chinese from Taiwan. J Forensic Sci 40: 287-290.

Imwinkelried EJ. 1990. The applicability of the attorney-client privilege to non-testifying experts: reestablishing the boundaries between the attorney-client privilege and the work product protection. Wash Univ Law Quart 68: 19-50.

Jacoby J, Handlin AH. 1991. Non-probability sampling designs for litigation surveys. Trademark Rep 81: 169-179.

Jakubaitis JL. 1991. Note, "genetically" altered admissibility: legislative notice of DNA typing. Clev St Law Rev 39: 415.

James G, James RC. 1959. Mathematics dictionary. Princeton, NJ: Van Nostrand.

Jeffreys AJ, MacLeod A, Tamaki K, Neil D, Monckton D. 1991. Minisatellite repeat coding as a digital approach to DNA typing. Nature 354: 204-209.

Jeffreys AJ, Pena DJ. 1993. Brief introduction to human DNA fingerprinting. In: Pena DJ, Chakraborty R, Eppelen JT, Jeffreys AJ. DNA fingerprints: state of the science. Basel, Switzerland: Birkhäuser Verlag. p 1-20.

Jonakait R. 1991. Forensic science: the need for regulation. Harvard J Law Technol 4:109-191.

Kahneman D, Slovic P, Tversky A. 1982. Judgement under uncertainty: heuristics and biases. Cambridge, England: Cambridge Univ Pr.

Kass R, Raftery A. 1995. Bayes factors. J Am Stat Assoc 90: 773-795.

Kaye DH. 1988a. Introduction: What is Bayesianism? In: Tillers P, Green EC, editors. Probability and inference in the law of evidence. the uses and limits of Bayesianism. Dordrecht, Netherlands: Kluwer Acad. p 1-19.

Kaye DH. 1988b. Plemel as a primer on proving paternity. Willamette Law J 24: 867-883.

Kaye DH. 1989. The probability of an ultimate issue: the strange cases of paternity testing. Iowa Law Rev 75: 75-109.

Kaye DH. 1990a. Improving legal statistics. Law Soc Rev 24: 1255-1275.

Kaye DH. 1990b. DNA paternity probabilities. Family Law Quart 24: 279-304.

Kaye DH. 1990c. Presumptions, probability and paternity. Jurimetrics J 30: 323-349.

Kaye DH. 1991. The admissibility of DNA testing. Cardozo Law Rev 13: 353-360.

Kaye DH. 1993. DNA evidence: probability, population genetics, and the courts. Harvard J Law Technol 7: 101-172.

Kaye DH. 1995a. The forensic debut of the NRC's DNA report: population structure, ceiling frequencies and the need for numbers. Genetica 96:99-105.

Kaye DH. 1995b. The relevance of matching DNA: Is the window half open or half shut? J Crim Law Criminol 85: 676-695.

Kaye DH, Freedman DA. 1994. Reference guide on statistics. In: Reference manual on scientific evidence. Washington DC: Federal Judicial Center. p 331-414.

Kaye DH, Kanwischer R. 1988. Admissibility of genetic testing in paternity litigation: a survey of state statutes. Family Law Quart 22: 109-115.

Kaye DH, Koehler JJ. 1991. Can jurors understand probabilistic evidence? J Roy Stat Soc 154A: 21-39.

Kidd JR, Pakstis AJ, Kidd KK. 1993. Global levels of DNA variation. In: Fourth international symposium on human identification 1993: Proceedings. Madison, WI: Promega. p 21-30.

Kirby LT. 1992. DNA fingerprinting: an introduction. New York: WH Freeman.

Klimpton CP, Gill P, Walton A, Urquhart A, Millican ES, and Adams M. 1993. Automated DNA profiling employing multiplex amplification of short tandem repeat loci. PCR Meth Applic 3: 13-22.

Koehler JJ. 1993a. Error and exaggeration in the presentation of DNA evidence at trial. Jurimetrics J 34: 21-39.

Koehler JJ. 1993b. DNA matches and statistics: important questions, surprising answers. Judicature 76: 222-229.

Koehler JJ, Chia A, Lindsey S. 1995. The random match probability (RMP) in DNA evidence: irrelevant and prejudicial? Jurimetrics J 35 : 201-219.

Krane DE, Allen RW, Sawyer SA, Petrov DA, Hartl DL. 1992. Genetic differences at four DNA typing loci in Finnish, Italian, and mixed Caucasian populations. Proc Natl Acad Sci USA 89: 10583-10587.

Kreiling KR. 1993. DNA technology in forensic science. Jurimetrics J 33: 449-487.

Krontiris TG. 1995. Minisatellites and human disease. Science 269: 1682-1683.

Lander ES. 1989. DNA fingerprinting on trial. Nature 339: 501-505.

Lander ES, Budowle B. 1994. DNA fingerprinting dispute laid to rest. Nature 371: 735-738.

Latter BHD. 1980. Genetic differences within and between populations of the major human subgroups. Am Nat 116: 220-237.

Lee H, Gaensslen R, editors. 1990. DNA and other polymorphisms in forensic science. Chicago, IL: Year Book Medical.

Lempert R. 1977. Modeling relevance. Mich Law Rev 75: 1021-1057.

Lempert R. 1991. Some caveats concerning DNA as criminal identification evidence: with thanks to the Reverend Bayes. Cardozo Law Rev 13: 303-341.

Lempert R. 1993. DNA, science, and the law: two cheers for the ceiling principle. Jurimetrics J 34: 41-57.

Lewontin RC. 1972. The apportionment of human diversity. Evol Biol 6: 381-398.

Lewontin RC, Hartl DL. 1991. Population genetics in forensic DNA typing. Science 254: 1745-1750.

Li W-H, Sadler LA. 1991. Low nucleotide diversity in man. Genetics 129: 513-523.

Liebeschuetz J. 1991. Statutory control of DNA fingerprinting in Indiana. Indiana Law Rev 25: 204-223.

Mange EJ, Mange AP. 1994. Basic human genetics. Sunderland, MA: Sinauer.

McCormick. 1992. McCormick on evidence. 4th ed. Strong J, editor. St Paul, MN: West.

Maringer EF. 1993. Note. Witness for the prosecution: prosecutorial discovery of information generated by non-testifying defense psychiatric experts. Fordham Law Rev 62: 653-683.

Meaney JR. 1995. From Frye to Daubert: Is a pattern emerging? Jurimetrics J 34: 191-199.

Meyer E, Wiegand P, Brinkmann B. 1995. Phenotype differences of STRs in 7 human populations. Int J Legal Med 107: 314-322.

Moenssens AA, Starrs JE, Henderson CE, Inbau FE. 1995. Scientific evidence in civil and criminal cases. 4th ed. Westbury NY: Foundation.

Monckton DG, Tamaki K, MacLeod A, Neil DL, Jeffreys AJ. 1993. Allele-specific MVR-PCR analysis at minisatellite D1S8. Hum Mol Genet 2: 513-519.

Monson KL, Budowle B. 1993. A comparison of the fixed bin method with the floating bin and direct count methods: effect of VNTR profile frequency estimation and reference population. J Forensic Sci 38: 1037-1050.

Montoya J. 1995. A theory of compulsory process clause discovery rights. Indiana Law J 845: 880-884.

Morton NE. 1992. Genetic structure of forensic populations. Proc Natl Acad Sci USA 89: 2556-2560.

Morton NE. 1994. Genetic structure of forensic populations. Am J Hum Genet 55: 587-588.

Morton NE. 1995. Alternative approaches to population structure. Genetica 96: 139-144.

Morton NE, Collins A, Balazs I. 1993. Kinship bioassay on hypervariable loci in blacks and Caucasians. Proc Natl Acad Sci USA 90: 1892-1896.

Mosteller F, Youtz C. 1990. Quantifying probabilistic expressions. Stat Sci 5: 2-34.

Mosteller R. 1986. Discovery against the defense: tilting the adversarial balance. Cal Law Rev 74: 1567-1685.

Mourant AE, Kopeac AC, Domaniewska-Sobczak K. 1976. The distribution of the human blood groups and other polymorphisms. London: Oxford Univ Pr.

Mudd JL, Baechtel FS, Duewer DL, Currie LA, Reeder DJ, Leigh SD, Liu HK. 1994. Interlaboratory comparison of autoradiographic DNA profiling measurements. 1. Data and summary statistics. Anal Chem 66: 3303-3317.

Nagylaki T. 1993. The evolution of multilocus systems under weak selection. Genetics 134: 627-647.

Nei M. 1965. Variation and covariation of gene frequencies in subdivided populations. Evolution 19: 256-258.

Nei M. 1973. Analysis of gene diversity in subdivided populations. Proc Natl Acad Sci USA 70: 3321-3323.

Nei M. 1977. F-statistics and analysis of gene diversity in subdivided populations. Ann Hum Genet 41: 225-233.

Nei M. 1987. Molecular evolutionary genetics. New York: Columbia Univ Pr.

Nei M, Li WH. 1973. Linkage disequilibrium in subdivided populations. Genetics 75: 213-219.

Nesson CR. 1979. Reasonable doubt and permissive inferences: the value of complexity. Harvard Law Rev 92: 1187-1199.

Nesson C. 1985. The evidence or the event? On judicial proof and the acceptability of verdicts. Harvard Law Rev 98: 1357-1392.

Neufeld PJ, Colman N. 1990. When science takes the witness stand. Sci Am 262: 46-53.

Nisbett RE, Krantz D, Jepson C, Kunda Z. 1983. The use of statistical heuristics in everyday inductive reasoning. Psychol Rev 92: 339.

Nisbett RE, Ross L. 1980. Human inference: strategies and shortcomings of social judgment. Englewood Cliffs, NJ: Prentice-Hall.

NRC. 1992. DNA technology in forensic science. Washington, DC: National Acad Pr.

O'Brien JP. 1994. Note. DNA fingerprinting: the Virginia approach. Wm Mary Law Rev 35: 767.

Olaisen B, Bekkemoen M, Hoff-Olsen P, Gill P. 1993. Human VNTR mutation and sex. In: Pena SDJ, Chakraborty R, Eplen JT, Jeffreys AJ, editors. DNA fingerprinting: state of the science. Basel, Switzerland: Birkhäuser Verlag. p 63-69.

Palmerini M. 1993. The illusion of knowing. Chichester, England: J Wiley.

Pena R, Chakraborty R, Epplen JT, Jeffreys AJ, editors. 1993. DNA fingerprinting: state of the science. Basel, Switzerland: Birkhäuser Verlag.

Perkin Elmer Corp. 1995. Forensic DNA technology implementation update, forensic forum: updates on PCR in casework and research. Norwalk, CT: Perkin Elmer.

Poulton EC. 1989. Bias in quantifying judgements. Hillsdale, NJ: Lawrence Erlbaum.

Promega. 1995. Fifth international symposium on human identification 1994: proceedings. Madison, WI: Promega.

Reeves T, Lockhart R. 1993. Distributional versus singular approaches to probability and errors in probabilistic reasoning. J Exper Psychol Gen 122: 207-226.

Risch NJ, Devlin B. 1992. On the probability of matching DNA fingerprints. Science 255: 717-720.

Rivas F, Cerda-Flores R, Zhong Y, Chakraborty R. 1995. Intra- and inter-population genetic diversity at the HLA-DQA locus and their implications for parentage analysis and human identification. Am J Hum Genet 55: A163.

Robertson A, Hill WG. 1984. Deviations from Hardy-Weinberg proportions: sampling variances and use in estimation of inbreeding coefficients. Genetics 107: 703-718.

Roeder K. 1994. DNA fingerprinting: a review of the controversy. Stat Sci 9: 222-278. (Comments by Balding, Berry, Lempert, Lewontin, Sudbury, Thompson, and Weir and rejoinder by Roeder.)

Roeder K, Escobar M, Kadane JB, Balazs I. 1995. Measuring heterogeneity in forensic databases using hierarchical Bayes models. Biometrika (submitted).

Saferstein R, editor. 1993. Forensic science handbook, Vol III. Englewood Cliffs, NJ: Regents/Prentice Hall.

Sajantila A, Budowle B, Strom M, Johnsson V, Lukka M, Peltonen L, Ehnholm C. 1992. PCR amplification of alleles at the DS180 locus: comparison of a Finnish and a North American Caucasian population sample, and forensic casework evaluation. Am J Hum Genet 50: 816-825.

Saks MJ, Koehler JJ. 1991. What DNA "fingerprinting" can teach the law about the rest of forensic science. Cardozo Law Rev 13: 361-372.

Scheck BC. 1994. DNA and Daubert. Cardozo Law Rev 15: 1959-1997.

Schwarzer W. 1994. Management of expert evidence. In: Reference manual on scientific evidence. Washington DC: Federal Judicial Center. p 7-35.

Sensabaugh GF. 1987. Genetic typing of biological evidence. Comments for the Cooper amicus brief. Cal Assoc Crim Newsl, July 1987, p 11-17.

Sensabaugh GF, Northey D. 1985. What can be learned from the proficiency trials? An analysis of the electrophoretic typing results, 1975-1983. In: International Symposium on Forensic Applications of Electrophoresis: proceedings Wash ington, DC· GPO, p 184.

Shaviro D. 1989. Statistical-probability evidence and the appearance of justice. Harvard Law Rev 103: 530-554.

Slimowitz JR, Cohen JE. 1993. Violations of the ceiling principle: exact conditions and statistical evidence. Am J Hum Genet 53: 314-323.

Sokal RR, Rohlf FJ. 1981. Biometry: the principles and practice of statistics in biological research. 2nd ed. San Francisco, CA: WH Freeman.

Stigler SM. 1995. Galton and identification by fingerprints. Genetics 140: 857-860.

Stoney DE, Thornton JI. 1986. A critical analysis of quantitative fingerprinting individuality models. J Forensic Sci 33: 11-13.

Sullivan PJ. 1992. DNA fingerprint matches. Science 256: 1743-1744.

Sutherland GR, Richards RI. 1995. Simple tandem DNA repeats and human genetic disease. Proc Natl Acad Sci USA 92: 3636-3641.

Symposium. 1991. Decision and inference in litigation. Cardozo Law Rev 13: 253-1079.

Therman E, Susman M. 1993. Human chromosomes: structure, behavior, and effects. 3rd ed. New York: Springer-Verlag.

Thompson WC. 1993. Evaluating the admissibility of new genetic identification tests: lessons from the "DNA war." J Crim Law Criminol 84: 22-104.

Thompson WC. 1995. Subjective interpretation, laboratory error, and the value of forensic DNA evidence: three case studies. Genetica 92: 153-168.

Thompson WC, Ford S. 1989. DNA typing: acceptance and weight of the new genetic identification tests. Virginia Law Rev 75: 45-108.

Thompson WC, Ford S. 1991. The meaning of a match: sources of ambiguity in the interpretation of DNA prints. In: Farley M, Harrington J, editors. Forensic DNA technology. Chelsea, MI: Lewis. p 93-152.

Thompson WC, Schumann EL. 1987. Interpretation of statistical evidence in criminal trials: the prosecutor's fallacy and the defense attorney's fallacy. Law Hum Behav 11: 167-187.

Tribe L. 1971. Trial by mathematics: precision and ritual in the legal process. Harvard Law Rev 84: 1329-1393.

TWGDAM. 1989. Guidelines for a quality assurance program for DNA restriction fragment length polymorphism analysis. Crime Lab Dig 16: 40-59.

TWGDAM. 1990a. Guidelines for a proficiency testing program for DNA restriction fragment length polymorphism analysis. Crime Lab Dig 17: 50-60.

TWGDAM. 1990b. Statement of the working group on statistical standards for DNA analysis. Crime Lab Dig 17: 53-58.

TWGDAM. 1991. Guidelines for a quality assurance program for DNA analysis. Crime Lab Dig 18: 44-75.

TWGDAM. 1993. A guide for conducting a DNA quality assurance audit. Crime Lab Dig 20: 8-18.

TWGDAM. 1994a. Notes from the Technical Working Group on DNA Analysis Methods. Crime Lab Dig 21: 9-13.

TWGDAM. 1994b. Notes from the Technical Working Group on DNA Analysis Methods. Crime Lab Dig 21: 69-74.

TWGDAM. 1994c. The Technical Working Group on DNA Analysis Methods (TWGDAM) consensus approach for applying the "ceiling principle" to derive conservative estimates of DNA profile frequencies. J Forensic Sci 39: 899-904. (Also Crime Lab Dig 21: 21-25.)

TWGDAM. 1995. Guidelines for a quality assurance program for DNA analysis. Crime Lab Dig 22: 21-50.

Walker RH, editor. 1983. Inclusion probabilities in parentage testing. Arlington, VA: Am Assoc Blood Banks.

Wallsten S, Budesco DV. 1990. Comment. Stat Science 5: 23-26.

Weir BS. 1990. Genetic data analysis: methods for discrete population genetic data. Sunderland, MA: Sinauer.

Weir BS. 1992a. Population genetics in the forensic DNA debate. Proc Natl Acad Sci USA 89: 11654-11659.

Weir BS. 1992b. Independence of VNTR alleles defined as floating bins. Am J Hum Genet 51: 992-997.

Weir BS. 1992c. Independence of VNTR alleles defined as fixed bins. Genetics 130: 873-887.

Weir BS. 1993a. Forensic population genetics and the National Research Council (NRC). Am J Hum Genet 52: 437-440.

Weir BS. 1993b. Independence tests for VNTR alleles defined as quantile bins. Am J Hum Genet 53: 1107-1113.

Weir BS. 1993c. DNA fingerprinting report. Science 260: 473.

Weir BS. 1994. The effects of inbreeding on forensic calculations. Annu Rev Genet 28: 597-621.

Weir BS. 1995a. A bibliography for the use of DNA in human identification. In: Weir BS, editor. Human identification. Dordrecht, Netherlands: Kluwer Acad. p 179-213.

Weir BS, editor. 1995b. Human identification: the use of DNA markers. Dordrecht, Netherlands: Kluwer Acad.

Weir BS, Cockerham CC. 1984. Estimating F-statistics for the analysis of population structure. Evolution 38: 1358-1370.

Weir BS, Gaut BS. 1993. Matching and binning DNA fragments in forensic science. Jurimetrics J 34: 9-19.

Weir BS, Hill WG. 1993. Population genetics of DNA profiles. J Forensic Sci 33: 219-226.

Weir BS, Triggs CM, Starling L, Stowell LI, Walsh KAJ, Buckleton EST. 1996. Interpreting DNA mixtures. J Forensic Sci (submitted).

Wilson MR, Holland MM, Stoneking M, DiZinno JA, Budowle B. 1993. Guidelines for the use of mitochondrial DNA sequencing in forensic science. Crime Lab Dig 20: 68-77.

Wong Z, Wilson V, Patel I, Povey S, and Jeffreys AJ. 1987. Characterization of a panel of highly variable minisatellites cloned from human DNA. Ann Hum Genet 51:269-288.

Wooley JR. 1995. Why we will never all agree about DNA testing in criminal cases. In: Fifth international symposium on human identification: proceedings. Madison, WI: Promega. p 1-4.

Wright S. 1951. The genetical structure of populations. Ann Eugen 15: 159-171.

Wrogemann K, Biancalana V, Devys D, Imbert G, Trottier Y, Mandel J-L. 1993. Microsatellites and disease: a new paradigm. In: Pena SDJ, Chakraborty R, Epplen JT, Jeffreys AJ, editors. DNA fingerprinting: state of the science. Basel, Switzerland: Birkhäuser Verlag. p 141-152.

Index